SECONDARY SCHOOLS

AT THE TURN OF THE CENTURY

Theodore R. Sizer

SECONDARY SCHOOLS AT THE TURN OF THE CENTURY

GREENWOOD PRESS, PUBLISHERS
WESTPORT, CONNECTICUT

Library of Congress Cataloging in Publication Data

Sizer, Theodore R
Secondary schools at the turn of the century.

Reprint of the 1964 ed. published by Yale
University Press, New Haven.
Based on the author's thesis, Harvard University.
"Report of the Committee of Ten on Secondary
School Studies, with the reports of the conferences
arranged by the committee": p.
Bibliography: p.
Includes index.
1. Education, Secondary. 2. Education--United
States. I. National Education Association of the
United States. Committee of Ten on Secondary
School Studies. Report. 1976. II. Title.
[LB1607.S54 1976] 373.73 76-43028
ISBN 0-8371-8972-1

Originally published in 1964 by Yale University Press, New Haven

Reprinted with the permission of Yale University Press

Reprinted in 1976 by Greenwood Press, Inc.

Library of Congress Catalog Card Number 76-43028

ISBN 0-8371-8972-1

Printed in the United States of America

TO MY FATHER, THEODORE SIZER

ACKNOWLEDGMENTS

In a search for manuscript materials, one depends much on the kindness of many persons, and the present author is no exception. I am particularly indebted to Bruce McClellan, Albert R. Evans, and Gerrish Thurber of the Lawrenceville School; to Eleanor H. Mackenzie, the daughter-in-law of the famous headmaster; to the Misses Helen I. and Frances M. Tetlow, daughters of John Tetlow; to Donald M. Love of Oberlin, who searched in the Henry Churchill King Papers on my behalf; to Alice H. Bonnell of the Columbiana Library for help with the Butler Papers; to Lewis G. Vander Velde and F. Clever Bald of the University of Michigan for collecting relevant letters from the Angell Papers; and to Kimball Elkins of the Harvard University Archives who spent several hours helping with the search in the Eliot Papers.

Others were generous with their help. Lawrence Cremin of Teachers College, Columbia University, Edward Krug of the University of Wisconsin, and Richard Whittemore of the Western Washington State College of Education gave invaluable advice. At the National Education Association, I received the assistance of Mildred S. Fenner and Irene Wolz. Vynce A. Hines of the University of Florida made available a manuscript of his that dealt with the Committee of Ten. And my nephew, Theodore S. Cochran, then of the University of Colorado, did yeoman service digging for material on James H. Baker.

Frederick Rudolph of Williams College and Robert Ulich of Harvard gave more encouragement and direction than I am sure they were aware of. Three persons immersed themselves in the manuscript and to them I owe a particular debt: Bernard Bailyn, of Harvard, who carefully read a succession of drafts and who gave valuable advice; my father Theodore Sizer, Professor of the History of Art, *Emeritus,* at Yale; and my wife, Nancy F. Sizer, who as editor and historical critic read several drafts and who quietly suffered interminable meal-time anecdotes about Charles W. Eliot.

I should also record my appreciation to Helen Garrison, Carol C. Sullivan, Angela Sniffen, and Karen Zurcher, who prepared the manuscript with accuracy and good humor above the call of duty.

T. R. S.

Cambridge, Massachusetts
March 1964

CONTENTS

ix

PREFACE

This monograph is the biography of a document—its setting, its composition, its distribution, and its effect. Why the *Report of the Committee on Secondary School Studies* deserves such attention needs justification, for documents by the bale were published on the subject of the schools at the turn of the century and to isolate one demands explanation. This *Report*—commonly referred to as "the Report of the Committee of Ten"—has had a profound influence on American education. For fifteen years after its publication it served as gospel for the curriculum writers of the burgeoning high schools; in our own time it serves as the explicit rallying point for those who feel that our secondary schools have forgotten their central role in training the intellect. Called in 1894 "the educational sensation of the New Year,"[1] it was termed in 1958 "the embodiment of the most profound, practical, and democratic philosophy of education ever enunciated in America."[2] While there were and are those who contest these assessments, it is clear that the *Report* carved a niche for itself in American school history, something that its scores of cousins written by similar committees and conferences failed to do. A description of the *Report*, the reasons for its success, and the limit of its effect can thus be justified.

The Committee of Ten was assembled to make order out of the widespread chaos in secondary education; it provided a system, if not a lasting one, at least the first, most difficult stand-

1. F. H. Kasson, editorial in *Education, 14* (1893–94), 431.
2. J. F. Latimer, *What's Happened to Our High Schools?* (Washington, 1958), p. 116.

xi

ardization. At the close of the nineteenth century a national system of education clearly was evolving in the country, as society increased its demand for a ladder of formal schooling from grade school through university, the rungs of which an ever increasing percentage of Americans would climb. As the schools grew, nationally accepted curricula developed and the one recommended by the Committee of Ten was the first widely followed by the secondary schools.

This Committee, like many, had mundane, bureaucratic beginnings. It was the child of the National Council of Education, a unit of the National Educational Association. The NCE called for a study of the subjects of the secondary school curriculum: it moved in 1892

> That it is expedient to hold a conference of school and college teachers of each principal subject which enters into the programmes of secondary schools in the United States and into the requirements for admission to college—as, for example, of Latin, of geometry, or of American history—each conference to consider the proper limits of its subject, the best methods of instruction, the most desirable allotment of time for the subject, and the best methods of testing the pupils' attainments therein, and each conference to represent fairly the different parts of the country.

It further created a central group to organize these conferences and to prepare a final report: "That a Committee be appointed with authority to select the members of these conferences and to arrange their meetings, the results of all the conferences to be reported to this Committee for such action as it may deem appropriate, and to form the basis of a report to be presented to the Council by this Committee."[3] This committee was the Committee of Ten.

The ten men selected were nationally influential figures. The chairman was Charles W. Eliot, then in his twenty-third year

3. *Report of the Committee on Secondary School Studies* (Washington, 1893), pp. 3–4.

as president of Harvard University and the acknowledged leader of college and university reform in America. Joining him were four other college presidents, James B. Angell of Michigan, James M. Taylor of Vassar, James H. Baker of Colorado, and Richard H. Jesse of Missouri. A sixth member, Henry Churchill King, a professor at Oberlin, was shortly to become president there as well. Four schoolmen were on the Committee, the most distinguished of which was the United States Commissioner of Education, William Torrey Harris, internationally known both for a brilliant career as superintendent of the St. Louis public schools and for his studies of Hegel. James C. Mackenzie of Lawrenceville, John Tetlow of Boston Girls' High and Girls' Latin Schools, and Oscar D. Robinson of the Albany High School were all heads of their several institutions. The Committee was distinguished in its membership and representative of the various parts of the country, desirable characteristics for a group with the task of preparing a report for national consumption.

The need for such a report was understandable, for at that time one could not clearly define an American secondary school. The upper limit of the elementary school was hazy. Some schools were not "graded" in a standard form—the students progressing from first grade to second, and so forth, on the basis of their achievement—and graduation from them reflected no meaningful standard. Other so-called elementary schools, however, provided their scholars with considerable work in the higher branches of learning. The existing academies and high schools varied markedly in terms of size, quality, course offerings, and even aims. Furthermore, the lower limit of college work was itself unclear. The freshmen at Harvard were doing work at a standard above that expected of graduates of some other colleges. In fact, the title "college" was no help: some state superintendents even lumped colleges, academies, and high schools together in their statistical summaries—tacit recognition of the low standards of the hopefully titled tertiary institutions. The country obviously needed, then, some authority to specify the scope and content of secondary education.

The Ten started their work by meeting in November 1892 at the home of a young Columbia philosopher, Nicholas Murray Butler, who was in time to become their most effective herald and propagandizer. They appointed "conferences" on the various school subjects, which were held in December 1892. Reports from these meetings came to Eliot early in 1893, and the Ten met again at Columbia in November of that year, signing their own report in December. This document and the Conference reports were published in January 1894, Commissioner Harris claiming that the *Report* was "the most important educational document ever published in this country."[4]

4. Ibid., p. 2.

I · TRADITION AND CHANGE

Schools, as all social institutions, reflect the pulling and hauling of tradition on the one hand and the changing of circumstances on the other. The American secondary schools of 1892 showed to an especially pronounced degree the marks of this tugging. As the public high school began its rapid growth in American communities, the inevitable questions of its function and design came very much into prominence. Increasingly and for ill-defined reasons, Americans began to see education beyond the rudiments as something desirable. As the high school thus became more important to a more representative group of citizens, its purpose needed clarification.

Although the high school was a hybrid, a pastiche of practices gathered from a variety of forebears, two distinct and non-complementary academic traditions were seen in the secondary schools of the early 1900s. On the one hand, commanding great prestige, was the classical-humanistic tradition represented institutionally in the Latin Grammar School. The classical languages of Greek and Latin were the core of its curriculum, which dates back well into the England of the thirteenth and fourteenth centuries. Mathematics found a small place in more recent years, and the pattern thus set was transferred to the American colonies as early as 1635. The Latin School or its equivalent was the dominant form of education beyond the rudiments offered in colonial America; classical studies were the condition of admission to the small but important colleges, such as Harvard and Williams, in pre-Revolutionary America.[1]

The classical languages, so clearly "vocational" in fourteenth-century Europe (whose means of discourse in diplomacy, law, medicine, and, indeed, in virtually all intellectual areas, was Latin), did not cease to be the heart of the curriculum as vernacular tongues slowly replaced them. The classics, even in the early history of the raw and practical United States, still formed the center of the collegiate course of study for which the secondary schools of the day had to prepare, and they were defended as such. Probably the most eloquent defense was made by the Yale faculty in 1828, a defense that had great influence in its day. Yale's President, Jeremiah Day, and his colleagues, first skirted the edge of the matter, asserting that knowledge of classical thought was the traditional mark of an educated man and that study of Latin and Greek provided help in memorizing modern languages and in working within the professions. The heart of their argument was simple: "familiarity with Greek and Roman writers is especially adapted to form the taste, and to discipline the mind, both in thought and diction, to the relish of what is elevated, chaste, and simple . . ."[2] The carefully inflected and polished words of the great classical writers provided the means for the sharpening and refining of the mind—this was the core of their position. True education and classical studies were virtually synonymous.

In 1892, the college-bound secondary school pupil prepared for entrance in a manner not wholly unlike that approved by Yale in 1828. More important, however, was the fact that Latin appeared to need even less defense than it had in antebellum days: it was still one of the most popular courses in the curriculum, even for children who had no thought of going on to college. Its appeal was not only that it supposedly refined the taste and disciplined the mind, since, as countless European visitors from de Tocqueville to Mrs. Trollope hastened to point

1. See R. Middlekauff, *Ancients and Axioms: Secondary Education in Eighteenth Century New England* (New Haven, 1963).
2. "Yale Report of 1828" in R. Hofstadter and W. Smith, *American Higher Education: A Documentary History* (Chicago, 1961), *1*, 289.

out, most Americans had little concern for these virtues. Its appeal was in its tradition of culture, its symbolic mantle of refinement. A smattering of Latin, hardly enough to satisfy President Day, was considered sufficient to make its owner somehow better able to get on in the world. Nowhere more poignantly is this symbolic value of the classical languages seen than in the pathetic efforts of the newly freed slaves to memorize some Greek and Latin: "There was a . . . feeling that the Greek and Latin languages would make one a very superior being, something bordering almost on the supernatural," wrote Booker T. Washington;[3] and where else could the ex-slave learn this reverence if not from his white master? The strong tradition of linguistic study, especially in ancient languages, was clearly seen in the curricula of many of the secondary schools that the Committee of Ten was charged to study, and the defenders of this tradition saw it in a highly emotional context.

The American, however, has never been noted for his firm support of models implying social class, or of matters of intellectual or aesthetic importance. The American seeking to rise in the late eighteenth and nineteenth centuries saw formal education in almost paradoxical terms: he wanted the symbol of "culture," i.e. classical studies; but at the same time he wanted "practical" instruction in order to make his way better in the world. This here-and-now demand is the second of the two academic traditions that were obvious in the school of 1892.

To satisfy the "practical" need, a host of small, private schools offering a variety of what present educators might call vocational subjects sprouted in late colonial and nineteenth-century cities and towns. They offered studies in English, the modern languages, commerce, navigation, bookkeeping, surveying, and similar matters. In the passage of time, these relatively ephemeral establishments were put into more permanent institutional form within academies, where they were married in a vast curriculum to the classical studies of the Latin School. The academies had a dual purpose: to prepare their college-bound students for collegiate studies, as the Latin schools had done;

3. B. T. Washington, *Up from Slavery* (Cambridge, 1900), p. 81.

3

and to prepare those who were not going on for more formal education for (as they termed it) "life." The academy provided for both wants of the American: his desire for the label of "culture" and his desire for "practical" tools. The results of this blend were more often than not deplorable, as the language courses for most of the students who were not college-bound were compressed into absurd "six-week" packages; and the so-called practical subjects, in the myopia of the pedagogues, were taught wholly out of books, with little recourse to the world in which they were to be useful. The academy movement, however, had great vigor, eclipsing the Latin grammar school as the predominant pattern of formal education beyond the rudiments in the United States. By 1850 there were probably more than 6,000 academies, spread widely through every state. Here the classical tradition was carried on, and to it was added the tradition for more practical studies.[4]

The public high school, the predominant form of secondary education in 1892, was the direct descendant neither of the Latin School nor of the academy. In contrast with eighteenth-century New England Latin Schools, which had been town controlled and supported, the academies had taken the institutional form of privately controlled schools, albeit with some public support. In addition, most were country boarding schools, an unsurprising fact considering the rural nature of the country and the relatively limited appeal of higher studies generally.[5] As public pressure, particularly in the cities and towns, militated for the accommodation of larger numbers of children in studies beyond the rudiments, the solution was the extension upward of the existing public common (elementary) schools rather than in the expansion of private, boarding establishments or the re-creation of town Latin Schools. As states after the Civil War provided for their own public universities

4. These sweeping generalizations may do ill to the grand variety within the academy movement. See my introductory essay to *The Age of the Academies* (New York, 1964).

5. Ibid., Part VI.

as well as for their common school systems, the provision at public expense for the intervening level of the ladder, the secondary schools, seemed obvious and appropriate. The academies in the form they took in antebellum times withered away in the face of this new competition, and the public high schools passed them in number of students enrolled during the 1880s.

As more children stayed longer in the common schools, the elementary curriculum of the "three R's" simply expanded. Algebra was added to arithmetic. English study followed the alphabet. Here and there Latin was started, along with French and German. As the schools grew in size, the one-room establishments were "graded," and the more advanced students separated from the beginners. Grading continued, and in due course "high school" branches of the common schools sprouted, though often housed in the same building with the elementary branches. The curriculum that evolved was "practically the systematic expansion through a four-years' secondary course of the modern studies mapped out for the elementary schools," as one high school principal remarked.[6] English, mathematics, modern foreign languages, history, some rudimentary science—these were the staples, the "modern" branches. Added to them was Latin in large doses, for the same reasons that had obtained for its retention in the academy (although Greek suffered a serious decline). The multitude of vocational, practical courses of the academy, such as navigation and surveying, never gained a firm foothold.

The high school was saddled with two traditions, then, in much the same way as the academy had been. The classics remained, particularly for the increasing number of students who desired to go to college. Parallel with them were the "modern" subjects, which had evolved from the common school or been taken over from the academy. These two traditions, for obvious reasons, were in many respects antithetical, as Presi-

6. R. G. Huling, in discussion of the *Report* of the Committee of Ten, New England Association of Colleges and Preparatory Schools, *Addresses and Proceedings* (1894), p. 5.

dent Day and his Yale faculty had argued in the 1820s. Both, being well established, presented a difficult task of compromise for the Committee of Ten.

Such was the tradition; but it is well to note that within it the schools had, up to 1890, remained outside the main stream of American life. The secondary school counted for little as the social sorting device that the nineteenth century American used. To complete a course beyond the rudiments actually appeared to have little effect on rapid advancement, and while the complete proof of this argument may never be at hand, one need only look at the leaders in the political and economic sectors of American life to see that formal secondary education played no consistent part in their rise.

With the 1890s, however, this situation was to change. Formal education was to become a more important factor in the functioning of society than it had been heretofore—indeed within fifty years after the publication of the report of the Committee of Ten formal education had become not one but the principal sorting device the society used.

The growth of cities and the shift in the sources of intellectual authority are the two most significant factors explaining the rise in the importance of formal education. In 1860, of a total population of 31,443,321, slightly over 6,000,000 lived in urban communities—that is, with populations over 2,500. In 1890 the population, now numbering 62,947,714, showed over 22,000,000 urban dwellers. In 1860 there had been but 392 communities of over 2,500 population; in 1890 the number had increased to 1,348.[7] The Civil War had spurred industrial growth, and the development of large, closely-populated communities of people to man this industry naturally followed.

The fact of urbanism is important for the schools, in that changes in education most often have been fostered in communities of concentrated settlement. This is understandable: wherever there is a reasonable number of children to be educated

7. U.S. Bureau of the Census, *Historical Statistics of the United States, Colonial Times to 1957* (Washington, 1960), p. 14.

6

who live within several miles of a central point, it is possible to have a school that offers more than a glorified tutorial. Large concentrations of population allowed for elaborate graded schools.

Education had been the principal expense of local communities since colonial days. When it became obvious that common schools were in demand, local tax moneys were found to support them. This was also true as the pressures for formal training beyond the rudiments began to be felt, resulting in political support for general taxation in order that secondary schools could be opened and operated. Consequently, only communities with an adequate property tax base could have educational facilities. The sparsely populated rural towns and counties, which were in serious financial trouble before the turn of the century, were unable (and unwilling) to support an expanding school system. The cities, on the other hand, with their concentrated population and relative wealth, were both able and willing to provide for fully graded public school systems. Besides, in the cities there were children with time to spare, there was an increasing number of jobs that called for formal education, and there always existed for the middle-class American the intoxicating possibility of rising into the well-paid ranks of the managers.

The family on the farm employed all hands. There was a great deal of menial labor, and the eight-year-old was useful in picking beans, hoeing potatoes, or watching sheep. Large families were economically advantageous. But when the family moved to the city, this was no longer so. Father labored in the factory; mother served as a domestic; sister was a waist maker; brother went to sea. The family as a cohesive economic unit, a group devoted to a single task, lost its meaning. For the children this breakup implied the end of an education of a practical sort at father's or uncle's knee and the prospect of work disassociated from other members of the family. The city with its industry found a place for the child, a place that reformers as early as the '90s found shameful. At the same time, more sensitive parents and children saw a better future in studying

7

in school than in doing piecework in a factory. While the family farm, passed on from father to son, promised the boy his future as well as agricultural training, in the city the school was the most useful form of apprenticeship for the varied careers open to the youth.[8]

With the growth of manufacturing and the relative decline of agriculture, the composition of the labor force as a whole was changing. In 1860, of the 10,533,000 "gainful workers" in the country, 6,208,000 were on the farms and 4,325,000 were in nonfarm occupations. In 1890, of the total labor force of 23,-318,000, 9,938,000 were at farming and 13,380,000 at other tasks. Furthermore, within nonfarming occupations, the available data suggest that jobs for white-collar clerical workers and skilled and semiskilled labor increased proportionately faster than did unskilled jobs.[9] Clearly the labor force in the period after the Civil War became more diverse, demanding an increasing number of skills not traditionally taught within a family or small operator-centered apprenticeship system. To provide for this transition, industry and office had to institute informal training for its new employees, and the public supported schools had to introduce suitable curricula. Informal training was more useful for most jobs in this period, but demand for formal studies in secondary schools was clearly present.

The principal factor, other than the growth of cities, that explains the rising importance of secondary education was the breakdown of the traditional sources of authority. Mechanization and an altered economic life not only broke up the traditional, self-sufficient farm with its tight family unit; the same factors eventually resulted in a rearrangement of the values determining social and, to a lesser extent, political leadership in American life. Of course this movement was afoot as early as the 1820s, as witness the electoral defeat of John Quincy

8. The extent to which this demand was reflected by a wide variety of groups in American society has been traced by Rush Welter, *Popular Education and Democratic Thought in America* (New York, 1962), Part III.
9. *Historical Statistics*, pp. 72, 74.

Adams; but it is well to note that the spokesmen for Americans up to the Civil War were men of means and traditional education more often than they were in the later decades of the century. The war, the shift of political influence from southern leaders to northern city politicians, and the change in economic influence from the small entrepreneur to the national business corporation together provided the American people with a new set of leaders. By the end of the century, the routes to social and economic power were opened to a wide group of people whose common characteristic was a ruthless ability to succeed. This was not lost on observant Americans: men bent on success could now realize their aim through their own talents rather than by birthright. The school was to provide the skill and polish that allowed a man to climb in life.

It became increasingly apparent that schooling was necessary in selecting people for positions of responsibility. The high school diploma per se began to have value in the market place for employment in a way it had not had previously. That its recipient knew anything about the tasks he was to perform was less important than the fact that he had survived the course of study and received a diploma. Since he had demonstrated the ability to master the academic curriculum, the chances were that he would respond well to the "informal" training his employer would provide. The diploma, more than the substance of his formal education, acquired important symbolic value on the labor market.

In this way formal education bestowed authority upon its recipients. Moreover, by 1890 the development of experimental science, best popularized by the works of Charles Darwin and Herbert Spencer, had shaken the traditional authority of the clergy with its vision of revealed truth. Although most Americans were ignorant of the evolutionary doctrine, it had a profound effect in the centers of industrial growth and in academia. Darwinism thus touched upon those persons in American society—the city dwellers and the academicians— who were most concerned with the expansion of the secondary schools. Paradoxically, this had little effect upon the teaching

9

of biology; increasing respect, however, was paid to the "expert" who divined truth by rational methods in contrast to the spiritual processes the theologian had used earlier. Truth for many was now a relative thing, a complex problem demanding sophisticated proof. The man who could provide proof was the man disciplined in experiment, the scientist.

Evolutionary theory had a profound impact on American society and intellectual life in the nineteenth century.[10] Most striking was the rapid acceptance of Darwinian and Spencerian ideas by scientific leaders in the colleges and universities, a fact all the more remarkable when one considers the assumptions upon which the old-time colleges rested. What Walter Metzger has called "a new rationale for academic freedom" was clearly evident in many American colleges and universities by 1892, and certainly those that produced the members of the Committee of Ten. "Disciplined inquiry" had become a source of truth; by its very nature, it could tolerate error. The important task in the search for truth was the manner of quest: the rules, as Metzger calls them, were crucial. Everything was open to honest doubt; truth was relative and subject to continuing search and research. Parallel to these dicta was the assumption that its seeker be objective. The only dependable criteria for proof were demonstrable facts, and the unsupported beliefs of the scholar were irrelevant to his work.[11]

Metzger argues these developments had important implications for academic freedom; but they had even more important, if subtler, implications for society as a whole. "With its rapid expansion, its exploitative methods, its desperate competition, and its peremptory rejection of failure, postbellum America was like a vast human caricature of the Darwinian struggle for existence and survival of the fittest." What the *Atlantic*

10. A full discussion of evolutionary thought and education is not possible here. For the movement as a whole, see R. Hofstadter, *Social Darwinism in American Thought* (rev. ed. Boston, 1955). For its impact on education, see Welter, *Popular Education and Democratic Thought in America*, chap. 14; and R. Hofstadter and W. P. Metzger, *The Development of Academic Freedom in the United States* (New York, 1955), Part II, chap. 7.

11. Hofstadter and Metzger, pp. 363–66.

Monthly called the scientific spirit of the age led to general acceptance of evolutionary thought; those sections of the country
most touched by rapid expansion and growth were the most affected.[12] The scientific spirit gave authority to the disciplined
inquirer as a source of truth. As the universities grew, so did
the prestige of their top scholars. By 1903 Eliot could speak of
his own Harvard University as "the most effective institution of
learning in the world."[13] Its graduates and those of other colleges replaced the clergy as the sources of knowledge. The universities were involved not only in matters of life and the explanation of the universe, but also, to an unprecedented extent,
in government and business. President Angell, for instance,
served in several key diplomatic posts under a variety of admin-
istrations. Eliot was offered ambassadorships (which he turned
down), and his influence on matters from prohibition to international peace was considerable. Butler became the friend
and confidant of presidents. And a participant in one of the
Committee of Ten's Conferences, Professor Woodrow Wilson of
Princeton, became President in 1912 and attempted to solve the
peace in 1919 with a delegation to Paris drawn almost wholly
from the scholarly community.

The rise of the educated expert—most often a scholar at a
college or university—to a position of prominence in society explains a great deal about the movement of formal education
closer to the center of American society in the late nineteenth
and early twentieth centuries. The influence of university scholarship and the scientific approach on the secondary schools was
to cause them to develop and articulate new areas of knowledge, each assured of its place in the academic sun and ready
to challenge the traditional classics and mathematics for an
equal portion of the students' time. The natural and physical
sciences expanded as knowledge of them grew. Scientific
method resulted in the call for laboratories planned essentially
for teaching. President Eliot, a chemist, prided himself on pro-

12. Hofstadter, *Social Darwinism in American Thought,* pp. 33, 44.
13. C. W. Eliot to A. B. Hart, August 25, 1903. Eliot Papers, Harvard
University.

ducing what he considered the first textbook in chemistry using the laboratory method.[14]

History, too, shifted its view, swinging to the Herbert Baxter Adams approach. Parson Weems' and McGuffey's view of Washington ("Little George . . .") gave way to the cold precision of the scientific historian. Once again method was a dominant factor. Books of readings and collections of documents were supplied for schools, and children were asked to carry out simple historical explorations in their own local districts. Economics was developed, in an effort to explain on scientific grounds the vicissitudes of the nation's finances, and efforts were made to reduce the vagaries of the market place to precise formulas. Politics and government were not immune to research; Woodrow Wilson's *Congressional Government* exemplifies the kind of objective study of the political system that was evolving in the post-Civil War period. As economic and political truths were bared, it was felt that they should be taught to children, as an additional responsibility of the schools.

The individual and his society were also subjects of study. Led by G. Stanley Hall of Clark University, the child study movement gained great popularity, causing even a schoolman of the caliber of Harris to exclaim that "these folks [Hall and others] that have got into the current of evolution, and are going so fast, make one dizzy to look at them."[15] This movement inevitably touched the schools. "The influence of the new doctrine of evolution . . . began to be apparent, and a conception of the child as a slowly developing personality, demanding subject matter and method suited to his stage of development, now began to take the place of the earlier pouring-in of information conception."[16] Efforts to define the curriculum by examining

14. C. W. Eliot and F. H. Storer, *A Manual of Inorganic Chemistry, Arranged to Facilitate the Experimental Demonstration of the Facts and Principles of the Science* (New York, 1862).

15. W. T. Harris to N. M. Butler, October 9, 1896, Butler Papers, Columbia University.

16. E. P. Cubberley, *Changing Conceptions of Education* (Boston, 1909), p. 43.

the needs and abilities of the child, however, did not originate with Hall's group; object teaching, a development from Pestalozzian theory, had had wide acceptance in American schools, particularly after it had been popularized by Edward A. Sheldon at his Oswego, New York, Normal School in the late 1850s. More important by the 1890s were the teachings of Johann Friedrich Herbart, whose doctrines of apperception and correlation found many American enthusiasts. Herbartian thought was disseminated by the Normal Department of NEA and by such men as Charles and Frank McMurry. The discipline of psychology was dignified by inclusion into university curricula and by the work of such pioneers as William James, whose *Talks to Teachers* gained national fame. Sociology, the study of society itself, developed under men like Lester Ward, William Graham Sumner, and Albion W. Small, and in time, it provided schools with a concrete new aim: social efficiency.[17]

Sociology and psychology had as yet no claim to the time of the secondary school pupil. The other subjects, though, demanded increased time and revised pedagogy; many of them were the erstwhile "modern" subjects of the extended common school—history, the sciences, economics. The rush of scientific study thus complicated the efforts of the Committee of Ten to reform the curriculum.

Darwinism and scientific thought, then, not only raised the academic man to a more prominent place in society, but also provided pressure for more studies, more disciplines, to be offered in the schools. While the latter factor was a complicating one for educators, the former provided distinction and prestige to the formally educated, inspiring others to follow in their footsteps. The pressure for expanded formal education in scientific fields was evident. The fact that such diverse evolutionary thinkers as William Graham Sumner, Lester Ward, and Andrew Carnegie all supported the notion of public education added more fuel.[18] Sumner's advocacy remains somewhat paradoxical, as does that of others, including Eliot himself. But the

17. Ibid., chap. 3.
18. Welter, *Popular Education*, pp. 228–35.

important point is that the intellectual movement clearly over-lapped with the popular demand: education was not only a good thing, but a centrally important thing; its aim was to rec-ognize talent, to allow for the survival of the fittest student. This notion of equality was still somewhat ill formed in 1892; indeed, together with evolutionary doctrine itself, it was to be transformed and refined by the pragmatists in the twentieth century. But the fact remains that the demand for schooling of the city dweller coalesced with the notions of the new scientific thinkers, the influentials who were members of the Committee of Ten.

As formal education since the earliest days on this continent had been very much a local responsibility, one striking fact about the appointment of the Committee of Ten was that it was expected to appeal to the secondary schools nationally. It was assumed that a pattern of studies could apply equally well in all parts of America. This assumption did not cause a ripple of disagreement or even comment when the Committee was formed, for the conception of America as a single nation had been fundamentally grasped in the decades after the Civil War. A Committee to preach to the nation on education was new, to be sure, but not at all surprising.

Improved communications, the rise of national industrial corporations and business organizations having nationwide in-fluence and control, the increasing dependence of the individ-ual American upon the goods and services of others, the rise of the standard and complexity of his living all had served to weld the nation together. Americans could observe the strength of their country growing in relation to that of foreign nations, and they came to see positive value in things that were uniquely American. At the same time this nationwide economic and psy-chological unity was developing, a similar kind of unity—or, better, homogeneity—was seen in the schools. While by 1892 the educational scene still appeared chaotic, there were signs of an emerging national pattern. Indeed, this pattern was largely in the minds of schoolmen; but what is important is that for the first time they were articulating their beliefs and spreading their word. One vehicle for this was the National Teachers' Association, founded in 1858, which changed its name soon after to the National Educational Association.[19] Annual meetings gave its leaders an audience of national breadth. Regional associations also provided platforms, as did a number of journals. As certain textbooks—notably the Mc-Guffey readers—became widely used, they created a kind of uniformity. Local flavor was still apparent, but the basis for a national standard was clearly emerging. In 1874, for instance, it was possible to publish a pamphlet entitled "A Statement of the Theory of Education in the United States of America as Approved by Many Leading Educators."[20] Prepared for the use of the Commissioner of Education at an international conference, this short work, written by W. T. Harris, set forth thirty areas on which seventy-seven men, including most of the state school officers and many college presidents, could agree. The areas ranged from the rationale for the common school and its curriculum to corporal punishment. The significant factor was the awareness of educators that theirs was an *American* system, not merely a group of state systems. At the same time, there was no public pressure for federal control of education. The tradition of state and local responsibility for the schools was well established, and there was no effort to change it. (Indeed, the need for federal control of business was more pronounced than that for education, and the nation saw little support for ways of checking the excesses of corporations and of individuals until the twentieth century.) Autonomy at the lowest level was considered sacred in the United States, and, while a national uniformity of standards was desired, these standards in a Darwinian era were to be achieved without any kind of national coercion.

These feelings, of both national consciousness and disinterest

19. The name was to change once again, to National Education Association, as the organization is now termed.

20. Washington, 1874. While the document itself does not credit Harris with sole authorship, his own copy, now at the Library of Congress, bears the citation—in his handwriting—"by W. T. Harris."

in national control, had clear effects on the schools. Patriotism was a major goal for education and became even more so toward the end of the century. This was strengthened by the native attitude—either aversion or concern—toward the so-called new, that is non-North European, immigrants. By the Spanish-American War this national drum beating had taken on an ominous aspect.

While no nationally directed scheme of public education evolved in the United States as it did in Germany, France, and, to an extent, Great Britain at this time, it cannot be said that there were no efforts to involve the government in school improvement. A Federal Bureau of Education was set up in 1867, with Henry Barnard as its first Commissioner; his job was to collect and publish statistics and offer advice, on the pattern of the state commissioners. The Bureau, once founded, was then ignored, starved for funds, and moved around within the executive branch almost at whim. By 1892 it was a unit under the Secretary of the Interior. The Bureau was not the product of the post-Civil War nationalist feeling, but rather the result of the successes of antebellum state officers, notably Horace Mann and Barnard himself. From its inception it has been ignored almost to the present day. No federal commissioner, Harris included, ever had as much influence as Mann, the servant of an individual state, and while a national system of education came of age, the national office of education only stood feebly by, taking its pulse.

More important were the early efforts by members of Congress to use federal funds and influence to improve schools. There was of course a precedent for this: in the Ordinances of the 1780s and in the 1862 Morrill Act, the national government had demonstrated a responsibility for education. From 1865 to 1900, however, all efforts to continue this policy failed. A proposal by Senator George F. Hoar of Massachusetts to force minimum educational standards on backward states—notably those in the South—failed in the Congress. More significant were the series of bills introduced by Senator Henry W. Blair of New Hampshire, calling for funds intended to reduce illiteracy.

These were considered five times by Congress during the 1880s; all failed to pass both Houses. It seemed that the country was not in the mood for federal participation in schooling. The postwar years brought to Americans a more precise sense of national identity, but no concurrent demand for national direction, in education or in any other sphere of society.

Schools, as we said earlier, are a peculiar blend of tradition and change. Tradition in the secondary schools of 1892 was represented by the twin and to some extent contradictory approaches of, on the one hand, classical education on the pattern of the Latin Grammar School and, on the other, the demand for modern, useful studies as represented in the extended common school. Change was represented by the quickening intellectual revolution caused by evolutionary doctrines and scientific advance, by vast demographic growth and shifts in the country, and by an altering labor market. It was also symbolized in the readiness of educators for the first time to sponsor a committee that would speak to the schools of the country as a whole.

Even a brief look at the history of Western education gives evidence enough of the glacial rate at which schools and universities change. Societies seem to tolerate, for considerable periods of time, schools that are quite out of tune with contemporary needs and beliefs. As long as education is a symbol rather than a substance, a premium is placed on its changelessness. And formal education always has had and continues to have symbolic importance in the United States.

Schools do change; but they seem to change only when the gap between schools and society is extreme and at the same time the demand for formal education is growing.[21] In 1892 the pressures that inevitably affect education clearly were great; change was inevitable. The appointment of the Committee of Ten in 1892 was propitious.

21. On the point of "disjunction" see O. Handlin, *John Dewey's Challenge to Education* (New York, 1959).

II · A WIDE GAP

Between the elementary schools and the colleges there "is a wide gap very imperfectly bridged by a few public high schools, endowed academies, college preparatory departments, and private schools, which conform to no common standards and are under no unifying control."[1] This fact was stated to a National Educational Association audience in 1890 by President Eliot, and few would have disputed it. Two years later, an unhappy school superintendent went so far as to say that the school "is poor enough to justify almost anything said of it by its enemies."[2] Education, particularly secondary education, was in chaotic condition.

The chaos in the secondary schools can be demonstrated in a variety of ways. First, the elementary schools were not by any standard supplying the secondary institutions with trained scholars, and without prepared students the high schools could not perform their intended role. Second, laymen exerted considerable control over the schools, often as a means for political and personal ends that were hardly in the interest of high academic standards. A third indication of the gap was the schools' financing: amounts spent by communities on education varied markedly and in the same proportion as did their provision for secondary education.

1. C. W. Eliot, "The Gap between the Elementary Schools and the Colleges," National Educational Association *Proceedings and Addresses* (1890), p. 522.

2. L. H. Jones, "The School and the Criminal," NEA *Proceedings* (1892), p. 208.

The sad state of elementary education was fully realized by President Eliot, who felt that the elementary schools were critically important—and said so on the occasion of his inaugural address as President of Harvard in 1869. He had many reforms to recommend.[3] He believed, as he wrote to Charles Kendall Adams, that "the most lamentable deficiency in our systems is in the schools which have to do with the boy before he comes to be 15 years of age."[4] Eliot once had two persons read aloud the entire list of books required for a six-year grammar school course (presumably grades 3 through 7) while he kept track of time; his conclusion was that the entire course could be read in no more than forty-six hours. He then gave a recent high school graduate all the arithmetic problems that exhausted one-fifth of the students' time in grammar school; the work was finished in fifteen hours.[5] With this little experiment completed, the story goes, Eliot prepared his speech to the NEA entitled "Shortening and Enriching the Grammar School Course."[6] In this speech, Eliot struck at the memorization of "facts which cannot be retained and which are of little value if retained,"[7] and argued vigorously for subjects of substance in the grammar school. He wanted arithmetic sharply cut and algebra and geometry added. He was in favor of eliminating much rote geography work and teaching physical geography along with natural history and political geography in a regular history offering. He would "dip down," in the phrase of the day, to introduce language instruction, optionally at least, at age ten. Bright children would be allowed to skip grades. Eliot clearly felt that the elementary school work of the day was dry, often useless, and even wasteful. His correspondent Adams agreed: "We chop our

3. C. W. Eliot, *Educational Reform* (New York, 1898), pp. 4–5.
4. C. W. Eliot to C. K. Adams, June 2, 1894, Eliot Papers, Harvard University.
5. W. D. Hyde, "President Eliot as an Educational Reformer," *Atlantic Monthly, 83* (1899), 355, and C. W. Eliot, "An Average Massachusetts Grammar School" in *Educational Reform*, 185–87.
6. NEA *Proceedings* (1892), 617–25. Also in Eliot, *Educational Reform*, 253–69.
7. C. W. Eliot, "Shortening and Enriching," p. 618.

mental pabulum up into little bits and feed it out in such a way that there is next to no development of the mind."[8] Eliot wanted to add new subjects while pruning and tightening up the old.

The speech caused a great furor. Frank Kasson of *Education* sniped that "President Eliot of Harvard University is 'at it again,' in his persistent attempt to discredit the American Common School."[9] More reasonable men such as George H. Martin[10] and William H. Maxwell[11] felt that Eliot was being a bit too severe, that he appeared to ignore the vast problems faced by the lower schools and their genuine efforts to improve themselves. But Nicholas Murray Butler put it succinctly and prophetically: Eliot was "a practical reformer. He is satisfied that the course of study is wrong. It must go. He will be on hand to diagnose and treat other diseases of the body scholastic when this one is out of the way."[12] Eliot's blunt proposals were child's play compared to the blast that J. M. Rice, a reporter for *Forum* magazine, loosed in a series of hostile articles published serially in 1893 and later as a book.[13] Eliot and Rice stirred up a storm because much of their criticism was entirely justified.

If the elementary school contributed to the gap by sending up to the secondary institutions scholars of poor quality, the laymen who controlled and supported the schools were equally responsible in determining the quality of the education their

8. C. K. Adams, "Impressions of the Report (of the Committee of Ten)," New York Regents *Bulletin, 28* (1894), 315.

9. F. H. Kasson, editorial in *Education, 12* (1892), 372.

10. G. H. Martin, speech to Massachusetts Schoolmasters' Club, reprinted in *Journal of Education, 35* (1892), 149.

11. W. H. Maxwell, "The Grammar School Curriculum," *Educational Review, 3* (1892), 472.

12. N. M. Butler, editorial in *Educational Review, 3* (1892), 308–09.

13. J. M. Rice, *The Public-School System of the United States* (New York, 1893). In connection with Rice see L. A. Cremin, "The Progressive Movement in Education: A Perspective," *Harvard Educational Review, 37* (1957–58), 251, more recently published as chapter 1 of Cremin's *The Transformation of the School* (New York, 1961); also O. Handlin, "Rejoinder to the Critics of John Dewey," *New York Times Magazine, 46* (May 15, 1958).

children received. The overwhelming majority of American schools were directed by school boards or boards of trustees made up of citizens who were in no way professional educators. Their influence on education in America has been and still is immense.

State legislatures had called for the establishment of secondary schools for many years. The Connecticut law of 1798 was quite specific. Schools of "a higher order" were to be set up,

> the object of which shall be to perfect the Youth admitted therein in Reading and Penmanship, to instruct them in the Rudiments of English Grammar, in Composition, in Arithmetic and Geography, or, on particular desire, in the Latin and Greek Languages, also in the Morality, and in general to form them for usefulness and happiness in the various relations of social life. . . . No Pupil shall be admitted into the said school except such as have passed through the ordinary course of instruction in the common Schools and shall have attained to such maturity in years and understanding, as to be capable of improvement in said school.[14]

There was, of course, a difference between passing a law and putting its requests into practice. At the time the Committee of Ten was deliberating, only Massachusetts required that towns either operate high schools or provide children with the means of attending one at a neighboring city. Few states had laws providing aid to secondary education, the majority being silent on the subject.[15] States varied widely in their provisions for education. Tennessee, like some others, felt obliged to specify what was meant by "secondary education," passing in 1891 a law that defined secondary schools as the sixth, seventh, and eighth

14. *Acts and Laws*, State of Connecticut, 1798. Quoted in S. Hertzler, *The Rise of the Public High School in Connecticut* (Baltimore, 1930), p. 226.

15. J. E. Canfield, "The Opportunities of the Rural Population for Higher Education," NEA *Proceedings* (1889), pp. 370 ff.

grades of a graded common school.[16] Other states were far more energetic. Indiana organized a State Board of Education consisting of the Governor, the State Superintendent of Public Instruction, the Presidents of the University of Indiana, Purdue, and the state normal school, all ex officio, and three citizens appointed by the governor. This group inspected all schools, and the institutions it "recommended" were allowed to admit their pupils to the State University on the presentation of a certificate attesting to honorable graduation. A system of accreditation of this sort, seen first at the University of Michigan prior to the Civil War, was adopted by many mid-Western states after the War and by Indiana in 1871. Indiana's Boards of Education set particular standards for their school inspections. High school work consisted of at least thirty months of study following the eighth grade of the common school. At least two teachers in each school—most high schools occupied the same buildings as common schools—had to be employed full time at teaching the higher subjects. A course of study was recommended by the Board; this, or its equivalent, had to be adhered to.[17] The pattern of state inspection was followed in several other states, often with members of the state university staffs making the visits.

Minnesota, in 1881, tried a similar but more elaborate scheme. The law passed in that year provided for an annual grant of $1,000 to all "state high schools." An institution could achieve such status and collect the money if it had "regular and orderly courses of study, embracing all the branches prescribed as requisite for admission to the collegiate department of the university."[18] The schools had to be coeducational and were to be inspected regularly by the Minnesota High School Board, which consisted of the Superintendent of Public Instruction, the President of the University, and a city school superintend-

16. *Annual Report of the Superintendent of Public Instruction for Tennessee* (1906), p. 103.
17. E. E. Brown, *The Making of Our Middle Schools* (rev. ed. New York, 1905), pp. 378–79.
18. Quoted without citation by R. G. Boone, *Education in the United States* (New York, 1889), p. 346.

ent. Provision was also made for the administering of state examinations.[19] President Eliot thought very highly of this scheme, calling it the best method of inducing common high standards employed by any state.[20]

Wisconsin laws also allowed for state subsidies to be granted to schools contingent on their passing state inspections. The Superintendent of Public Instruction in his annual report for 1894 shows how conformity was achieved through the power of the dollar:

> In some communities there is a desire to make [free high schools] commercial colleges, manual training schools, or otherwise warp them from their legitimate sphere. Too often this effort comes from the desire of the principal to "popularize" his school. It has sometimes been necessary to notify the authorities that the state has made no appropriation of public money for such purposes. A more common evil is the attempt of inexperienced teachers to expand the courses of study and to ride their hobbies. They seem to forget that the state does not purpose to support two hundred little colleges or universities. It is for this reason that it has required the state superintendent to prepare courses of study for them and made his approval a prerequisite to the apportionment of money.[21]

This same superintendent, in fact, withheld funds even if local school outhouses were not up to standard.

New York had a system that also drew praise from President Eliot. The University of the State of New York had five departments, one of them for high schools and academies. The state Regents, as they were called, administered examinations at the end of the secondary school course in an attempt to enforce, or

19. Brown, *The Making of Our Middle Schools*, p. 366.
20. Eliot, "The Gap between the Elementary Schools and the Colleges," p. 526.
21. *Biennial Report of the State Superintendent of the State of Wisconsin* (1894), p. 51.

at least encourage, uniform standards. Eliot, however, felt these exams were unfair and the examiners of poor quality.[22]

From these examples, several conclusions can be drawn. First, lay political groups were active in school matters, affecting standards by passing laws specifying certain curricula or certain inspection schemes. As a result, a school inspection system had been organized in several states; with only one or two notable exceptions, however, compulsion was lacking. In the state of New York, for example, parts of New York City were without any literary high school whatsoever. However, where the state boards had power, it was wielded to draw the schools into conformity with the curriculum desired for entrance to the state university. A Minnesotan put it clearly: "Where State boards exist, the tendency is to make the school a feeder to the university, and [the school's] curriculum correspondingly changed. When there is no such superior authority, public sentiment demands shorter courses; and the school becomes, as it were, a high grammar school."[23]

Local sentiment also exerted a significant influence on schools and teachers; it had in fact been responsible for the very founding of most early academies and, later, high schools. Its power over schools—in contrast with English parish authority and French and German state authority—was concentrated in town and city politics. Schools had to react to the wishes of their clientele, rather than to those of some central body of professionals or government bureaucrats. As a result, schools took on characteristics reflecting local fads. "The character of the public schools, therefore, and, in particular, of the public High School, registers quite well the degree of culture of each local community. In each case the opinions of the school board determine the course of study for the school. Teachers have nominally no power in the matter."[24] Then, as now, the pressure of

22. Eliot, "The Gap between the Elementary Schools and the Colleges," p. 526.

23. R. E. Denfield, "Discipline in High School," NEA *Proceedings* (1892), pp. 341–42.

24. R. G. Huling, "The American High School," *Educational Review*, 2 (1891), 52–53.

local opinion reflects both the strength and the weakness of the democratic process: the strength in achieving popular goals, the weakness inherent in popular support of poor causes.

Local politics affected school standards, for, if the school boards were used as political pawns, then the best interests of the children and teachers were usually overlooked. An article published by the *Atlantic Monthly* in 1898 entitled "The Confessions of Three School Superintendents," is revealing.[25] The three authors profess satisfaction with their school boards, except in the appointment of teachers—which was, of course, the most important job the boards performed. One of the superintendents reported that the local boards felt teaching was "a dignified calling for anybody in indigent circumstances who is unable to do any other work."[26] A teacher's post was a good spot for a poor local lass or for a man temporarily out of work. It was also a place for political payoffs. The effect of this system on the quality of instruction in the schools can well be imagined.

The three superintendents' recommendations for improvement imply difficulties the authors did not explicitly outline. They wanted boards to be smaller and not based on ward representation: large groups representing different areas of a locality were unwieldy and difficult to satisfy. The business and educational departments of the school system were to be separated, for obvious reasons. The curriculum was to be in the hands of the superintendent, not under the jurisdiction of an ignorant "Committee in the Course of Study" that might pad departments to open up new jobs and add courses irresponsibly under the pressure of public whim. The superintendent should be given more power in all spheres, a not unexpected recommendation. The school budget was to be handled as an account separate from other civic departments, as teachers deserved to be placed on a different level from police, firemen, and other workers. Finally, school board members were to be prohibited by law from holding any other public office for at least two or

25. *Atlantic Monthly, 82* (1898), 644–53.
26. "Confessions," p. 647.

three years after retirement. This was to prevent politicians from using the schools as a rung, a first step for personal attention on the way up the ladder; climbing politicians considered a post on the school board as the first office to win, and what real interest would such officials have in educational standards? The condition of municipal government was poor indeed in the '90s, and the educational departments, particularly in the cities, were not immune from the disease of corruption.

The curriculum was the area most affected by outside pressures. State laws, written, argued, and voted on by laymen, often defined the secondary school course of study (a notable example was the 1789 Connecticut statute quoted above). Most often, state boards of education "recommended" syllabi that were generally in the pattern of those used by Indiana and Wisconsin. Sometimes—in Iowa, for example[27]—schools, colleges, and state officials agreed on a syllabus together. Sometimes states prescribed the course of study by legislating what was not acceptable: Washington Territory would not "recognize"—for financial aid—schools "in which languages other than English and mathematics higher than algebra are taught."[28] This area, along with parts of the South, appeared to support the common school, anticlassical extreme of the curricular dilemma.

State legislatures could and did require the introduction of specific courses. The most significant of these was "scientific temperance." The prohibition movement that was to culminate in the ratification of the Eighteenth Amendment had its noisy beginnings in the nineteenth century, and one area its enthusiasts assaulted was the schools. Their efforts resulted in laws like those passed in Michigan in 1883 requiring the teaching of "physiology and hygiene, with special reference to the effects of alcoholic drinks, stimulants, and narcotics generally, upon the human system."[29] By 1904 it was the only course required by

27. C. R. Aurner, *History of Education in Iowa* (Iowa City, 1920), *3*, 225.
28. Canfield, "The Opportunities of the Rural Population," p. 383.
29. D. Putnam, *The Development of Primary and Secondary Education in Michigan* (Ann Arbor, 1904), p. 171.

high schools of that state. Often more general requirements to teach "morality" were specified, as in North Dakota.[30]

Most states delegated responsibility for the schools to the local communities, which affected the curriculum adopted. Iowa's law of 1857 is an example. Communities of 600 or more inhabitants were to elect a board of six citizens whose job it would be to determine the course of study. A majority vote would decide all matters except introduction of any language other than English, when a two-thirds majority would be required.[31] Needless to say, such a provision cast its bias on the local lawmakers.

Clearly, then, the course of study the Committee of Ten had been charged to reform was controlled to a considerable extent by laymen at various governmental levels.[32] The standards Eliot and his colleagues hoped to set had to meet the approval not only of teachers but of the elected political representatives of the people.

The third obvious aspect of the gap between elementary schools and colleges was finance. Poorly paid teachers and shoddy buildings and equipment could lead at best to mediocrity. As might be expected, financial support of the schools varied greatly from community to community across the country. In general, children in city schools received better attention than those in the country: the average daily expenditure per child in 1894 was 15 cents in the cities and 11 cents in rural areas. The West spent most per child—23 cents a day, and the South the least—about 10 cents. Southern states depended more on state aid than those in other sections of the country: local taxes contributed only 16.4 per cent of the school income in Tennessee, 12.5 per cent in Texas, and 1.7 per cent in North

30. *Third Biennial Report of the Superintendent of Public Instruction* (of North Dakota) (1894), pp. 26–27.
31. Aurner, *History of Education in Iowa, 3,* 176–77.
32. The federal government was even urged to support curricular changes in the schools. An Illinois congressman introduced a bill to provide $250,000 to set up spelling schools around the country—under the direction of an Illinoisan. The bill met defeat. *Journal of Education, 35* (1892), 56.

Carolina. Wyoming, on the other hand, raised all its money from local sources, Ohio raised 76.4 per cent, and Massachusetts 98.1 per cent. Southern communities, still suffering from war damage and poor agriculture, had to depend on moneys the state raised by general taxation; the more stable Far West and East could afford local support. Nationally, school income was drawn 67.8 per cent from local taxes, 18.7 per cent from the state, 5.6 per cent from permanent funds and rents, and 7.9 per cent from other sources.[33] Some states like California still refused to grant any aid at all to secondary schools, but these were few.[34]

Thus, while the disparity among different parts of the country was not as high as might be expected, there was enough variation to affect standards. City schools offered more to children than rural schools; the South, wracked with severe economic and political problems, could give its children less than the affluent, more densely populated Northeast.[35] The Committee of Ten was asked to supply a national standard. Could a norm be applied to all sections of the country in the face of the obvious inability of some areas to support schooling on the same scale as others?

Public secondary education in the South was virtually non-existent; the only schools that did exist were essentially private, no matter what they called themselves.[36] A historian summarizing the situation in 1900 painted a black picture. Secondary education drew little public interest or support; state laws were

33. F. W. Hewes, "The Public Schools of the United States," *Harpers Weekly, 39* (1895), 1068–69.

34. *Biennial Report of the Superintendent of Public Instruction* (of California) (1895–96), p. 8.

35. Private philanthropy helped to correct the disparity. The Peabody Fund provided $3,000,000 for the aid of those Southern schools which could meet certain minimal standards. The Slater Fund added another $1,000,000. After the turn of the century even larger grants were made, for example Russell Sage, $10,000,000, and the General Education Board, $46,000,000. See E. C. Moore, *Fifty Years of American Education* (Boston, 1917), pp. 85–88.

36. J. H. Canfield, "The Opportunities of the Rural Population for Higher Education," NEA *Proceedings* (1889), pp. 378 ff.

silent on the subject of high schools; no common standards existed and the curriculum was wholly ad hoc; the only real work being done at all was in the private academies and a few city high schools. To cap the scene, the author was thoroughly dubious about the standards at any of these institutions.[37] The existing schools for the Committee of Ten to consider were primarily Northern and Eastern; but the Committee could not avoid the compelling problem in the South, the problem of the very existence of secondary education at all.

In describing this chaotic situation, one must make several important distinctions. First, there were marked differences between urban and rural schools. Second, there were disparities in the standards and aims of private and public institutions. Finally the colleges themselves, in maintaining so-called preparatory departments, competed with other forms of secondary schools, thus influencing the quality of the latter.

The urban-rural comparison is a complex one, and the problems presented by the differences between city and country schools occurred in all parts of the United States. Using government census reports, one author in 1895 concluded that about one-third of Americans could be classed as city dwellers. This fraction varied widely by geographical area. The North Atlantic states were 55 per cent urban, the North Central 30 per cent, the West 35 per cent, and the South about 15 per cent.[38] It is no surprise to find the secondary schools concentrated in the urban states, where a demand was felt for them and where there was sufficient wealth to support them.

New York City, the largest metropolis in the country, stands out as an exceptional case. Manhattan and the Bronx had no high school at all before and during the years of the Committee of Ten's activity, unless one counted the City College and the Normal College. Pressure for a city high school intensified until, in 1897, the first high school was opened. By 1902, five years

37. W. C. Ryan et al., *Secondary Education in the South* (Chapel Hill, 1946), p. 115.
38. Hewes, "The Public Schools of the United States," p. 1141.

later, almost 10,000 students were enrolled.[39] This kind of public demand—though belated—was in marked contrast to that in the rural South.

Urban high schools tended to be large, with graded classes and teachers organized into academic departments. State governments in densely populated states were often active, and some uniformity of curriculum was achieved.[40] The situation in rural areas, a wholly different one, was described in a report to the National Council of Education in 1889 by James H. Canfield. Canfield's conclusions are blunt and unequivocal:

I. The State systems are still very generally partial and chaotic.

II. For all secondary education, the mass of the rural population is generally dependent upon chance, or the favor of some city.

III. With few exceptions no opportunities or inducements worthy of the name in the way of secondary or higher education are offered the rural population.

IV. Where efforts in the way of systematic secondary education have been reported as made, outside of cities and towns, but are not and cannot be considered as even fairly successful, it is because—

1. They are too limited as to territory, population, and resources; or,

2. The organization is not sufficiently close and complete—there being too much irregularity in the work of the lower schools; or,

3. The people of the rural districts have no voice in the management or control of such schools, and hence indifference takes place of interest.[41]

Whether or not schools were graded was a fact of considerable importance, for the academic standards of the ungraded

39. Brown, *The Making of Our Middle Schools*, pp. 407–08.
40. See, for example, the uniformity achieved in Rhode Island, W. T. Peck, "The High School and High School Programs," in *Twenty-Fourth Annual Report of the Rhode Island State Board of Education* (1894).
41. Canfield, "The Opportunities of the Rural Population," p. 387.

institution are open to question. A single teacher in such a school taught children of diverse ages and varying academic achievement. The pedagogical problem of coordinating different subjects in a single classroom is a complex one and probably overwhelmed most teachers, ill trained as they were. Even if this difficulty was overcome, there remained the problem of the teacher's academic excellence. He had to be classicist, mathematician, historian, economist—all at the same time. Clearly only a genius could successfully conduct an ungraded secondary school or a common school with a few pupils on a secondary level. The city school, large enough to allow for grading and for the division of labor among teachers by academic competence, had a clear-cut advantage. However the ungraded school was not only more common,[42] but also died hard: no less an authority than Commissioner Harris believed in it.[43] Even he, though, when pressed by his opponents, agreed that departmental and graded teaching was superior for secondary school subjects. What concerned the Committee of Ten was the fact that most rural schools were ungraded, including those which professed to teach secondary school subjects. Statistics are available for Illinois: in 1890 49 per cent of all the children in school were in ungraded situations, taught by 64 per cent of the teachers.[44] If the Committee of Ten was to raise secondary school standards, it had to come to grips with this situation.

All this is not to say that efforts were not being made to extend secondary education into rural areas. Local country groups struggled to found their own schools. Some states, particularly those in the North Central area, gave state aid to local ventures. Others attempted to found country high schools with state assistance. The cities helped by allowing country pupils to at-

42. No statistics are available to show what percentage of the schools reported to the Commissioner of Education as "secondary" were ungraded; statistics are available only for all schools.

43. W. T. Harris to N. M. Butler, September 6, 1895, Butler Papers, Columbia University. The ungraded primary school, if not the one-room schoolhouse, is returning into vogue in our own day.

44. H. Raab, "The Rural School Problem," NEA *Proceedings* (1892), p. 572.

tend their schools—for a fee—and the growing railroad system made commuting a possibility for those who could afford it. Colleges provided preparatory departments furnishing resident students with a secondary education.

None of these ventures, however, was really successful. The private academies, started by local initiative, died out for a variety of reasons, mostly economic. State aid to public schools was often inadequate, and the county high school plan tried in Kansas was a failure. The 1886 law there had led to the opening of only three institutions.[45] The city high schools were costly to attend; moreover, some felt that they brought the clean-living farm youth into contact with bad city influences.[46] The "prep departments" of colleges and universities enrolled few.

Conservatism was a further factor accounting for the lack of rural secondary schools. "The country school has done little or nothing to adapt itself to the changed conditions of our life," wrote one Westerner.[47] The farmer clung hard to his traditions, which, in schooling, called for the rudiments and little beyond. The demands of the industrialized city dweller appeared a little farfetched to country folk.

The two most discussed school problems of the '90s were rural education, both elementary and secondary, and moral education. The NEA spent numerous hours on both subjects, and solutions of a wide variety were offered. The standard of secondary education in America depended on how well they were solved.

A distinction as important as that between urban and rural schools was that between public and private institutions. President Eliot insisted time and again, in his speeches and correspondence during this period, on treating private and public schools separately. His reason for so doing stemmed from the fact that America, like England, had a dual system of schools,

45. *Ninth Biennial Report of the Department of Public Instruction* (of Kansas) (1893–94), p. 61.
46. E. E. White, in discussion of the Canfield Report, NEA *Proceedings* (1889), p. 393.
47. Cubberley, *Changing Conceptions of Education*, p. 41.

and in 1892 each part of the system, public and private, had distinct characteristics. However, as any viewer of Commissioner Harris's *Reports* could see, these characteristics were becoming blurred, and the public secondary school was rapidly outstripping the private—at least in terms of numbers.

In 1894 Harris listed 3,964 public high schools and 1,982 private institutions. Geographical areas differed markedly: North Central states reported 2,043 public secondary schools and only 354 private, Southern states showed 683 public and 841 private. Public schools were predominant in the Northeast, but not in the West.[48]

Eastern private schools, however, had importance out of proportion to their numbers in that they provided a large percentage of the entrants to the most respected private colleges. Harvard's statistics are illuminating, both on this fact and on others. In 1871, of 203 entrants, 70 came from public schools, 86 from private and endowed schools, and 39 from studies with private tutors. In 1894, of 470 entrants, 126 came from public schools, 220 from private and endowed institutions, and 34 from tutors. Less than a third of Harvard men came from public schools, and their percentage was decreasing.[49] In 1893, 64 per cent of Wesleyan's entrants came from nonpublic sources; the University of Pennsylvania in 1895 admitted 72 per cent from private schools; Columbia in 1897 admitted 83 per cent from private schools. The Midwest and West, of course, were in marked contrast to this pattern, with over three-quarters of the students trained either in state university preparatory departments or in public high schools. The South, as might be expected, trained the fewest in public institutions.[50] Commissioner Harris reported national figures in 1894: 40.9 per cent of freshmen had come from public high schools, 39.9 per cent

48. *Report of the Commissioner of Education* (1893–94), p. 86.
49. *Annual Reports of the President and Treasurer of Harvard College* (1894–95), 2, 263–70. One should note that the Massachusetts Latin schools provided the overwhelming number of 1871 entrants, while the 1894 freshmen came from a significantly larger number of public high schools.
50. W. A. Wetzel, "Growth of High Schools, 1891–1900," *Educational Review, 24* (1902), 521, 524.

from college preparatory departments, and the rest from private schools.[51]

While privately operated institutions varied enormously, those with most prestige centered on the college preparatory task. President Jesse, a Midwesterner, asserted that "the chief aim of the private secondary school is to get students ready for college, its subordinate aim to fit them for life." He went on significantly: "In the public high school the chief aim is to fit students for life and preparation for college is subordinate."[52] This distinction between "prep" schools and high schools is one that Eliot had in mind.

Private schools were increasing. The Episcopalians, for example, were very active in the East, and James Mackenzie of Presbyterian Lawrenceville remarked that "in increasingly large numbers everywhere, save in New England, our more prosperous citizens have been sending their children not to the public schools, but to schools and academies essentially private."[53] Many of the schools Mackenzie referred to were the new boarding schools which got their students from the newly wealthy, a clientele that wanted its sons and daughters to be polished in the East and then sent to one of the long-established colleges. President Eliot also testified to the growing importance of the private schools, claiming that the "increased heterogeneity of the population" spurred parents to avoid public schools that were forced to admit everyone indiscriminately. Private schools trained their charges better, he maintained,

51. *Report of the Commissioner of Education* (1893–94), 106.
52. R. H. Jesse, "What Constitutes a College and What a Secondary School?" *Proceedings* of the North Central Association of Colleges and Secondary Schools (1896), p. 25.
53. J. C. Mackenzie, "Supervision of Private Schools by State or Municipal Authorities," NEA *Proceedings* (1893), p. 183. Mackenzie, one of the Committee of Ten, gained considerable notoriety in certain circles by making the suggestion, in the address quoted above, that, since private schools were increasingly numerous, they should be subject to state supervision. He compared the private school teacher to the harbor pilot: each should be under the check of the public, as the service each performed was vital to public welfare. Needless to say, Mackenzie's plan found no fruition, but it caused a stir, his speech on the subject even appearing in the British press.

and responded to educational improvements more promptly than did public institutions.[54] One could still report that in those areas where public education was languishing, private ventures were continually started: "it is far within the truth to say that less than twenty per cent of the total enrollment of the private secondary schools come from towns that maintain a high school giving even passable preparation for college."[55]

All of this was true; more important, however, was the simple fact that the private schools were being dwarfed by a veritable explosion in the number of public secondary schools. The Bureau of Education statistics from 1870 to 1890, crude as they were, could at least demonstrate the trend of an increasing percentage of secondary school pupils attending public rather than private institutions. One historian puts 1888 as the year in which public secondary enrollment exceeded private for the first time,[56] and Eliot himself saw significance in the larger number of public high schools able and willing to send boys up to Harvard.[57] In 1890, 32 per cent of the secondary school pupils were in private schools, according to Bureau of Education statistics, but in 1900—although the independent schools were flourishing—this percentage had fallen to 18 per cent.[58] The Committee of Ten could not have been unaware of this tremendously important fact. While recognizing that the school population of 1892 represented only a small fraction of the age group entitled to secondary education, they also had to recognize that the schools were in the process of an enormous expansion. Seven per cent of the fourteen-to-seventeen-year-olds attended secondary school in 1890; by 1900, the percentage had risen to 11.4, and the increase was largely in public schools.[59]

54. C. W. Eliot to the Royal Commission on Secondary Education, August 7, 1894, Eliot Papers, Harvard University.

55. C. H. Douglas, "Status of the High School in New England," *Educational Review*, 5 (1893), 31.

56. Brown, *The Making of Our Middle Schools*, p. 400.

57. *Annual Reports of the President and Treasurer of Harvard College* (1894–95), p. 10.

58. *Report of the Commissioner of Education* (1904), p. 1729.

59. U.S. Commissioner of Education, *Biennial Survey of Education in the United States* (1950–52), *1*, table XIII.

If, as Eliot felt, there was a distinction in aim and method between public and private schools, those of the former would have to be considered as increasingly important ones in the eyes of the public.

Commissioner Harris, in reporting 408,000 secondary school students enrolled in 1892, chose to omit from this figure 52,552 students in college and university preparatory departments, 16,469 normal school enrollees, and 3,418 students at private manual training schools; if he had included them, the total secondary school enrollment would have reached 480,000.[60] Why he omitted them is not clear, for the manual training and normal school students were taking courses similar to those offered in many high schools; indeed, some normal schools were offering work at the standard of many colleges. Harris preferred to cite the preparatory department pupils under the figures for higher education, a policy that can be called, at best, confusing, for the children attending to their secondary studies on college campuses were clearly secondary school students. Furthermore, they were an important and influential group: they provided almost 40 per cent of the freshman body in American colleges in 1894.[61]

Colleges often had to found lower schools in order to supply themselves with students trained in the subjects they required. Boston Latin, Cambridge Latin, and Roxbury Latin Schools developed into Harvard prep schools early in American history. Colleges founded later had to find similar institutions: in the '80s Alice Freeman negotiated with various communities for "preparatory schools" leading to Wellesley College; Dana Hall School and eventually fifteen others resulted.[62]

Colleges in other less wealthy sections of the country could not do this. Either they had to become essentially secondary schools themselves, taking in boys and girls directly from the common schools, or they had to construct their own prepara-

---

60. *Report of the Commissioner of Education* (1893–94), pp. 92–94.
61. *Report of the Commissioner of Education* (1893–94), p. 106.
62. F. Converse, *Wellesley College 1875–1938* (Cambridge, 1939), p. 46.

tory departments. Michigan tried to develop prep schools in
various parts of the state, creating, in time, the state school system, but most institutions, particularly private ones,[63] started
secondary school courses on their own campuses. For example,
in 1867 Minnesota started a prep department before doing
anything else, and by 1869 enough pupils were ready to open
the college.[64] In 1889 James Canfield reported that "of nearly
four hundred institutions of higher learning in the United
States, only sixty-five have freed themselves from the embarrassment of a preparatory department."[65]

Canfield implied by the word "embarrassment" that the colleges might be ashamed of their lower-school appendages. He
had quizzed state university officials on the subject and received the following alarming replies, which he not surprisingly kept anonymous: "we maintain a preparatory department in order to keep up a show of numbers"; "we continue
our preparatory work, because a large number of those desiring to enter can have no other access to means of preparation."
Even more upsetting were these justifications: "Our university
still has a preparatory department, because it is more of a grammar school than a university"; "we have no preparatory department, because the freshman class is graded down to touch the
county district schools."[66] The colleges were maintaining these
departments—against their will—only because of the gap between the elementary school and the college.

Schoolmen disliked preparatory departments because, by
their very existence, they checked the growth of local secondary
schools. College men felt it undignified to have little children
around their universities. At the same time, the rowdy college
youths were a poor influence on youngsters; "many a young boy
comes fresh from the bosom of a pure family, with the mother's

63. Fully 47,000 of the 52,500 "prep department" pupils were in private
colleges. *Report of the Commissioner of Education* (1893–94), p. 94.

64. Moore, *Fifty Years of American Education*, p. 78.

65. Canfield, "The Opportunities of the Rural Population," p. 374. Canfield argued that few rural pupils gained admission to the preparatory departments.

66. Canfield, "The Opportunities of the Rural Population," p. 376.

kiss and benediction still aglow in his countenance, to be enticed into the ways of evil, and before the close of the session to be sent away a moral wreck."[67]

Such, then, were some of the dimensions of the gap that Eliot found in the American educational ladder: weak elementary schools underneath, political influence of an often injurious nature, and imbalanced and inadequate financing. The issue was further confused by the diversity between urban secondary schools and their rural counterparts, by the fact that private schools in some sections competed with public, and by the fact that in some parts of the country the colleges themselves, with their preparatory departments, undercut the development of the high schools. The pattern of secondary education was hardly systematic, and the few institutions that filled Eliot's gap in 1892 were in chaotic form.

67. J. W. Jackson, "The Demands of the High School for Severance from the College and the University," NEA *Proceedings* (1890), p. 631.

III · TEACHERS AND STUDENTS

To describe the extent of the chaos that characterized secondary education in the America of 1892, one must look at the classrooms themselves and at the teachers and students in them. Adequate classrooms were scarce, and the poorly trained instructors who labored there were expected to teach a wide variety of subjects. It is no surprise that standards were low. The students added to the confusion by attending school in ever-increasing numbers.

High schools were being built in large numbers in the early '90s; city, state, and federal school reports bulge with photographs and floor plans of the new fortress-like stone structures. Even so, it was impossible to keep up with the flood of students. Girls' High School in Boston, built for 925 students, housed 1,095 in 1895; Dorchester, Massachusetts, had nine teachers but only six classrooms—which meant that classes were conducted with two teachers in a room. Baltimore, Detroit, Minneapolis, and Buffalo were in similar situations.[1]

Most high schools (the private schools were a case apart) did not even have their own buildings. In 1893, of the fifty-nine high schools in Connecticut, only nine had their own buildings.[2] The state of Illinois, also a leader in education, could report little better: of 258 high schools, only thirty-eight had separate

1. J. H. Penniman, "The Criminal Crowding of Public Schools," *Forum*, *19* (1895), 289 ff.
2. *Report of the* (Connecticut) *Board of Education* (1892–94), pp. 132–33.

39

buildings.[3] This fact is of considerable importance. In one sense it testifies to the fact that high schools were the natural outgrowth of common schools: the two institutions still shared the same building. In another sense, it shows how impossible it must have been for principals to break away from the ways and habits of the elementary school in order to carry out satisfactory secondary programs. Strict, unthinking discipline was necessary. The teachers of secondary subjects were drawn from the lower grades and often continued along a course more suitable for eight-year-olds than teen-agers. The division of the staff into academic departments was unlikely. Facilities necessary for advanced work—libraries, laboratories, and so on—were often absent. The superintendent in Leominster, Massachusetts, a town in the wealthiest and educationally most progressive state, wrote to his school committee: "We feel that we have no alternative than to bring up again the need of different accommodations for the High School. It is in many ways a source of trouble to both schools, that a Grammar and High School should be in the same building"; he then listed all the difficulties he was experiencing.[4] Academic standards here were clearly diluted simply because of physical difficulties. Pawtucket, Rhode Island, a city in the most densely populated state, had its high school moved twice in one year; the superintendent could only report under the circumstances that "the high school has held its own."[5] If this was so in Leominster and Pawtucket, how did less fortunate areas fare?

The material demands on the schools were truly immense. As the students poured in, space became a primary requirement. The superintendents who should have been concerning themselves with their pupils' minds were forced to worry almost entirely about the roofs over the pupils' heads. Their published reports in the '90s reflect this imbalance. Indeed, extremes were

3. *Twenty-First Biennial Report of the Superintendent of Public Instruction* (of Illinois) (1894–96), p. 14.

4. *Annual Report of the* (Leominster) *Public Schools* (1894), p. 7.

5. *Twenty-Fifth Annual Report of the* (Rhode Island) *State Board of Education* (1895), p. 121.

reached: the poor condition of school outhouses became a major public concern. The *Pennsylvania School Journal* editorialized, "We are desirous of effecting some radical reform in the condition of *School Outhouses* in Pennsylvania. A large proportion of these houses are a disgrace to civilization, unspeakably abominable, moral plague-spots on the community."[6] Maine found its facilities "shocking,"[7] North Dakota, Tennessee, and Wisconsin all agreed, and efforts to improve the situation were promised in the *Reports* of the superintendents of these states. Tragicomical though this national concern over outhouses was, it did underscore one point: school authorities were swamped with work simply to preserve the status quo, without a chance of turning their attention seriously to innovations that the Committee of Ten or any other agency might offer. The improvement of academic standards would have to wait.

More important than buildings in their influence upon secondary school standards were the teachers themselves. It is difficult to measure the effectiveness of a teacher even through continual observation in his classroom; measuring his worth without this opportunity is even more difficult. However, one can look for indications of the standard of excellence of instructors by examining those who became teachers—what drew them to teaching, the training they received, and what their former pupils thought of them.

Salaries indicate something about the teaching force. If jobs are not plentiful and the pay for instructors is reasonably high, many men and women of high caliber will be drawn to the classrooms. Such a situation was seen in America in the 1870s and 1930s, during periods of economic depression. However, when educational salaries are low and other less strenuous and more favored vocations are beckoning to outstanding men and women, the ranks of teachers thin and their quality declines.

6. Editorial in *Pennsylvania School Journal, 42* (1894), 347. Italics in original.
7. *Maine School Report* (1895), 49.

Teacher salaries had been rising substantially since 1865. The average weekly salary in that year was $11.70; in 1890, it was $16.41. In real terms, however, this was even better; the postbellum period was one of deflation, and the teacher's dollar continually bought more goods. In buying power, one study shows the rise in the average salary from the 1865 level of $11.70 to $26.25 in 1890; that is, the 1890 salary of $16.41 would have purchased $26.25 of 1865 goods.[8] This improvement of financial position was recognized by the "Many Leading Educators": "The salaries paid teachers indicate somewhat the estimate placed upon their work by the public. For some years there has been a steady increase in salaries. Better qualifications have been brought to the work, and teaching, particularly in cities, has become a regular occupation. Teachers mingle freely in the best social circles and enjoy the respect of the community."[9]

The Educators' use of the word "somewhat" is significant, for teacher salaries, although rising, still left much to be desired. Rural and especially Southern areas offered salaries only one-quarter the amount of those in Massachusetts, for example. A journalist could ask, "it must be a rather poor average man (teacher) who would not find some opening which would pay him an average of more than $5.67 per week (the national average for teachers) and . . . a very poor offer of marriage that would not induce the average schoolma'am to quit a job which paid her an average of only $4.67 per week."[10] In competition with other fields in the '90s, teaching was a poorly paid profession. Because it was, one can safely surmise that fewer people of quality were willing to enter it.[11] To be sure, the

8. W. S. Elsbree, *Teacher in America* (New York, 1939), pp. 431–32. A far bleaker picture indeed is painted by C. B. Dyke, *The Economic Aspect of Teachers' Salaries* (New York, 1899).

9. "A Statement of the Theory of Education," (Washington, 1874), p. 19.

10. F. W. Hewes, "The Public Schools of the United States," *Harpers Weekly, 39* (1895), 1041.

11. In some rural areas the prestige of the teacher, however modest

brilliant and altruistic exception could be found,[12] but the average must have been discouraging.

The effect of politics on the teaching force has already been discussed. Favoritism and irresponsibility were common, undermining academic standards. At a time when textbook publishers were engaged in a ruthless fight for markets, one observer reported that "the acquisition and loss of positions by teachers and officers is often determined by their opinions of certain text-books."[13] While little evidence remains on how teachers were hired and fired, one can speculate both from the experience of the present day and from the state of municipal politics in the '90s that academic standards were often considered of little importance in selecting teachers.

Another striking aspect of the American teaching force was its feminization. The Leading Educators applauded this: "The female character, being trained by experience in family-supervision to the administration of special details wherein division of labor cannot prevail to any great extent, is eminently fitted to control and manage the education of the child while it is in a state of transition from caprice to rationally-regulated exercise of the will; and the development of individuality is generally more harmonious up to a certain age if the pupil is placed under female teachers." But the Educators' closing sentence tells the larger part of the story: "The comparatively small cost of female-labor, also, largely determines its employment in all public schools."[14] The influence of women on school standards was important. Teaching became a "woman's

---

his attainment might have been, was notably high, for the teacher was a symbol of learning and, thus, success. Mark Sullivan, certified a teacher at the age of 15, became in a small Pennsylvania town "an honored figure in that community, second only to the judge." M. Sullivan, *Education of an American* (New York, 1938), p. 94.

12. See the testimony of one of the Conference members of the Committee of Ten: J. H. Dillard, "School of the Past," *Sewanee Review, 29* (1921), 410 ff.

13. J. W. Jenks, "School-book Legislation," *Political Science Quarterly, 6* (1891), 91.

14. "A Statement of the Theory of Education," p. 19.

job" and men avoided it.[15] Women often tended to view teaching as a stopgap before marriage rather than as a career; the large turnover that resulted led inevitably to lower standards. Rabbi Solomon Schindler found the women even "dangerous," asserting that "the flaw in our educational system is *the overwhelming preponderance of women's influence in our public schools*," and predicting that it would lead to the dissolution of the public school system.[16]

Henry Seidel Canby commented on the questionable level of academic standards when he wrote of his teachers in a Baltimore Friends' school in the '90s: "They had knowledge but, not knowing what to do with it, passed it on to us in its raw condition of fact. They knew facts, but could neither relate nor coordinate them. They believed in their subjects with the absolute conviction of the baker that his bread is the staff of life, but there was no passion in their belief, and, to tell the truth, not much reason."[17]

Roughly half of the secondary school teachers held bachelor's degrees. A California educator, after sending questionnaires to seventy-nine city school systems across the country, found that 72 per cent of the men and 30 per cent of the women were college graduates; probably the majority of these were teaching in the high schools.[18] In New England, 56 per cent of the high school teachers were college graduates, and an additional 21 per cent had done at least some work beyond high or normal school.[19] But even assuming that the A.B. degree was an index

15. Of Massachusetts' teachers, 90 per cent were women, the highest percentage in the nation. In Alabama, where in a time of economic unrest teaching offered security, only 47 per cent of the teachers were women. Nationally, 66 per cent of the teachers were female. Hewes, "The Public Schools of the United States," p. 1017.

16. S. Schindler, "A Flaw in Our Public School System," *Arena, 6* (1892–93), 60. Italics in the original.

17. H. S. Canby, *The Age of Confidence* (New York, 1934), p. 105.

18. E. E. Cates, "Report of High School Principal," pamphlet submitted to the city superintendent, 1895.

19. C. H. Douglas, "Status of the High School in New England," *Educational Review, 5* (1893), 33.

of scholarly competence—a dubious assumption in the United States[20]—teachers, even in progressive and well-paid New England, were not noted for their college preparation. While asserting that a large percentage of the teachers were ill prepared, one must repeat that these teachers were asked to teach a wide variety of subjects. Missouri offers some examples. Henry King at Albany, Missouri, was responsible for teaching botany, zoology, Latin, general history, English, etymology, and arithmetic. W. J. Rowley at Bowling Green taught all the subjects offered, from Latin through psychology to zoology. Except in large city schools, where departments had been set up, the situation was the same.[21] Under such conditions, how could Messrs. King and Rowley and the majority of their colleagues meet high standards of competence, ill trained and overscheduled as they were?

In order to cover their obvious weaknesses, these teachers—significantly—relied on the textbook. W. T. Harris, who was optimistic enough to state that "the teachers in the secondary schools are, on the whole, more skillful, so far as command of methods is concerned, than the teachers in the elementary schools or the professors in colleges,"[22] could still assert that textbooks were a "distinctively American feature of instruction." Harris agreed that Europeans were justified in accusing Americans of "doing little in our schools except causing the pupil to memorize (or 'cram') the text of the printed page."[23] Most teachers had no other recourse: there was probably no greater boon to teachers than the spate of free textbook laws

20. One is reminded of Sinclair Lewis' fictional Terwillinger College, "one of ten denominational colleges (in eastern Kansas), all of them with buildings and presidents and chapel services and yells and colors and a standard of scholarship equal to the best high-schools." *Elmer Gantry* (new ed. New York, 1960), p. 8.

21. *Forty-Sixth Report of the Public Schools of the State of Missouri* (1895), p. 163.

22. W. T. Harris, "The Curriculum for Secondary Schools," NEA *Proceedings* (1894), p. 500.

23. W. T. Harris, "Education in the United States," in N. S. Shaler, *The United States of America* (New York, 1894), 2, 340.

45

passed in the early '90s.[24] However rote teaching had grave deficiencies, which the Committee of Ten had to take into consideration and try to remedy. The reformer Rice wanted to do just that. Asked to speak before the Elementary Department of the NEA in 1895, he pointedly titled his address, "Substitution of the Teacher for the Text-book."

Other pedagogical devices were available to teachers, offered by such thinkers as Pestalozzi and Herbart and propagandized by their disciples in the NEA, in teacher institutes, and elsewhere; but there is little evidence that the average, overworked teacher could or did pay them much heed. "Not one teacher in a hundred has any call to vex himself over the psychology of Herbart or to pretend to be profoundly interested in the experiments on the nerve-system of frogs," reported Samuel Thurber of the Boston Girls' High School faculty; "we teachers have no vitality to spare."[25] James Baker found American teachers' ignorance of psychology a "disgrace."[26] This is not surprising. One need only look closely at the teaching methods of instructors sixty years after the publication of John Dewey's *School and Society* to realize that, though the titles, aims, and jargon of courses often change, the pedagogy of the teachers themselves shows little development. The doctrines of Herbart found currency among leading thinkers and in the best schools; but it is doubtful whether they penetrated into the small, average high school. The textbook and drill were the order of the day. In spite of all the talk of correlation and apperception, a historian could report that "the realm of the classroom in the 1890s was totally set off from the experience of the child who in-

24. Maine, Massachusetts, New Jersey, Pennsylvania, Nebraska, and Minnesota all had such laws, and legislation at least aiding parents to buy books was found in Iowa, Indiana, and California, among others. Where texts were scarce, even the Montgomery Ward catalogue served as a reader. See C. T. Whittenburg, "The Frontier Schoolma'am on Ranch and Homestead," *Educational Forum, 13* (1948), 78–89.

25. S. Thurber, "The Response of the Public School to the Demands of the Public," *Proceedings* of the American Institute of Instruction (1895), pp. 171–72.

26. J. H. Baker, "The High School as a Finishing School," NEA *Proceedings* (1890), p. 636.

habited it . . . learning consisted of the tedious memorization of data without a meaning immediately clear to the pupil."[27] Such learning could not produce students of high caliber.

In addition, the teacher was faced with large numbers of children. Of fifty-nine Connecticut high schools, thirty-three had staffs of one or at the most two men, who had to carry the whole curriculum.[28] Other states show a similar pattern; nationally, the Bureau of Education reported an average of only 3.1 teachers to each public high school and four teachers to each private secondary school.[29] Teacher-pupil ratios, however, were far more favorable for secondary school teachers than for elementary; each teacher in Boston's grammar schools had an average of fifty-two children,[30] but public high school teachers averaged only twenty-four and private secondary school masters only fifteen.[31] In spite of this, elementary school discipline appeared to have lasting effects. Eliot called this discipline a "semi-military machine";[32] it led one little girl, when asked why she went to school, to answer, "to sit in position."[33] Such strictness was hardly suitable to inspire adolescent minds. Canby described his school: "It was haphazard, makeshift, ill-ordered, yet regimented internally into a fairly efficient factory where pupils could march from study to assembly hall without much lost motion."[34]

A bleak picture of schooling indeed comes to light. Poorly trained and inexperienced, teachers instructed their secondary school students in an impossibly wide variety of subjects, aided

27. O. Handlin, *John Dewey's Challenge to Education* (New York, 1959), p. 42.
28. *Report of the* (Connecticut) *Board of Education* (1892–1894), pp. 132–33.
29. *Report of the Commissioner of Education* (1893–94), p. 85.
30. C. W. Hill, "What Can Be Done to Bring Pupils Further . . . ?" NEA *Proceedings* (1892), p. 652.
31. *Report of the Commissioner of Education* (1893–94), p. 85.
32. C. W. Eliot, "Undesirable and Desirable Uniformity in Schools," NEA *Proceedings* (1892), p. 88.
33. B. A. Dutton, "Discipline in Elementary Schools," NEA *Proceedings* (1889), p. 491. Similar findings were reached by H. A. Falk, *Corporal Punishment* (New York, 1941).
34. Canby, *The Age of Confidence*, p. 111.

by a pedagogy inherited from the elementary school and already under fire. High academic standards did not flourish under these conditions—a fact that the Committee of Ten well realized.

The variety, age, and aspirations of the children who attended the schools were also matters of concern to the Committee. The Commissioner of Education published a "Statistical Review of Secondary Education,"[35] for the years 1893–94, a detailed report that sheds some light on the situation across the country. He found 407,919 students in 5,946 schools instructed by 20,129 teachers. This represented, at best, only about seven per cent of the fourteen-to-seventeen-year-olds eligible for schooling; the overwhelming majority of American teen-agers were not in any kind of school at all.[36] This fact was of immense importance.

The Commissioner also broke down his enrollment figures by geographical area. Of approximately 408,000 students, 303,000 came from the North Atlantic and North Central states, the latter having over 165,000. The South could muster only about 83,000, the West but 21,000.[37] Unfortunately there is no accurate census according to age from which to compute the percentages of attendance for high school age pupils in each area, but one can safely generalize that the low figures of the South represented a paucity of schools, while the sparsely settled West was making a better effort.

A word should be said about the compulsory education laws. Few states required children to attend school after the age of fourteen; indeed, only twenty-eight of the forty-four states had laws at all, the Southern states not providing compulsion until the twentieth century. Connecticut, Minnesota, Ohio, and Wyoming went so far as to require attendance until the age of sixteen, but a commentator at the time had to confess that "the proportion of children of school age affected by [any of]

35. *Report of the Commissioner of Education* (1893–94), p. 33.
36. U.S. Commissioner of Education, *Biennial Survey of Education in the United States* (1950–52), *1*, table XIII. This percentage would rise rapidly. See below, p. 199.
37. *Report of the Commissioner of Education* (1893–94), 65, 74.

these laws is small. . . . Here and there through the country are isolated instances of enforcement, but for the most part, in more than a score of States, these laws have apparently not only failed to affect school attendance to any appreciable degree, but have tended by their very inefficiency to weaken the public school system itself in public confidence."[38]

Before leaving these various statistical studies, we should assess their accuracy. First of all, in making his graphs and tables, the Commissioner of Education had to decide what were secondary schools and what were not. His decisions were, of necessity, highly arbitrary. Tennessee's "grades VI to VIII," Boston's Latin School, and Indiana's extended common school were all lumped together, not to mention the admittedly wretched Negro high schools in the South, which a partisan in 1910 could still say "were sub-standard in every respect."[39] Even the most progressive states had secondary institutions that did not meet minimal standards. Frank A. Hill, Secretary of the Massachusetts Board of Education, admitted that "eleven of [Massachusetts'] high schools are not strictly high schools at all; they are grammar schools in which a few of the more advanced pupils take some high school subjects. They have been classed with high schools in deference to their humble but laudable beginnings."[40] Commissioner Harris tried hard to eliminate the borderline cases. These included, among others, schools called high schools but having no students taking high school subjects and common schools offering no more than one subject beyond the rudiments. At best he could eliminate only the extremely unqualified. But Harris' problem did not end there: to draw graphs he needed information, and information was often not available. When the Commissioner's aides made special efforts to gather secondary school data in 1893 they found an embarrassingly large group of new schools; Harris

38. W. B. Shaw, "Compulsory Education in the United States," *Educational Review, 4* (1893), 136–37, 140.

39. C. H. Ambler, *A History of Education in West Virginia* (Huntington, 1951), p. 409.

40. F. A. Hill, "The Report of the Committee of Ten," *Proceedings* of the American Institute of Instruction (1894), p. 177.

had to explain in the *Report* that the reason for the great leap forward from 4,246 schools in 1893 to 5,946 schools in 1894 was due to an improvement in data collection procedures.[41] For most of his information, Harris had to depend on the state superintendents, and their difficulties in collecting statistics were herculean. As a city superintendent in Baltimore wrote in 1895, "there are so many erroneous publications made with reference to the number of children of school age in our city that it would be desirable to have a correct census taken."[42] A Florida state superintendent reported on his attempts to elicit information from schools: "Some seemed to have regarded the request as another one of my numerous and unnecessary demands upon their time and attention, and did not treat the request with the courtesy of a reply."[43] Nicholas Murray Butler in *Educational Review* charged New Jersey with "padding" its returns, basing the accusation on the facts that the school census takers were paid on a per-capita-reported basis, districts reporting large enrollments would receive large state grants, and local pride demanded good school attendance.[44] While placing great store in statistics, Harris recognized the flaws in those collected by his Bureau, and particularly those of the period from 1871 to 1890. At best the Committee of Ten could expect only a rough estimate from the Commissioner's graphs; but even this was useful.[45]

Thus the children who attended American high schools in the '90s escape close categorization, as much of the information about them is lacking. However the reports from four-year es-

41. *Report of the Commissioner of Education* (1893–94), p. 33.
42. *Sixty-Seventh Annual Report, Board of Commissioners of Public Schools* (of Baltimore) (1895), p. xi.
43. *Biennial Report of the Superintendent of Public Instruction* (of Florida) (1894–96), p. 193.
44. N. M. Butler, editorial in *Educational Review, 4* (1892), 508.
45. See J. H. Blodgett, "Education in the Eleventh Census Year," *Educational Review, 2* (1892), 238 ff. Unfortunately, later Commissioners have not been as careful as Harris. Enrollments from 1869 to 1890—discredited by Harris in 1891—are still published with little qualification. While the figures as they are may show rough trends, they should be considered thoroughly suspect.

tablished city high schools yield some dependable data. The pupils' age is one factor of importance, as high standards depend somewhat on students' maturity. In Chicago high schools, for example, out of 6,189 secondary level pupils in 1894, 2,202 were seventeen or over. Only 212 students were under fourteen; it is clear, then, that the high school population in Chicago, at least, was a mature one, even by standards of a later day.[46] St. Louis reported a similar pattern: 73 per cent of its secondary school student body was between the ages of fifteen and eighteen; 5 per cent, interestingly enough, was over 20.[47] In the East, the average age of a Harvard freshman was almost nineteen.[48] While there were many exceptions, caused by such factors as adult evening schools and substandard secondary institutions, American high schools as a whole enrolled students no younger than their teens.

Another significant factor in the make-up of the secondary school student body is that girls markedly outnumbered boys. Commissioner Harris reported 176,988 boys and 230,000 girls as secondary students in 1894, and the imbalance was roughly consistent in all geographic sections and in both public and private schools.[49] Reports from certain localities give even more of an edge to the distaff side. Fully two-thirds of secondary students in Iowa in 1880 were girls.[50] New Bedford, Massachusetts, in 1891 reported a similar proportion, as did Cambridge High School in 1902.[51] For the Committee of Ten, however, the point was clear: over half the pupils in the secondary schools were female, in a country that provided little college education for girls or, indeed, any kind of intellectual career.

46. *Fortieth Annual Report of the* (Chicago) *Board of Education* (1894), pp. 204–05.
47. *Forty-First Annual Report of the . . . St. Louis Public Schools* (1895), p. 100.
48. *Annual Reports of the President and Treasurer of Harvard College* (1894–95), p. 271.
49. *Report of the Commissioner of Education* (1893–94), pp. 65, 74.
50. C. R. Aurner, *History of Education in Iowa* (Iowa City, 1920), *3*, 229.
51. R. G. Huling, "How English Is Taught in One High School," NEA *Proceedings* (1891), p. 632; R. G. Huling to C. W. Eliot, May 12, 1902. Eliot Papers, Harvard University.

It is difficult to generalize about the social status of the students. There were extremes, represented for instance by Phillips Andover and a country school in the West. One can say, however, that as far as city high school records show, American secondary schools were not maintained exclusively for the education of the rich. Wisconsin's superintendent could assert that "more than one-half of all the parents or guardians who have children in the high schools pay no tax or are assessed at less than one thousand dollars. The claim that these schools are maintained by the many for the benefit of a few rich cannot be maintained." He went on to report that the children of farmers were most numerous in the high schools, with those of "unclassified day laborers" next, and the offspring of "widowed mothers" fourth.[52] Superintendent Soldan of St. Louis made a similar study of the families of students in the normal and high schools under his charge. In 1894, although 524 out of 1,856 students were put in a hazy "unclassified" status, 264 of the total were children of merchants, 259 of clerks, 178 of mechanics, 37 of laborers, and 15 of seamstresses. These categories are vague, but one gains the impression that the schools had a broad clientele. Soldan in the same report referred to his high school as "the People's University"—an even more exalted title than that of the often mentioned People's College—and with certain justification, as the people of St. Louis were all represented, if not in due proportion.[53]

One large urban group not represented in the secondary schools appears to have been the new immigrants. Usually poor, and thus requiring the earnings of all family members irrespective of age, the immigrants often dodged even the compulsory elementary school laws. One reformer asserted that "in spite of the fact that Chicago is a city largely made up of foreign-born people, the school census of 1894 will show that

52. *Biennial Report of the State Superintendent of the State of Wisconsin* (1894), p. 50.

53. *Forty-First Annual Report of the . . . St. Louis Public Schools* (1895), pp. 101, 106. See also J. D. Philbrick, *City School Systems in the United States*, Bureau of Education, *Circular of Information* 1–1885 (Washington, 1885), 27.

nearly all the children now in the schools were born in this country."[54]

The standard of excellence reached by each individual student depended to a certain degree on the length of time he spent at school. The Commissioner of Education reported that the schools were open an average of 134.7 days in 1890 and that children actually attended them an average of 86.3 days.[55] Figures from other sources tend to support this, but show a regional variation. Students in the North Atlantic states attended school an average of 111 days, but in the South only about 61 days. Massachusetts school attendance topped the list—124.9 days—while North Carolina was at the bottom, with only 36 days.[56] The standard of instruction offered during the course of a year in the North clearly was superior to that in the South, at least in gross terms of time spent.

Important also was the fact that many students never completed a four-year course—if it was even offered. Chicago statistics reveal a sharp drop-out rate: in 1894 there were 2,699 ninth graders, 1,709 tenth graders, 1,050 eleventh graders, and 731 twelfth graders.[57] Huling's New Bedford High experienced the same situation; classes averaged 120 to 140 pupils on admission but only forty to fifty on graduation.[58] One can guess that economic pressures caused much of this dropping out, and the rate was considered serious enough to warrant close study by an NEA committee; the committee, in time, recommended a vigorous extension service to provide opportunities for day laborers.[59]

One way of categorizing students is to see how many were working in a college preparatory course. If schools were expected to lead to college, then the Committee of Ten might

54. A. P. Stevens, "Child Slavery in America," *Arena, 10* (1894–95), 129.

55. U.S. Commissioner of Education, *Biennial Survey of Education in the United States* (1952–54), *1, 20.*

56. Hewes, "The Public Schools of the United States," p. 1094.

57. *Fortieth Annual Report of the* (Chicago) *Board of Education* (1894), pp. 204–05.

58. Huling, "How English is Taught," p. 632.

59. See NEA *Proceedings* (1892), pp. 355–56. The night school extension course was, of course, not at all new to the American scene, and it would continue in popularity to the present day.

view their preparatory function as central; if they were expected to be terminal institutions, on the other hand, the Committee might emphasize another aspect of the curriculum. Commissioner Harris' 1894 statistics showed 14,988 college preparatory students graduating in the class of 1894, a class that totaled 48,479.[60] Further refinement of existing statistics shows the trend clearly: of the students in public high schools during 1893–94, 14.3 per cent were in college preparatory curricula. Only 12.9 per cent of the students graduated, but of these 26.7 per cent had been in college preparatory courses. The pattern is even more extreme in the private high schools and academies. There, slightly over one-quarter of the students were working in preparatory curricula. Only 9.4 per cent of the students graduated, but of these over half were trained in college preparatory classes.[61] Thus, while less than one-quarter of the students in American high schools were studying in college preparatory curricula, they tended to drop out less frequently than did pupils working in other programs. Viewed in this light, college prep work gains relative importance. At the same time, one must remain aware that in both public and private secondary institutions the majority of pupils were not concentrating on college preparation.

A close study of the American secondary school body by the Committee of Ten, then, should have brought home several hard facts. First of all, only a small fraction of the eligible population was in school at all. Every social class, though not in proportion to its number, was using the high schools. Most students neither planned nor studied to go to college, and a majority left before reaching the twelfth grade. And girls, who could expect only a limited career, outnumbered boys in school. Implicit in Harris' statistics was the promise of even greater secondary school enrollments, with an obviously altered student body. As a larger percentage of the eligible age group started attending the schools, some change would be necessary in order to meet their particular requirements.

60. *Report of the Commissioner of Education* (1893–94), *1*, 66, 75.
61. *Report of the Commissioner of Education* (1893–94), *1*, 70, 79, 86.

IV · THE CURRICULUM

To describe the "gap" that Eliot had so clearly seen, one must finally examine the curriculum. It was the specific function of the Committee of Ten to bring about reforms in this area and to examine college entrance requirements, as requested by the National Council.

The issue of the relationship between school and college had received considerable airing in the National Council of Education of the NEA during the 1880s, there being no less than six committee reports on some aspect of the subject. A report on "Harmonizing of Higher, Secondary, and Elementary Schools" was received in 1882, two reports on college admissions in 1884, a report on "The Relation of High Schools to Colleges" in 1887, and the James H. Baker committee report on requirements for admission to college in 1891. The standing committee on secondary education of the NCE had presented a total of eight reports to the Council, four of which dealt with the relation between colleges and secondary schools. Thus, the issue of college entrance requirements was not new, for either the NEA or the members of the Committee of Ten.

The reason for this emphasis on admission requirements was that these requirements significantly affected secondary school curricula. If children wished to enter a college, they had to complete a specified course of study; the schools they attended were called upon to supply it to the letter. The effect of these detailed requirements can be gathered from the tenor of an editorial by Professor Butler in *Educational Review:* "How tyrannical and how petty some college entrance examinations are, the general public does not know. There are colleges, not all of them so very far from New York, in which conditions at entrance are actually imposed on minor subdivisions of a prescribed subject: for example, on one book or a part of a book in geometry, on a single process or rule in arithmetic. . . . This is an almost inspired method of encouraging cramming on the part of the student, and routine, mechanical teaching on the part of the secondary school."[1] Mackenzie of the Committee of Ten was even more vigorous: "The utter chaos into which college entrance requirements have fallen—the revealed idiosyncrasies of the college faculties often ruthlessly enforced upon long-suffering, protesting schoolmasters—is a railing reflection upon the intelligence, good sense and fair play of the American people."[2] Butler and Mackenzie could agree on two important points: that the college admission requirements of the early '90s were poor, and that they directly affected the secondary schools. William C. Collar, headmaster of the Roxbury Latin School, spelled out the extent of this effect on preparatory schools. When Harvard started to require sight translation in Greek on entrance examinations, Collar reported, his students had to study twice as long as before to prepare themselves. Previously they had only to disgorge, in English, part of a passage announced by the college one year prior to testing, a task requiring far less effort than sight translation. Collar asserted as well that Harvard had greatly affected secondary school physics and geometry teaching.[3] Other college preparatory high schools exhibited their dependence in their catalogues; Worcester Classical High School announced that "the course of study . . . is subject to slight modifications. The work is practically determined by college requirements,"[4] and Cambridge Latin School said that "the course of study is almost wholly decided by re-

1. N. M. Butler, editorial in *Educational Review, 3* (1892), 513.

2. J. C. Mackenzie, "The Report of the Committee of Ten," *School Review, 2* (1894), 148.

3. W. C. Collar, "The Action of the Colleges upon the Schools," *Educational Review, 2* (1891), 439; see also editorial, *Educational Review, 2* (1892), 414.

4. *Report of the Worcester Schools* (1895), p. 18.

quirements for admission to Harvard College."[5] Midwestern high schools that depended on the university for accreditation tended to adhere to a university approved syllabus. Only in those areas where the colleges were weak, in either numbers or standards or both, did the high schools go their own way in determining the course of study. At the very least, college entrance requirements affected American secondary schools way out of proportion to the number of students who were college bound.

Entrance requirements varied widely by institution. Yale in 1892–93 required work in Latin, Greek, ancient history, mathematics, and a modern language. The areas to be covered in each field were specified: "Caesar—Gallic War, books i–iv . . . Roman History, to the death of Augustus . . . Xenophon—Anabasis, four books . . . Greek Grammar . . . Algebra—so much as is included in Loomis's Treatise, up to the chapter on Logarithms."[6] The University of Michigan in the same year considered candidates for the A.B. degree who were either graduates of a university approved secondary school or who passed an examination in English, history, mathematics, physics, botany, Latin, and Greek. Like Yale, Michigan specified the areas within each subject to be covered: "Physics.—An amount represented by Carhart and Chute's Elements of Physics."[7] Harvard made it possible for a boy to enter for work toward the A.B. without offering Greek, although its entrance requirements were both broad and deep. A candidate had to pass exams in eight "elementary studies"—English, Greek, Latin, grammar, French, history, mathematics, and physical science— and two "advanced studies," chosen from Greek, Latin, Greek and Latin composition, German, French, two areas of mathematics, and two areas of physical science. With three advanced examinations, a candidate could have his elementary German or French waived; with four, two in math and science, he could have his elementary Latin or Greek waived. Five advanced

5. *Annual Report of the* (Cambridge) *School Committee* (1894), p. 65.
6. *Catalogue of Yale University* (1892–93), pp. 33–34.
7. *Calendar of the University of Michigan* (1892–93), pp. 34–36.

studies would waive two languages, one classical and one modern.[8] A comparison of the requirements of these three leading institutions testifies to the variety of demands the colleges placed upon the preparatory schools. The confusion was worsened by the colleges' practice of awarding a variety of degrees besides the A.B. Most of these alternatives, called Ph.B., B.Sc., and so forth, called for different and often less strenuous admission requirements. Yale's Sheffield Scientific School, for example, required the following: English, United States history, geography, Latin, arithmetic, algebra, geometry, and trigonometry.[9] Scientific courses often demanded only two or three years of preparatory study, compared with the "collegiate" or classical course's three to four.[10]

The colleges approved candidates for admission by either of two methods, or a combination of both. The Eastern colleges generally gave written examinations. Students had to pass these to be admitted; schools therefore trained their charges for them specifically. President Eliot favored this system of admission as the most successful, but at best its accuracy and validity are questionable.

The second method for admission was accreditation; it was introduced by the University of Michigan in 1871, and by 1896 it was being practiced by 192 colleges, mostly Midwestern and Western.[11] The arrangement for accreditation in Indiana was outlined above.[12] Under this system, the secondary school rather than the individual was examined. If the institution passed, its students would be admitted to the college automatically. The university accredited schools by inspection rather than by written examinations on set topics. A curriculum was usually recommended by the college faculties, and any school desiring accreditation adopted it. In some states—Cali-

8. *Harvard University Catalogue* (1892–93), pp. 177–82.
9. *Catalogue of Yale University* (1892–93), pp. 93–94.
10. "Uniformity in Requirements for Admission to College," *Report* of the Committee on Secondary Education, NEA *Proceedings* (1891), p. 307.
11. *Report of the Commissioner of Education* (1894–95), pp. 1171–88.
12. Pp. 21 ff.

fornia, for one—the inspection was made by members of the various academic departments of the university. While accreditation clearly provided more freedom for the secondary school teacher, the curriculum was still subject to college control.

As a device for maintaining standards, the accrediting system was even more dubious than the examination system, for a school could not possibly be inspected thoroughly in a few short visits and no state could inspect regularly enough to assure that standards would not slip. While the system of accreditation had much to commend it, it was actually as crude a method of admission as the written examination.

College-school relationships presented several problems for the Committee of Ten. The first one was that posed by the new subjects in the college curriculum: the sciences, English, and history. Were they worthy of as much preparatory study as the classics and mathematics? Yale thought not, but Michigan thought they were. Harvard stood in the middle by admitting boys without Greek only if they could pass an examination in another field that was "harder than the Greek."[13] The old classical college curriculum had been easy to plan for, and admission requirements were reasonably predictable. The variety of subjects in the new disciplines that were now demanded by both students and scholars complicated the machinery of admission enormously. One person even figured out that there were 2,760 ways of entering Harvard![14]

A second problem facing the Committee of Ten was that the colleges were demanding more and more of the preparatory schools. At the same time that new subjects were added, the same amount of study was devoted to the old subjects; furthermore, as Roxbury Latin School's Collar ruefully reported, the old subjects were being examined at an even higher standard. This trend worried Commissioner Harris, who felt that this up-

13. C. W. Eliot, in discussion of college entrance requirements, *Proceedings* of the New England Association of Colleges and Preparatory Schools (1894), p. 29.

14. Reported in the *Proceedings* of the New England Association of Colleges and Preparatory Schools (1887), p. 38.

ward trend would soon leave most high schools behind.[15] He claimed that it took a student one-and-one-half to two more years to prepare for college in 1891 than it had in 1865. Harris wanted a return to the 1865 standard yet, at the same time, favored the introduction of a post-graduate university course in the German tradition.

A third problem was the mechanical one of uniformity. With every college requiring a different course of study, a single school had to offer a maddening variety of courses. The Baker committee reported the comments of schoolmasters on this system: "We are fitting boys and girls for twelve or fifteen colleges, and no two require the same preparation"; "the present diversity is distracting and demoralizing, unreasonable and unnecessary"; "a class containing pupils fitting for each of . . . three colleges must either be broken up into three classes in French, or must do at least double the amount of work required by any one college in the group." John Tetlow summarized the schoolmasters' feelings: "My brethren, these things ought not so to be."[16]

There were mechanical problems for the colleges also. Those involved with a system of accreditation had to undertake school inspections frequently, and one can well imagine the problems faced by a president as he tried to persuade his faculty members to spend uncomfortable weeks visiting high schools. Those colleges giving written examinations had to provide for their administration and correction; Yale, for example, gave its tests in New Haven and at least eleven other cities.[17] Various efforts were made by college presidents to pool resources and give common exams. Eliot struggled to reach agreement with Yale's Noah Porter, but without success, and he was no more fortunate with Porter's successor, Timothy Dwight.[18] The New

15. W. T. Harris, "The Present Status of Education in the United States," NEA *Proceedings* (1891), p. 140.
16. "Uniformity in Requirements for Admission to College," pp. 310–11.
17. *Catalogue of Yale University* (1892–93), p. 35.
18. C. W. Eliot to N. Porter, March 2, 1888, and C. W. Eliot to T. Dwight, May 26, 1894, Eliot Papers, Harvard University.

England Association of Colleges and Preparatory Schools, founded in 1885, held a series of sessions to achieve uniformity, but with limited success. Similar associations were at work in other parts of the country: North Central and Southern associations were founded in 1895; and the Association of Colleges and Preparatory Schools in the Middle States and Maryland, formed in 1892, led to the development of the College Entrance Examination Board in 1901.

The Committee of Ten, while not charged with specifying admission requirements, still had to consider two basic issues. How much freedom were secondary schools to be allowed in developing their own curricula? How important should the demands of the college be on secondary school courses of study, offered to pupils only a quarter of whom would even consider work at a higher institution of learning? But Eliot, for one, saw another dimension to the issue: he felt college entrance requirements were the most effective point of leverage for bringing about general secondary school reform.[19]

As the Committee of Ten was charged to study "each principal subject which enters into the programmes of secondary schools," it had to determine exactly what was being offered in American curricula, a task that appeared easy on the surface but was extremely difficult. "The high school course in Pennsylvania is like the letter X in algebra—an unknown quantity," reported the Superintendent of Public Instruction of that state in 1894;[20] if he was unaware of what was happening in his own schools, the Committee of Ten could not have been much better informed. A questionnaire sent out by the Committee produced a list of nearly forty subjects taught in the schools;[21] Eliot only a few months earlier had reported to the NEA that

19. H. James, *Charles W. Eliot* (Boston, 1930), *1*, 365.
20. *Sixtieth Annual Report of the Superintendent of Public Instruction of the State of Pennsylvania*, found in the *Pennsylvania School Journal*, 42 (1893–94), 287.
21. *Report of the Committee on Secondary School Studies* (Washington, 1893), pp. 4–5.

"all the subjects from which high school programmes are made up" totaled but thirty.[22] While the exact number is unimportant, it does symbolize the wide variety and confusion in secondary school curricula. Subject titles ran from "Greek" and "arithmetic" to "international law," "bookkeeping," and "moral philosophy." Even if the Committee could succeed in classifying by the titles, its work would be only partly done, for many titles actually obscured the content of the courses. Many schools taught history under the title of English; Eliot himself had recommended that geography be similarly subsumed. Such subject titles were little help to the Committee.

The situation was relieved by the practice of arranging subjects into "courses," and despite the labels given these, two "tracks" could be discerned: one leading to college, the other to "life." The college preparatory "course," descended from the Latin School, usually consisted of Latin, Greek, algebra, geometry, English, and other subjects required by particular colleges. The general or terminal "courses," reflecting their common school roots, offered some Latin and French or German, mathematics, natural science, English, and often a commercial subject.[23] The latter courses enrolled fully three-quarters of the students. There was a wide diversity of general courses, each emphasizing a variety of subjects. Some were a combination of the college preparatory and the general. Most were called English "courses," or Latin-Scientific, or English-classical, or, simply, Commercial.

A number of representative course samples should reveal the classical-practical dilemma and show the curricula with which the Committee of Ten were to deal. New Haven's Hillhouse High School had four "courses": Classical, Scientific, English, and Three Years Commercial. The Classical and English courses are worthy of comparison:

22. C. W. Eliot, "Undesirable and Desirable Uniformity in Schools," NEA *Proceedings* (1892), pp. 92–93.

23. R. G. Huling, "The American High School," *Educational Review*, 2 (1891), p. 51. See also B. Mehl, "The High School at the Turn of the Century," unpublished dissertation, University of Illinois (1954), p. 159.

	Classical	*English*
First Year	Algebra	Algebra
	Latin	Latin
	English	English
		Drawing
Second Year	Latin	Latin
	English	English
	Algebra	Algebra and Geometry
	Plane Geometry	General History
	Greek	Drawing
Third Year	Latin and Roman History	Latin
	German or French	German or French
	Greek and Greek History	Civil Government Lectures
		Botany and Zoology
		Physics
		Drawing
Fourth Year	Latin	English Literature
	German or French	German or French
	Greek	Astronomy
	Solid Geometry	Physical Geography
	English	Geology
		Physiology and Hygiene[24]

The similarity between the two is notable. The Commercial "course" included one foreign language (German), mathematics, English, and subjects like bookkeeping. The Scientific "course," a three-year program, was essentially a shortened English course.

The High School Department of the schools in Memphis, Tennessee, provided a contrast. Grades eight through eleven were included, and only one "course" was offered. Reading, spelling, writing, composition, elocution, and music were offered each year. The only foreign language available was Latin,

24. *Annual Report of the Board of Education of the New Haven City School District* (1892), p. 64.

and that optionally. History, mathematics, and physiology dominated the first three years; in the final year, arithmetic, geometry, physical geography, English grammar, English literature, and bookkeeping were added.[25] Clearly Memphis took the practical side of the curriculum dilemma and offered what were actually extensions of common school subjects. All this was in marked contrast with New Haven.

Will S. Monroe, the superintendent of the Pasadena Public Schools, reported two courses in the high school of that city, a Scientific Course and a Literary Course. English and mathematics were included throughout both programs. The Literary Course provided Latin, four terms of history and civics, and three terms of science. Students in the Scientific Course took only German or French in addition to their science subjects. Pasadena's curriculum was somewhat of a compromise, not demanding as much linguistic study as did New Haven, but also not providing the variety of common school and commercial subjects seen in Memphis.[26]

A close study of high school curricula in the North Central states reveals a general pattern for that area. During the years 1891–95, a great variety of "courses" were offered. Out of a total of sixty schools, twenty had English "courses," seventeen Latin, nine Scientific, and two Commercial. Twenty-eight schools offered only one "course." Thirteen offered two, and nine, three; two schools offered no less than six "courses." Of forty schools, all offered algebra and most offered arithmetic and geometry. Some form of English instruction—rhetoric, composition, grammar, literature, or a combination of these—was almost universal. Physiology, physics, and botany were seen in over 80 per cent of the schools. Latin, after algebra, was the subject most often offered: 95 per cent of the schools provided it, 63 per cent of them for four years. A tremendous variety of history and civics subjects were given. Bookkeeping, the most popular

25. *Manual of the Board of Education of the City of Memphis* (1894–95), pp. 38–39.
26. *Report of the Public Schools of the City of Pasadena* (1891), pp. 24–25.

commercial subject, appeared in 48 per cent of the curricula, pedagogy in 20 per cent, and psychology in 15 per cent. Dozens of other subjects appeared, with few takers.[27] This study of Midwestern secondary schools shows several things. Latin and mathematics remained traditionally strong, but scientific and English subjects were becoming increasingly important. As considerable confusion in titles existed, categorization was very difficult; and uniformity was conspicuously absent.

What the students were to gain from their various academic studies was another matter entirely. Whether preparing for college or preparing for life, students would be acquiring "power," the first step of which was the ability to think properly. There were a variety of ways of attaining this; students were to develop their wills, their abilities to observe, their ethical selves. However this "power" did not consist of vocational proficiency in the manual sense; it was an intangible quality, that of intellectual strength. Educators disagreed about the subjects that would achieve this aim, but they did agree that the schools should teach their charges to think. The social and industrial roles of the schools were to come later.

Because of this tacit agreement, a distinction could be made between "disciplinary" and "informational" studies. The former trained the mind, the latter filled it; and the former were to be favored in secondary school studies. Children were to be taught "thoroughly": they were to master their work completely before moving on. The Latin sentence was fully dissected; all the capitals of American states were learned, not only for the information but for the discipline of memorization; all the arithmetic rules were committed to memory. This thoroughness was thought a fetish by many, including Eliot and Harris,[28] but it remained a central characteristic of American teaching.

27. J. E. Stout, *The Development of High-School Curricula in the North Central States from 1860 to 1918* (Chicago, 1921), pp. 48–49, 71–74. Some of Stout's figures were seriously questioned by the late Alexander Inglis, for reasons not altogether clear.

28. W. T. Harris, undated notes titled "Length of Grammar School Course," Harris Papers, Library of Congress.

Because mental training was desired by all, whatever their views on the classical-practical controversy, it is not surprising to see how widely Latin was offered in American schools, for Latin was looked upon as an excellent vehicle to train the mind. When one considers its absolute lack of use for the average American, however, one is struck by the fact that, in Commissioner Harris' best statistical judgment, fully 44 per cent of American secondary school pupils were studying it.[29] This does not mean there were no critics of the classics and mental training. There were. Charles Francis Adams, Jr., caused a considerable furor in a speech prepared for the Harvard chapter of Phi Beta Kappa in 1883.[30] Arthur L. Goodrich of Salem probably best reflected the sentiment of some of the public high school patrons: "In a vague, uncertain way, the general public feels that the classical schools and courses do not equip the youth with either the knowledge or the power he ought to have. Unable through ignorance to make itself effective in any other way, this feeling generally finds expression in obstruction."[31] And in those areas of the country where the influence of the colleges and their alumni were slight—the rural South and the new West—anticlassicism was found in its most extreme form. On a nationwide scale, though, the subject of Latin—if no longer Greek—was well entrenched.

The defenders of the classics, who were aware of the new and increasingly popular disciplines that had developed over the last fifty years, reacted vigorously. Chicago's school superintendent A. F. Nightingale thundered that "we must stand as educators, shoulder to shoulder, an unbroken phalanx, in maintaining the incomparable superiority of the thorough

29. *Report of the Commissioner of Education* (1893–94), p. 90. This percentage was only exceeded by algebra, which drew 53 per cent of the students. History drew 36 per cent, physics 24 per cent, and Greek but 5 per cent.

30. C. F. Adams, Jr., *The College Fetich* (Boston, 1883). See also W. G. Sumner, "Our Colleges before the Country," in *War and Other Essays* (New Haven, 1911), pp. 355 ff.

31. A. L. Goodrich, in discussion of college entrance requirements in history, *Proceedings* of the New England Association of Colleges and Preparatory Schools (1895), p. 10.

knowledge of the classics for the attainment of that broad, intellectual discipline, which the higher interests of science, religion, education, and politics will always demand."[32] Harris agreed entirely. Charlies Eliot was less sympathetic. A chemist by profession and president of Harvard University, he had already incurred the deep hostility of his own Greek department through his successful efforts to drop Greek from the college entrance examinations. The ancient languages were threatened, and their supporters met the enemy with high emotion.

The modern languages, also widely offered, were taught to be read, not spoken. To speak the languages would be a skill; what was wanted was the discipline of translation and manipulating grammar. Utility, again, was not of primary importance. English as a school subject was gaining stature; even traditional Yale started in 1894 to require its candidates for admission to pass an examination in the subject. English had not achieved the prestige of the classics, however, and the Department of Secondary Instruction of the NEA felt it necessary to adopt a resolution in 1887 asserting that "in the opinion of this department, the English language should be given at least an equal place with that of the classics and science, in high school courses of study."[33]

History, designed to inculcate patriotism and at the same time to teach historical method, was taught by the process of memorization: "the teacher assigns a fixed number of pages in the textbook to be memorized; pupils repeat the text in recitation; they are examined in the text, and the subject is dropped —usually willingly."[34] The texts were full of factual material on sovereignties and wars and contributed to this pedagogically inefficient procedure. The sciences, on the other hand, hopefully taught by the "laboratory method," were often reduced to simple recitations from a single text. "We went to school for

32. A. F. Nightingale, "The Claims of the Classics," NEA *Proceedings* (1887), p. 416.

33. NEA *Proceedings* (1887), p. 395.

34. F. N. Thorpe, "American History in Schools, Colleges, and Universities," in H. B. Adams, *The Study of History in American Colleges and Universities* (Washington, 1887), p. 231.

facts and got them. Facts about Latin, facts about history, facts about algebra, which gave us a valuable experience in taking intellectual punishment without a quaver. But of education there was very little."[35] Educators had high hopes for their methods and curricula, but one must question—as the Committee of Ten in its soberest moments must have questioned—the validity of these hopes.

A subject on the threshold of the curriculum but not as yet permitted to enter in any full sense was manual training. As has been mentioned, school leaders did not yet want to provide institutions for direct and utilitarian vocational training. In 1890 only thirty-seven cities offered work in manual training.[36] The arguments in favor of the subject were voiced by those experienced in the practical, common school tradition. Most of these persons were not in the NEA or in any other educational association. They were the laymen who saw no rhyme or reason to linguistic studies, and they simply did not patronize the high schools of the early '90s.

The NEA heard many speeches on the subject of manual training, mostly from men like James H. Baker and Harris, who were tolerant but not convinced. The Commissioner favored trade schools, but only after general, liberal studies. "Cultivate the humanities first," he urged in a speech provocatively entitled "The Intellectual Value of Tool-Work," "and afterwards the industrial faculties. . . . Above all, we must never yield to the economic spirit that proposes to curtail the humanizing studies in our schools for industries. Rather we must do what we can to extend the period of study in pure science and the humanities, knowing as we do that all which goes to develop the ability of the youth to see possibilities and ideals, goes to make him a more productive laborer in the fields of industry."[37] Baker agreed: "Education is the development of the

35. H. S. Canby, *The Age of Confidence* (New York, 1934), p. 104.

36. E. C. Moore, *Fifty Years of American Education* (Boston, 1917), p. 58.

37. W. T. Harris, "The Intellectual Value of Tool-Work," NEA *Proceedings* (1888), p. 173.

soul activities, Knowling, Feeling, and Willing; its aim is man-hood. . . . The highest use of studies is to develop the mental powers. . . . The popular demands [for practical education] are really demands for special education before the mind is suffi-ciently developed."[38] There were, however, a few superintend-ents at the meetings of the NEA who protested that intellec-tual subjects dominated the schools excessively,[39] and Nicholas Murray Butler could well argue at a meeting of the American Institute of Instruction that "Industrial Education is a protest against this mental oligarchy, the rule of a few faculties."[40]

Of all subjects in the curriculum, art stands out as a good example of the discipline the schools desired to nurture. Art meant drawing; and drawing meant imitation, the copying of other, ready-made forms. Art was not a subject for release of the imagination, but a means of directing the powers of ob-servation, forcing the student to record what he saw. Canby, characteristically, condemned this narrow conception, recall-ing that his "school was not concerned with self-expression; [and] knew it only as a form of naughtiness."[41]

American secondary schools were, at best, doing an imperfect job. They enrolled few; they provided their students with in-structors the majority of whom were barely competent. The schools' strength was sapped by politics and by the need for buildings and equipment. They provided no clear philosophy for education, as they were split by two relatively antithetical philosophies. They could only agree on a desire for mental power, whether it be gained from the grammar of the classics or from a study of contemporary political economy. Their peda-gogy in the hands of inept teachers was one of rote memoriza-tion and recitation, hardly popular with the students. "In our

38. J. H. Baker, "Practical Education: The Psychological View," NEA *Proceedings* (1888), p. 173.

39. See, for example, W. E. Shield, "The Schools Fail to Give a Proper Preparation for Active Life," NEA *Proceedings* (1888), pp. 148 ff.

40. N. M. Butler, "Manual Training," *Proceedings* of the American In-stitute of Instruction (1888), p. 222.

41. Canby, *The Age of Confidence*, p. 47.

town," one of these students would later report, "certainly the best educated were outside of the schools."[42]

These were the dimensions of Eliot's gap. The reasons for its existence were of great importance, for by isolating and remedying these, the Committee might achieve some constructive reform. The first reason was the nature of the control of American schools. School boards were provincial and often lacked a sense of balance and standards. Local conditions affected their actions to a major degree: witness the difference between the curricula of the New Haven and the Memphis schools. If one assumes there is some basic common standard in secondary education—as the Committee of Ten did—then one must question the hit-or-miss system whereby curricula were developed in many schools. Furthermore, it is clear that many school districts could not afford secondary education to any real extent, and without state or national aid they could not hope to improve their schools. Local control, then, kept the schools close to the people, but at the same time often denied them a good education because of the school boards' myopic ignorance or because funds were lacking.

Another reason was political corruption. Of this, the cities had a major share. As Superintendent Seaver of Boston wrote to John Tetlow in 1904—just after Seaver had been eased out of his long-held post for political reasons—"the principles of Civil Service Reform must be applied to the public schools in all our cities and large towns. There is no other way to rid them of politics and favoritism."[43] Until teachers' appointments, school budgets, and school administration could be kept free from corrupt politics, no chance of a major reform of the secondary schools was possible.

The third reason was the pressure of numbers upon the schools. To meet the demand, schoolmen had to cut corners everywhere: classroom space, teaching staff, books and materials. A school system with enough rooms with desks and

42. Ibid., p. 103.
43. E. P. Seaver to J. Tetlow, July 18, 1904, Tetlow Papers, Harvard University.

enough teachers of sufficient standards had reason to congratulate itself. But improved standards often had to wait while the physical demands upon the educational system were somehow met.

Needless to say, low teacher competence was another reason for the gap. Teachers had a low social status, and the profession was hard put to compete for able men and women. Until good teachers were found, reform of the curriculum was academic.

Finally, there was the grip of conservatism. "There is no subject which is to-day so submerged in cant and humbug as education. Both primary and secondary education are suffering from this cause, but in different ways. Primary education is afflicted by the cant and humbug of progress and innovation, and secondary education is afflicted by the cant and humbug of conservatism and toryism." Such was William Graham Sumner's conclusion, and he went on to blame the colleges: "In no civilized country is mandarinism so strong as in the United States. Its stronghold is in the colleges, and they use such control as they possess to establish it in the schools."[44] Those colleges that in 1890 still refused to recognize the existence of academic subjects of any standing save the classical languages and mathematics were far out of step with the intellectual life of the country. Biological and physical science, history, sociology, vocational training, and the modern languages were all in demand, and to deny these subjects equal status with the traditional classics was to block even moderate reform. The hard truth is that many educational leaders had their heads in the sand and were oblivious to the changes taking place in society. One can legitimately criticize the National Council of Education on this point, for their charge to the Committee of Ten, although of considerable scope, failed to specify most of the causes of the chaos and low standards in the secondary schools.

The reasons for this oversight, this failure to diagnose accurately the disease in education, are not clear. It is plain, however, that the schoolmen of the National Council of Education

44. W. G. Sumner, "Our Colleges before the Country," pp. 355–56.

71

saw the problems of their institutions and the means for re-forming them only within the context of the institutions them-selves; they failed to notice the pressures on the schools that society was exerting from without. Thus the NEA talked of poor teachers, but never of corrupt lay control. It talked of cur-ricula, but never of the complex power structure within and without the schools that helped shape them. The men of the '90s did not see the school as a social institution, one among many in the larger culture. They saw it rather as a proud, iso-lated ideal, detached from the worst crudities of the world. In their intense concern to improve the internal mechanics of their schools, they forgot to assess the more important influence of external forces upon their structure. The narrow approach is understandable but deplorable, although later reformers were guilty of the same thing.

Thus the NCE, while seeing Eliot's gap, failed to direct the new committee to the heart of its causes, and turned their at-tention solely to the details of the secondary school curriculum.

V · THE COMMITTEE

The formation of the Committee of Ten was due largely to a movement within the National Educational Association to make college entrance requirements uniform. James H. Baker had chaired the Committee on Secondary Education of the National Council of Education at Toronto in 1891 when it gave its report on "Uniformity in Requirements for Admission to College," and one of its recommendations was that "a committee be appointed by this Council [the NCE] to select a dozen Universities and Colleges and a dozen High and Preparatory Schools to be represented in a convention to consider the problems of Secondary and Higher education."[1] This recommendation was adopted, and in due course the meeting of school and college men at the convention of the NEA in Saratoga, New York, was held, with Nicholas Murray Butler of Columbia as chairman. No record of proceedings was kept, but apparently the group reached the conclusion that a separate association should be formed, devoted exclusively to school-college articulation. "At this point in the discussion," one observer reported,

> President Eliot, who had entered late, was invited to state his views. He spoke in disapproval of the proposed formation of a new association, and expressed the belief that there were associations enough already existing ... but he added that he had observed in New England that, when representatives of the colleges and secondary schools came together in conference, good

1. NEA *Proceedings* (1891), p. 316.

73

was apt to result. He recommended, therefore, that a committee, duly representative of colleges and secondary schools and of the different sections of the country, be appointed, with authority to call conferences, similarly representative, of experts in each of the subjects or groups of subjects required for admission to college, and that the committee so constituted after conferences should make a final report to the national Council. President Eliot's proposal met with prompt and hearty acceptance.[2]

The conference then recommended Eliot's plan to the NCE and included the names of the ten. The National Council, in turn, approved, and sent formal recommendations to the directors of the NEA with Butler, Harris, and W. E. Sheldon as a committee of three to press the matter. Although several directors balked over the expense involved,[3] it was finally approved, twenty-one to nine.

The NEA, the forum from which the Committee of Ten would speak, was an organization of growing prestige. Founded in 1857, the Association had had lean years until the '80s. As improved transportation made it easier to attend meetings, its influence grew, and there developed within its ranks a group of members who attended the conventions religiously, manned its offices regularly, and spread its word. Of these, William Torrey Harris was the most outstanding.

By the '80s the NEA was attracting more of the influential college men, probably because these leaders had awakened to the obvious split between secondary schools and higher education. Harvard's Eliot, Yale's Porter, Johns Hopkins' Gilman, and Princeton's McCosh, among others, were speakers during the '80s, and their interest in the organization lent it considerable prestige. Even so, and despite improved rail transporta-

2. J. Tetlow, "The Colleges and the Non-Classical High Schools," undated manuscript, Tetlow Papers, Harvard University. N. M. Butler, writing many years later, claimed credit for suggesting the form of the Committee. *Across the Busy Years* (New York, 1935), *1*, 17.
3. See below, pp. 107–08.

tion, the Association's membership fluctuated widely according to the site of the annual meeting. When the Association met in San Francisco in 1888, for example, 4,974 Westerners were enrolled members; the next year, at the convention in Nashville, only 38 Westerners were on the books. Average membership from 1884 to 1900 was 6,169, half coming from the North Central states, with the South poorly represented.[4]

By 1892 the NEA could truthfully say that its meetings and published *Proceedings* had considerable national effect. The superintendents who attended the meetings returned to their cities and lectured their teachers at the inevitable Saturday morning teachers' meetings. Harris and others became nationally known among schoolmen, and their ideas were widely repeated. While the NEA had no large influence on the lay public, it was acknowledged to be a forum of growing stature. The presidents of long-established colleges were attending NEA conventions and, as Butler put it, "for the president of Yale or of Harvard to be seen in such company twenty years ago would have seemed as incongruous as to find Daniel Webster present and taking part in the debating society of a country school."[5]

The NEA approved the NCE's recommendations for membership on the Committee of Ten, although only five of the ten were members of the Association at the time. This, though unprecedented, could be explained in two ways. First, several of the Ten, even though they were not members, had attended the Saratoga convention at the school-college conference. Second, and more important, the names had been chosen by Nicholas

4. NEA *Proceedings* (1900), p. 801.

5. N. M. Butler, editorial in *Educational Review*, 5 (1893), 94. See also E. B. Wesley, *N.E.A.: The First Hundred Years* (New York, 1957); M. S. Fenner, "The National Education Association, 1892–1942," unpublished dissertation, George Washington University (1942), also available in shortened, printed form as *N.E.A. History* (Washington, 1945); and F. R. McKenna, "Policy Evolution in the National Education Association," unpublished dissertation, Harvard University (1954). The Association asked President Harrison and his Cabinet to the 1892 meeting; Harris urged the Secretary of the Interior to come and to "present the matter favorably to the President." W. T. Harris to the Secretary of the Interior, February 28, 1892. Bureau of Education Records, U.S. Archives.

Murray Butler with a specific strategy in mind. Eliot, Harris, Angell, and the rest were not selected at random: they were picked because they were nationally influential. Only they could sway both colleges and secondary schools. The reports of lesser men—regardless of their merit—were not even given a reading by most educators outside of the NEA. To reach schools of the stature of Andover and Roxbury Latin School on the one hand and unknown, struggling high schools on the other, the Committee had to have prestige; and this meant naming influential men to its membership.

Butler felt his most successful coup was to secure both the appointment of President Eliot as chairman and Eliot's agreement to carry the burden.[6] Eliot's blunt speeches on elementary and secondary education before the NEA and elsewhere had given him a reputation as a reformer, not only of Harvard but of education in general. At fifty-nine, he was by far the most powerful voice in higher education. As a balancing influence, Butler offered Harris, the teachers' teacher and the real leader of the NEA. College and school would get equal spokesmen if both Eliot and Harris were on the Committee. Baker was named out of courtesy for his labors in 1891–92; he also represented the West on the Committee. Angell, by contrast, could speak for the state universities and for the North Central states, which of course enrolled the largest number of secondary school students. Midwesterners might mistrust Eliot, but they would surely read what Angell proposed, a fact Butler shrewdly recognized. The other men were added to fill gaps: Taylor for the women's college, King for the small private college, Jesse for the Southwest, and Tetlow, Mackenzie, and Robinson for various kinds of schools.

Interesting indeed is the exclusion of certain men. Not a single superintendent was on the Committee, and men like Illinois' Nightingale and Missouri's Sabin and Greenwood were passed over. Considering the influence of superintendents in

6. N. M. Butler, *Across the Busy Years* (New York, 1935), *1*, 17. However, in the light of John Tetlow's recollections, it is hard to see how Eliot could have refused. Butler probably overstated the extent of his own role.

the NEA, this is remarkable; but in education and in the country at large, their influence, in Butler's view, was limited.

Yet Butler did not select his men solely because they had national prestige. The men he chose had, without exception, high qualifications to speak on educational matters. Several had been induced by President Baker to come to Saratoga for the college-secondary school conference. Although no attendance records were kept, Eliot, Harris, and Baker—all members of the National Council of Education—were surely there. King attended, representing Oberlin.[7] Butler suggested that Taylor might have been included,[8] and Baker had written to Eliot prior to the meeting to say that President Angell needed "some extra inducement" to attend, such as a letter from Eliot.[9] John Tetlow, in the light of his statements, most probably was there. Jesse of Missouri, like King of Oberlin, was listed as a member of the NEA at the 1892 meeting, evidence that he too may have been at Saratoga. In any event, a reasonable number of the Committee were aware of the nature and content of the discussions already under way at the NEA.

Of the Ten, Eliot was by far the most important, for he wrote the *Report* (though with the approval of the other nine). The role of chairman gave him the initiative, and experience showed that, given initiative, Eliot was a strong advocate of his views.

Charles William Eliot was born a Boston patrician. He grew up on Beacon Hill, attended the Boston Latin School, and went to Harvard, graduating second in the Class of 1853. The following year he joined the Harvard faculty—which at that time totaled thirteen—as a tutor in mathematics. In 1858 he became Harvard's first assistant professor, holding the chair in mathematics and chemistry; but in 1863, failing to be ap-

7. D. M. Love, *Henry Churchill King of Oberlin* (New Haven, 1956), p. 60.

8. N. M. Butler, editorial in *Educational Review, 4* (1892), 203.

9. J. H. Baker to C. W. Eliot, February 11, 1892, Eliot Papers, Harvard University. Angell was at Saratoga anyway, to address the annual convention of the American Institute of Instruction.

pointed to the coveted Rumford chair, he resigned in disappointment. After more than a year in Europe, he returned to Cambridge, this time to the new Massachusetts Institute of Technology as a full professor. He moved up the river again to Harvard as president in 1869.

Eliot was not a philosopher. His reforms at Harvard and in education in general resulted not from a closely reasoned educational rationale, but rather from a simple belief in efficiency. He wrote and spoke in concrete, practical terms, and his efforts were all directed toward practical ends. He was a scientist and reflected the mood of science, interpreted it, and translated it into action. He was a Unitarian and an idealist, but he did not sermonize on these subjects. Eliot was a doer, a man whose reputation rests in the institutions he fashioned. No one today reads Eliot; his influence remains rather in the kinds of colleges and secondary schools he had a hand in shaping.

There is little indication that Eliot was a reader of philosophy. Although he wrote an introduction to an English edition of Herbert Spencer's *Essays on Education,* in 1910, there is no evidence that he was a militant Spencerian. This introduction, significantly, emphasizes not Spencer's theory but rather the institutions fashioned from that theory. His letters to educators are notable for their paucity of theoretical discussion; Eliot stayed close to facts.[10]

As a scientist, Eliot was content to question the status quo. If a traditional practice was found wanting in results, it had to go. At Harvard, Eliot saw professional schools not worthy of the name. Harvard's doctors were inefficient and unfortunately sometimes killed their patients: accordingly, the medical school was reformed. Harvard's students were clearly not being made

10. Typical was a short speech Eliot wrote at the request of John Heyl Vincent for delivery at an 1893 Chautauqua chapel service. Expected, surely, to present a philosophical piece, Eliot talked of children and how they were mishandled. He suggested how good teachers were needed to correct the bad situation, as well as understanding parents. While its message was important, the short talk was phrased in uncommonly concrete and often homely phrases. The text of the speech may be found in the Eliot Papers, Harvard University.

into thinkers of high quality under an exclusively mathematical and classical curriculum: therefore, they were given the chance to develop in another direction according to their interests. Students taught by texts alone learned less efficiently than those taught by actual experience: ergo, the laboratory method. Eliot's reforms at Harvard—the reform and extension of the various professional and graduate schools, the elective system, the promotion of nonlinguistic studies and the relative demotion of the classics—were all reforms of a practical nature, taken because the end products of the classical tradition were inadequate. Of course, Eliot's changes were not completed in a vacuum: men had been preaching the doctrines behind the Harvard reforms for some time. The theories of Silliman, of Eliot's predecessor President Hill, and of Herbert Spencer all found practical expression in Harvard's curriculum. Eliot was a devotee of no one, but rather a man caught in the stream of science and the new intellectual currents of his day. His energies were directed at concrete improvement of the existing order.

Eliot had always had an interest in educational administration; in fact this interest may have won him his post as president. While a junior faculty member at Harvard, he had carried out clerical tasks for various college committees.[11] Unhappy with the mechanics of the oral exams used at the college, he and James Mills Pierce introduced written tests.[12] He was known as a man who got things done; possibly this, too, swung the vote to him over the opposition of several Fellows who feared the somewhat radical views he had expressed in two articles in the *Atlantic* in 1869.[13] Once at the helm of his college, Eliot developed the office of Dean to a large extent and streamlined the efficiency of the administration.

Although Eliot served as a college teacher and administrator, he always retained an interest in the lower schools. In 1854 he

11. H. James, *Charles W. Eliot* (Boston, 1930), *1*, 69–72.
12. Ibid., p. 68.
13. C. W. Eliot, "The New Education: Its Organization," *Atlantic Monthly*, *23* (1869), 203, 358.

was on a primary school committee for Boston and taught during the evenings at the Pitt Street School.[14] His speeches and articles, including his inaugural address, paid attention to the importance of elementary and secondary schools. On his two trips to Europe, the first during the Civil War and the second in the '70s, Eliot visited schools, studied their administration, and talked with their teachers; he made similar trips in this country.

Many of Eliot's views on education have been examined above. But the best expression of his ideas was seen in a high-school curriculum he prepared for the Chelsea, Massachusetts, public schools. Requested by the Chelsea school committee to design a "course," he plotted a four-year curriculum, with English, mathematics, and natural science to be taken each year. English studies would also embrace work in history. Latin was started in the second year, but only for students planning to finish high school. Those who were to leave at the end of this class took extra English instead. French, which was also part of the curriculum, was replaced by advanced science for those leaving. Greek was started in the third year, with German as an alternative. Music, gymnastics, and drawing were offered in small quantities throughout the four years.[15]

Several matters here are of particular interest. First of all, the course adhered to the traditional linguistic pattern, at least for those completing the full four years. Students took three languages in addition to English. Second was the provision for English, history, and science throughout each year of the course; in contrast to traditional curricula, these new subjects had near parity with the languages. The mathematics courses were difficult: the students were asked to absorb algebra, plane and solid geometry, and trigonometry. Also noteworthy is Eliot's provision for a balanced education for children who left school without finishing the course. Finally, the President provided for only two years of Greek. When the Committee of Ten made

14. James, *Charles W. Eliot, 1,* 56–58.
15. *Annual Report of the School Committee of the City of Chelsea* (1884), pp. 51 ff.

the same decision, the wrath of the classicists was aroused for a full decade, as they considered three years to be an irreducible minimum. The most striking aspect of the Chelsea curriculum is that it contained only one course that was flexible enough to provide a few elective choices—for example, between German and French—and that gave all children a well rounded education. If Eliot had his way, all students—whether preparing for college or not—would have the same education. Chelsea is a good example of Eliot's point of view, and the respect to which this curriculum would parallel that of the Committee of Ten is striking.

Eliot was fully capable of antagonizing those who disagreed with him. He was a tall, energetic person who inspired considerable awe (John Tetlow's daughter recalls being struck speechless, as a young girl, upon meeting him).[16] He was thought by many to be cold and somewhat heartless, but others disagreed.[17] Yale's John Ferguson Weir, for instance, found Eliot not only a hospitable guide in Cambridge, but also an unusually agreeable companion.[18] Blunt in both his speech and his writing, he may frequently have given offense. Such directness was not customary in that day: witness Frank Plummer's opening statement to the Department of Secondary Education of the NEA at Saratoga in 1892:

> "*Ladies and Gentlemen, and Fellow Teachers of Saratoga and of this Continent:* I greet you, I give you welcome, free and warm. What a great gathering this! How representative! How significant! How important! From every section of the Union, and from the remotest parts of this Continent, ye come. New England is here—New England with her olden civilization. . . ."[19]

16. Helen Ingersoll Tetlow described this incident to the writer.

17. See B. Perry, *Life and Letters of Henry Lee Higginson* (Boston, 1921), p. 133.

18. T. Sizer, ed., *The Recollections of John Ferguson Weir* (New York, 1957), p. 77.

19. F. E. Plummer, "President's Opening Address," NEA *Proceedings* (1892), p. 338. Italics in the original.

And on and on. Eliot wrote the following—quoted here in its entirety—to N. M. Butler in 1890:

> My dear Sir,—Why not advance your requirements for admission at Columbia about a year's worth, and so get older Freshmen? The right age for going to college seems to me to be eighteen, at least for boys who have had good advantages. The advancing of the standard of Columbia would be, of course, a great help to other institutions. Very truly yours—[20]

Not only is this letter short, but it is direct. Eliot was no mincer of words, a fact Butler appreciated and valued. Eliot was controversial, and he knew it;[21] he considered himself a reformer not only of Harvard, but of American education in general. In 1900 upon receiving a copy of a report on Columbia's new and liberalized curriculum, Eliot, with characteristic belligerence, exclaimed simply, "Now for Yale!"[22]

Ralph Barton Perry has called Charles Eliot "in his day the most influential leader in the educational activities of the country."[23] The '90s were Eliot's day; and his beliefs found their way into the *Report* of the Committee of Ten.

William Torrey Harris was a far different kind of reformer. "In a superficial view, how unlike Eliot and Harris! Eliot's approach to the educational problem is from the side of practical valuation; Eliot's question is, 'Is it good?' Harris' approach to the educational problem was from the side of philosophy; his question was, 'Is it true?' Yet in Harris, as there is in Eliot, was a union of the philosophical and of the practical, of the scientific and of the metaphysical, of the teacher and of the

20. C. W. Eliot to N. M. Butler, March 4, 1890, Butler Papers, Columbia University.
21. Ibid., June 9, 1892.
22. Ibid., February 14, 1900.
23. R. B. Perry, "Charles William Eliot," in *Dictionary of American Biography* (New York, 1931), *6*, 71. See also Butler, *Across the Busy Years, 1*, p. 9.

student."[24] This assessment by a man who knew both men demonstrates the areas where Eliot and Harris diverged and those where they agreed. The President and the Commissioner both led practical reform movements, the former at Harvard and the latter at St. Louis. Harris started from a philosophical rationale, Eliot from a quest for efficiency. Eliot would say more than "Is it good?"—he would ask, "Does it work?" Harris would have more in mind: he would ask, "Does it conform with nature's laws?"

William Torrey Harris was born in rural Connecticut in 1835, the same year that Charles Eliot was born. Harris attended country schools and academies and finally prepared for college at Phillips Andover. He entered Yale in 1854, but left in 1856 feeling that the college had taught him all it could and that continued work in the classical languages was wasteful.[25] Rather at loose ends, Harris went West and eventually found himself teaching in an elementary school in St. Louis, Missouri. Within a year, he was made principal and in 1867 he became the city school superintendent.

Harris' interests were not solely pedagogical. After leaving Yale, he developed an interest in philosophy, and together with a St. Louis friend, Henry Conrad Brokmeyer, he immersed himself in the subject, particularly in the work of Hegel. In 1867, besides becoming superintendent in St. Louis, Harris began to publish the *Journal of Speculative Philosophy,* a periodical that brought him national prominence as a scholar.

The superintendent-philosopher made a national mark on education as well. Harris' annual reports concerning the city schools were widely read and even published in foreign languages. Not only was St. Louis' educational plant expanded by Harris, but a kindergarten was added to the system; and the city library facilities were expanded. Harris handled his teachers with skill and achieved a reputation as a thoughtful educator. In 1875, he became President of the NEA.

24. C. F. Thwing, *A History of Education in the United States since the Civil War* (New York, 1910), p. 309.
25. K. Leidecker, *Yankee Teacher* (New York, 1946), p. 70.

In 1880 Harris resigned his superintendency, spent several months traveling in Europe—representing the United States at the Brussels Congress of Educators—and returned to New England, where he joined in founding and teaching at the Concord, Massachusetts, School of Philosophy and Literature. Typically, while devoting his time to philosophy, he still kept up his pedagogical interest and served as Concord's superintendent of schools. In 1889, he was appointed United States Commissioner of Education, a post he held until 1906.

Harris was a voluminous writer, but most of his best work has been published in bits and pieces and thus lacks coherence. He published four books: *The Spiritual Sense of Dante's Divina Commedia* (1889), *Introduction to the Study of Philosophy* (1889), *Hegel's Logic* (1890), and *Psychologic Foundations of Education* (1898); he also published no less than 475 articles in periodicals and magazines.[26] These were on all sorts of topics, from "The Need of Women in Politics" and "Beethoven's Sixth Symphony" to "The Educational Lessons of the Census," "The Effect of Exercise on the Vital Organs," and "Ought Young Girls to Read the Daily Newspapers?" He gave 145 speeches at the NEA—more than any other person before or since.[27]

Out of this mass of material, much of Harris' philosophy of education can be drawn. He has been called a "conservator" rather than a radical;[28] this assessment is demonstrated by Harris' own definition of education as "the process by which the individual is elevated into the species." He placed "a very high value on the accumulated wisdom of the race."[29] Unlike Eliot, Harris had a philosophical plan for the school and college curriculum, one that colored most of his judgments on school prob-

26. "Bibliographical Note" in the W. T. Harris Papers, Library of Congress.

27. Wesley, *N.E.A.: The First Hundred Years*, p. 45.

28. M. Curti, *The Social Ideas of American Educators*, (2d ed. New York, 1935), p. 310.

29. From a draft by Harris for a chapter in O. Lang, *Educational Creeds of the Nineteenth Century*, W. T. Harris Papers, Library of Congress, pp. 1–2.

lems. He saw "five great divisions of the life of man," five areas of knowledge that man needed in order to live fully. Harris called them "the five windows of the soul." The first was a grasp of quantification and computation; this was represented by arithmetic. Next was man and his physical environment; the relevant facts in this area were provided by geography. This was distinct from man's past; history, the third window, reveals how man has evolved, how nations have developed. Fourth came logic and reason as represented by language. Finally, there was "the fullest and completest expression of the sentiments, opinions, and convictions of a people"—their literature.[30] Harris' five windows were imprecise, and they were not coordinate. He lumped together substantive knowledge (history, for example), ways of thought (as within language), and matters of aesthetics and emotion. Their differences were obscured by being tied in with the current course labels of recognized disciplines: geography, arithmetic, literature, and so forth. Harris' philosophy of knowledge is either difficult to understand or superficially developed; most probably, it is both.

For the purposes of the Committee of Ten, these convictions, however imprecise they might have seemed, were clear, as his five windows opened on five areas of knowledge well established in school curricula. Harris favored a broad curriculum, containing mathematics, geography, history, language, and literature. As long as studies were difficult enough to promise "will-culture," the discipline of the mind, they should be selected on the basis of their usefulness in teaching the student the facts of his environment. Discipline of the mind meant persistence, alertness, and dedication, and was taught by a "firm and mild" pedagogy;[31] discipline of the intellect was achieved when man understood the facts of his world. "In order to be

30. W. T. Harris, "On the Relation of the College to the Common School." *Proceedings* of the American Institute of Instruction (1883), pp. 150–51. See also the work of Eliot's predecessor as President of Harvard: Thomas Hill, *The True Order of Studies* (New York, 1875).

31. W. T. Harris, "Excessive Helps in Education," *Education, 9* (1888–89), 215. For Harris' views on manual training, see above, pp. 105–06.

in possession of intellectual power the mind must have in its grasp the keys of nature and human society."[32] Harris, then, linked—rather than separated—the disciplinary and informational studies.

If Harris had seen the Chelsea High School curriculum planned by Eliot, he would probably have criticized it on a number of counts. Geography was neglected excepting what was taught under the label of natural science. History, tied in with English studies, also was neglected. The languages, surprisingly, he may have found neglected, particularly insofar as the classics were not required. "Language study . . . lies at the foundation of school education as the discipline which makes possible all others and which leads to the knowledge of one's self, . . . the nature of reason itself, the logical structure of thought and the ethical structure of the will."[33] Harris fought hard for Latin and Greek, arguing that since they were the basis of all modern languages and the classical cultures the foundation of modern society, they required close study.[34] But Harris did agree with Eliot's concept of a broad general secondary education for all children, regardless of their postgraduation plans.

Although Harris was "one of the most overlooked figures in American education . . . few men have equalled his influence."[35] His relatively conservative view on broadening the curriculum to embrace five general studies was, in a fashion, a solution to the classical-practical dichotomy. While he defended the classics with the vehemence and logic of the Harvard Greek department, he also asserted that "the high-school education is, and

32. W. T. Harris, manuscript of a speech(?) prepared in 1886, W. T. Harris Papers, Library of Congress.

33. W. T. Harris, "What Shall the Public Schools Teach?" *Forum, 4* (1887–88), 574.

34. W. T. Harris, "Latin and Greek in Modern Education," *Journal of the* (London) *Women's Education Union, 8* (1880). Harris spoke and published so often in defense of the classics that on at least one occasion he simply cut paragraphs out of his old printed articles, pieced them together with connecting sentences, and presented the glued-together result.

35. N. J. McCluskey, *Catholic Viewpoint on Education* (Garden City, 1959), p. 58 n.

must be, based largely upon the three moderns, science, history, and language."[36] Ideally, he saw a balance between the old subjects and the new, a balance also accepted by the administrator Eliot, who, although in favor of more modern courses, endeavored to compromise with the classics on an equal basis.

The three state university presidents were far less influential than either Harris or Eliot in the deliberations of the Committee of Ten. While all three were pioneers of education in their respective states, not one of them had both the personal vigor and distinctive educational policy characteristic of Harvard's president and the Commissioner of Education. Nor did they disagree basically with the ideas of the two leaders; although Baker did file a minority report, it reflected as much misreading of the *Report* as disagreement with the facts.

Of the three, James Burrill Angell was the best known. In 1892 he was already sixty-four years old but barely halfway through his thirty-eight-year reign as president of the University of Michigan. Angell was born a Rhode Islander and attended Brown University during the enlightened administration of Francis Wayland, graduating in 1849. Top man in his class, he was offered by Wayland his choice of two chairs at the college, that of Civil Engineering or that of Modern Foreign Languages. Angell, who traveled in Europe after his graduation, accepted the latter and returned to Providence in 1852. Wayland's replacement by Barnas Sears in 1855 boded ill, for Angell was a disciple of the liberal ex-president. Consequently, he left the college for a journalistic career. In 1866 he returned to his former profession by accepting the position of president of the University of Vermont. Five years later he went to Ann Arbor.

While Angell was not an educator with the dedication of an Eliot or a Harris, he was a wise man with broad interests who instinctively recognized sound policies. Particularly fortunate was his espousal of the high school-university accreditation tie

36. W. T. Harris, in discussion of the "Report on Academies," NEA *Proceedings* (1885), p. 457.

that had been started by his predecessor, Acting President Henry S. Frieze. Angell agreed that the plan's strength rested in the visits to schools by University faculty, and he made many of these visits himself, becoming acquainted with the problems of secondary school education in a way that would prove useful for the Committee of Ten. Significantly, he said that the "University was also enabled to see what was possible to the High School and was guarded against the danger of asking too much of the students as the condition of admission."[37] Angell's views on a suitable secondary school course are best shown by the entrance examinations the University offered for students from nonaccredited high schools; the breadth of studies required is not out of step with the opinions of Harris and Eliot.[38]

Angell built his University with the help of several distinguished men. Edward Olney in mathematics, Charles Kendall Adams in history, Alexander Winchell in science, Martin L. D'Ooge in Greek, and Thomas M. Cooley in law all had national reputations, and the eminence Michigan achieved was the result of their—and Angell's—efforts. Angell himself had many interests outside of university administration. From 1880 to 1882, he served as a United States Commissioner to China to negotiate new treaties, principally those having to do with the emigration of Chinese to America. In 1887 he served on an international commission to settle the disputes between the United States and Canada over fisheries, and in 1897–98 was the United States Minister to Turkey. While not active in the NEA during his tenure as president of Michigan, he was a founder of the American Historical Association and its president in 1893–94. Angell's scholarly and administrative interests were catholic.

Angell's energies were not centered on educational matters, and the emphasis he himself placed on his extracurricular work is exemplified by his *Reminiscences,* which deal largely with his public functions and in which his work on the Committee of Ten is not even mentioned. A writer who knew Angell as

37. J. B. Angell, *Reminiscences* (New York, 1911), p. 238.
38. See above, p. 57.

"Uncle Jim" recalls him as a friendly, elderly person who would have been overwhelmed by the aggressive assurance of Charles W. Eliot.[39] Brilliant and important as he was, his influence on other members of the Committee of Ten did not equal that of either Eliot or Harris.

One would have expected James Hutchins Baker to be a key man on the Committee of Ten. In 1892 he was not only on the National Council of Education, the Committee's sponsoring body, but was its president. He had been chairman of the NEA group that was the Ten's direct forerunner. But although Baker was deeply committed to education in a more obvious way than Angell, he was not an original thinker. He was very much an advocate of Harris' five windows of the soul and his speeches on the curriculum reflect this.[40] He was a devotee of the mental power argument:

> The mental power, the development of the mental faculty—that higher purpose of education—must be constantly kept in view. Properly employed, mathematics trains the abstractive and deductive powers; science the perceptive, conceptual and inductive powers; history the ethical and the higher personal emotions; literature the aesthetic and the ethical emotions; all studies exercise memory and imagination more or less; proper school requirements cultivate right emotion and train the will; all physical training, as reading, speaking, music, drawing, exercise, give the mind power over the body and thus train the will.[41]

The high school curriculum that he and five others presented in 1891 to the Colorado State Teachers Association was liberal by Yale's standards, but quite ordinary by those of Angell's

39. The recollection of Pierre Hazard, stated to the writer in 1960.
40. See, for example, J. H. Baker, "Practical Education: The Psychological View," NEA *Proceedings* (1888), pp. 168 ff.
41. J. H. Baker, "The High School as a Finishing-School," NEA *Proceedings* (1890), p. 636. Parts of this address also closely reflect the thinking of W. T. Harris.

Michigan and other Western colleges. Baker called for three "courses," Classical, Latin Scientific, and Scientific. The first consisted of Latin, Greek, and either French or German, as well as one year of physics. The Latin Scientific and Scientific courses differed only in that Latin and French or German were required in the former and Latin or German in the latter. English was required—in the form suggested by the New England Association of Colleges—in all three "courses," as was a subject called "general history." Baker and his colleagues put into words what Eliot implied in his Chelsea curriculum: "The course of study that best prepares for higher education should also be, in the essentials, the best preparation for intelligent citizenship and the active duties of life."[42]

James Baker was forty-four in 1892. He was born and raised in Maine and graduated from Bates College in 1873, having worked his way through by teaching school during the holidays. Upon graduation he became principal of the Yarmouth, Maine, schools, but when ill health forced him to take the advice of doctors and move to a drier climate, he traveled to Denver, Colorado, in 1874. There he became principal of the city high school and, in January 1892, president of the University of Colorado, an embryonic institution with sixty-six students. By this time he had to his credit one book entitled *Elementary Psychology*, published in 1890.

A biographer has described Baker's personality as being characterized by "shyness and stubborn aggressiveness."[43] He was stiff and inflexible, and hard to understand. Baker's efforts, after leaving the Committee of Ten, to form a committee on the "culture element in education" exasperated Eliot, who, after an exchange of letters, still could not see just where Baker wanted to go.[44] James Grafton Rogers describes spending an

42. *Ninth Biennial Report of the* (Colorado) *Superintendent of Public Instruction* (1894), p. 117.

43. H. M. Barrett, "James Hutchins Baker," in *Dictionary of American Biography* (New York, 1928), *1*, 522–23.

44. C. W. Eliot to E. A. Alderman, June 15, 1904, C. W. Eliot Papers, Harvard University. On James H. Baker, see also P. H. Hanus, *Adventuring*

entire morning with Baker in a committee meeting and finding with surprise that Baker had completely forgotten his name by that afternoon. Rogers asserts that Baker did not have a keen mind and was acutely conscious of it.[45] Serving on the Committee of Ten, he probably deferred to Eliot and Harris and at the same time confused and irritated them.

Richard Henry Jesse was far more amenable. The president of the University of Missouri was but forty in 1892, but had already pursued a varied career in schools and colleges. He was born in Virginia and graduated from its university in 1875. He taught French and mathematics at academies for two years and in 1878 became dean of the academic department of the University of Louisiana, which soon thereafter was renamed Tulane. From 1884 to 1891 he was given the title Professor of Latin at Tulane and in 1891 was appointed president of the University of Missouri.

President Jesse had tremendous problems, most of them stemming from increasing enrollment. Three hundred ninety-three students attended his University in 1889–90; by 1894–95 the number had risen to 615. In 1907–08, Jesse's last year, the figure reached 2,307. Jesse worked hard to raise the academic standards not only of his University but also of the state high schools. He closed the college preparatory department within a year after his appointment. His administration contributed over $5,000 a year to the high schools, and Jesse claimed that he spent three-quarters of his time away from Columbia, riding in his buggy from town to town, visiting schools and urging higher standards and greater efforts.[46]

Jesse, a handsome, bearded scholar, was called "first of all,

---

in Education (Cambridge, 1937), pp. 47–52. Hanus' description of the Denver high school and of the fledgling university are also revealing of primitive educational conditions in the west.

45. J. G. Rogers' recollections were recounted to the writer in 1960.

46. H. O. Severance, Richard Henry Jesse: President of the University of Missouri (mimeographed) (Columbia, Mo., 1937), pp. 135 ff.; and R. H. Jesse to N. M. Butler, November 1, 1897, Butler Papers, Columbia University.

and always, a gentle man."[47] His views on the articulation of high schools with the state university could not have varied markedly from those of Angell. Though a classicist, he was also fully aware of the popular demand for English studies. He probably was highly flattered to be appointed the southern representative to the Committee of Ten. He had a tremendous respect for and allegiance to Eliot; Jesse's views did not differ from those of the chairman, and even if they had, he would not have pushed them with vigor.[48]

The two men who represented endowed colleges on the Committee of Ten agreed by and large with the ideas of the chairman; for Vassar's Taylor and Oberlin's King were raised in much the same tradition as Eliot and Harris. Taylor was a summer friend of Eliot at Bar Harbor and Mt. Desert, Maine, sharing the Harvard president's love of that area. King was able to attend only the first meeting of the Committee; he was studying in Berlin when the second was held. Although he was absent from the discussions of the *Report* drafts, he was kept informed by Eliot and wanted his name signed to the Committee's findings.

James Monroe Taylor, forty-five years old in 1892, was born in Brooklyn. He graduated from the University of Rochester and, in 1871, from the Rochester Theological Seminary. After a year in Europe, he held pulpits in Baptist churches in Connecticut and Rhode Island and in 1886 accepted the presidency of Vassar College. There, his biographer asserts, he was known as a "promoter, rather than an intellectual leader."[49] He rid the college of its preparatory students, energetically raised money, and taught psychology, ethics, and philosophy; in 1892 he published *Elements of Psychology*. Active in school-college affairs,

47. W. Williams, in introduction to Severance, *Richard Henry Jesse* (no pagination).
48. See the correspondence between R. H. Jesse and C. W. Eliot in the Eliot Papers, Harvard University, and R. H. Jesse, "Some Helpful Educators," *Educational Review, 42* (1911), 20–22.
49. H. N. MacCracken, "James Monroe Taylor," in *Dictionary of American Biography* (New York, 1936), *18*, 329.

he was President of the College Association of the Middle States and Maryland during its transformation into the Association of Colleges and Preparatory Schools. It was in this capacity that he went to the Saratoga meeting of the NEA, and this probably was a factor in his selection for the Committee of Ten. It is not surprising that he was a good friend of Nicholas Murray Butler. The correspondence between the two men reveals Taylor's warm, humorous, and often urbane personality. His educational views were conservative, and lacked originality; he could be expected to defer to Harris, if not to Eliot, on the Committee of Ten.

Henry Churchill King at thirty-five was the youngest of the Committee. Because he was absent from the more important of the two meetings, he probably exerted little influence on the proceedings. Born in Michigan, he studied at Oberlin for both A.B. and B.D. degrees. In 1883 he studied philosophy at Harvard and returned the following year to Oberlin as Associate Professor of Mathematics. His true interests were philosophical and theological, and when he was appointed a full professor in 1891, it was as a philosopher.

King's interest in school-college relations stemmed from a proposal by the Oberlin faculty in 1888 to study ways of bringing Ohio high schools into closer harmony with the colleges. King spent an entire academic term visiting schools, and even after his return to Oberlin, he often left it again to speak to teachers' groups or inspect still more schools. A report of his work, made to the Ohio College Association in 1889, called for a single standard high school course that all students would take and all colleges would accept for admission.[50] In 1889 he spelled this out to the NEA: "This is not to say that exactly the same studies must be pursued by all; but that in the education of each one, the five great branches of study—mathematics, science, language and philosophy, history, literature and art—should be fairly represented."[51] This was, of course, Harris all

50. Love, *Henry Churchill King of Oberlin,* pp. 58–62.
51. H. C. King, in discussion of a speech by E. W. Coy, "Uniform Course of Study for High Schools—a Report," NEA *Proceedings* (1889), p. 532.

over again, with the logic of Eliot's single course for Chelsea thrown in.

The three schoolmen on the Committee of Ten were all vigorous and respected teachers, and the views of at least two of them carried much weight. John Tetlow was named secretary of the Committee and worked closely with the chairman, and James Mackenzie was active in whatever effective opposition to Eliot there was.

Tetlow was known as one of the few schoolmen who could stand up to the imperious president of Harvard and get away with it.[52] Born in Providence, he went to a local high school and then to Brown, where he graduated with highest honors in 1864. While an undergraduate, he commanded the college company of militia and spent one summer with his troops guarding Narragansett Bay from an expected Confederate invasion. Upon graduation, after a few months as principal of the Maple Street Grammar School in Fall River, he joined the faculty of the Friends' Academy at New Bedford. He remained there teaching classics until 1878, when he traveled to Germany for study. On his return he assumed the principalship of the New Bedford school, but left to start the Boston Girls' Latin School in 1878.

Tetlow was called "an ideal teacher." His school, a friend asserted, "belongs to the age of the millennium."[53] He was principal of Girls' Latin for thirty-two years, and, for a time, of Girls' High as well, and his many pupils were effusive in their praise of him.[54] He published a book entitled *Inductive Latin Lessons* in 1885, and another—an annotated edition of the eighth book of the *Aeneid*—in 1893.

52. The recollection of Helen Ingersoll Tetlow, recounted to the writer in 1960.
53. W. G. Bradbury, in discussion of J. Tetlow, "School Instruction in Morals and Manners," *Proceedings* of the American Institute of Instruction (1890), p. 136.
54. See the collection of letters of appreciation in the Tetlow Papers, Harvard University; also M. Antin, *The Promised Land* (Boston, 1912), pp. 292–93.

Tetlow's career paralleled that of many of the best school-masters. The qualities leading to his selection by Butler for the Committee of Ten were his candor and his considerable activity in New England for the improvement of school-college relations. Along with Roxbury Latin's William Collar and New Bedford's Ray Greene Huling, he had been a key school-man responsible for establishing the New England Association of Colleges and Preparatory Schools. In 1893 he was president of this Association and was re-elected the following year. Tetlow was a strong classicist and a vocal advocate of equality for women. His school followed the requirements for admission to Harvard's "Annex" (which eventually became Radcliffe), and to Wellesley and Vassar. He argued that the stiff work demanded by colleges was neither too difficult for women's talents nor too strenuous for their constitutions. While Tetlow did not disagree markedly with Harris or Eliot, his views coincided with those of Taylor, also a vigorous spokesman for the weaker sex; girls, after all, were the preponderant element in the secondary schools' student body. Moreover, Tetlow and Taylor wanted no special treatment for their girls.

One of the most interesting men on the Committee of Ten was James Cameron Mackenzie. Mackenzie had had the rare experience of founding a school without having to worry about funds. At the age of thirty, he was asked by the trustees of the John C. Green Foundation to spend a year traveling around to determine a plan for an ideal secondary school. This Mackenzie did; and in 1883 he became the first headmaster of Lawrenceville School.[55] His most important innovation, the "house" system in the pattern of the English public schools, has had nationwide influence.

Mackenzie was born in Scotland, and came as a boy with his mother to Wilkes-Barre, Pennsylvania. After a tremendous struggle to achieve an education, he entered Phillips Exeter Academy and graduated in 1873 with top honors. After a year

55. The John C. Green Foundation essentially "founded" the school, but on the site and with a handful of students from an old institution which had existed since 1810.

of teaching, he went to Lafayette, graduating again at the top of his class in 1878. He became principal of the Wilkes-Barre Academy and held this position until he was called to Lawrenceville. He received a Ph.D. from Lafayette in 1882 and a B.D. from Princeton Theological Seminary in 1885. His reputation was very high; during his tenure at Lawrenceville, from 1882 to 1899, he was offered teaching and administrative posts at a large number of schools, including the presidency of Lafayette, the headmastership of Exeter, and the principalship at Central High School, Philadelphia.

Like Tetlow, Mackenzie had an interest in school-college relations. Lawrenceville had been founded in 1882 as a preparatory school for Princeton,[56] and a member of the University faculty was on the Board of Trustees. Mackenzie was active in the Association of Colleges and Preparatory Schools of the Middle States and Maryland, succeeding Taylor as president in 1893. In that same year he was both a founder of the Headmasters' Association and President of the Secondary Department of the NEA. He corresponded with Butler and welcomed President and Mrs. Eliot to his campus. Eliot approved of his school —the only fault he found with it in 1892 was that it had only eight bathtubs for over 200 boys.[57] On a later occasion, Harvard's president called Lawrenceville "the best endowed preparatory school in the United States."[58]

As headmaster of Lawrenceville, Mackenzie had more difficult problems than those of mere bathtubs. His Board of Trustees, of which he was not a member, even ex officio, breathed down his neck, even reserving the right to approve of the textbooks used in the classrooms. Mackenzie's most controversial

56. Its curriculum contained three "courses," classical, scientific, and English—the last being dropped in 1893. The syllabi were not at wide variance with those of Hillhouse High School at New Haven (see above, pp. 62–63): Lawrenceville School *Register* (1893–94), pp. 9, 14–19.

57. R. J. Mulford, *History of the Lawrenceville School, 1810–1935* (Princeton, 1935), p. 108.

58. C. W. Eliot, "The Report of the Committee of Ten," *Educational Review*, 7 (1894), 105.

innovation was to allow senior boys considerable freedom and self-government in a house of their own; this practice was severely criticized even by his own faculty. He persisted in trusting his boys, setting an example that is now widely copied. He was a man of imagination and strength, and of great use to the Committee of Ten.

Oscar D. Robinson had neither the national nor the regional reputation of the other nine members of the Committee. An alert, full-bearded man with a refreshing humility, he had served as a teacher at the Albany High School and may have been there since its opening in the late 1860s; in 1879, at any rate, he was a teacher of Latin and Greek.[59] In 1887 he became principal, holding in addition the title Professor of Mental and Moral Science.

Robinson was the spokesman for the public high school on the Committee and found that role difficult. It was not that his views on the ultimate aim of the schools differed from those of the rest of the Committee; it was more that he saw certain subjects, such as manual training, stenography, and drawing, in a rather different, more important light than his colleagues.[60] The Albany High School had three courses, English, Latin-English, and Classical, the English course including some subjects of a vocational nature. In 1893 thirty-two students graduated from the English course, fifty-one from the Latin-English, and nine from the Classical. Of those taking the Regents' Examinations, 339 took the American history test, 117 algebra, and 360 one or both of the English tests. Only thirty-five papers were written in the four Greek exams, but 259 were submitted for eight Latin exams.[61] Robinson, classicist that he was, argued both for those subjects that Harris would call informational rather than vigorously disciplinary, and for the accepted English subjects. While he was highly flattered to be included

59. *Report of the Principal of the Albany High School* (1879), p. 40.
60. See below, p. 143.
61. *Twenty-Fifth Annual Report of the Albany High School* (1893), pp. 82–83, 42.

among the Ten and, indeed, altered his school's curriculum to meet the Committee's recommendations,[62] he had grave misgivings about the omission of the more practical subjects that a reasonable proportion of his own students elected to take.

The members of the Committee of Ten, then, despite their varied backgrounds and academic posts, had much in common. All had had experience in either college or school teaching and several in both. Nine—and possibly all ten—had been active in regional and national organizations that were striving to make a closer and more reasonable articulation between school and college. Even the loftiest of the university men was well aware of and well informed on the problems of the lower schools. All agreed that mental training was the general aim of education. And, most surprising, all were in substantial agreement as to how the dilemma posed by the classical and practical traditions was to be met. Their solution was a comprehensive curriculum that retained Latin, often Greek, and always algebra and added the "English" subjects of English composition and literature, history, and the natural sciences. Neither the die-hard linguists like those among the members of the Harvard Greek department nor the rabid vocational-training enthusiasts that were found in many city high schools had a single man on the Committee. Butler, in a sense, stacked the deck with his Ten, and was well aware of what he was doing. His selection shaped the *Report* itself.

62. *Twenty-Sixth Annual Report of the Albany High School* (1894), p. 52.

VI · THE CONFERENCES

In the November 1892 meetings at Columbia, the Committee of Ten had to decide what the principal subjects of the secondary school curriculum were, to select members for conferences on each subject, and to provide the conferences with some kind of common direction. Probably the most important of the decisions was determining the principal subjects, for once these were decided upon many areas of controversy would be eliminated. "The Committee of Ten, after a preliminary discussion on November 9th, decided on November 10th to organize conferences on the following subjects: 1. Latin; 2. Greek; 3. English; 4. Other Modern Languages; 5. Mathematics; 6. Physics, Astronomy and Chemistry; 7. Natural History (Biology, including Botany, Zoology, and Physiology); 8. History, Civil Government, and Political Economy; 9. Geography (Physical Geography, Geology, and Meteorology)."[1] This list is striking for a number of reasons. First, Latin and Greek received separate committees. Considering that Greek enrolled less than 5 per cent of all American secondary school students, one may wonder why it received so much of the Committee's interest. The reason was that Greek, despite its small enrollment, was still a major college entrance requirement and was also the subject of much debate in educational circles. The Committee of Ten, with an eye to influencing the strong traditionalists, was wise to give Greek an important place. Latin, of course, deserved its prominent position. It is highly probable that the Ten consid-

1. *Report of the Committee on Secondary School Studies* (Washington, D.C., 1893), p. 5.

99

ered combining Latin and Greek into one conference as it did
with physics and chemistry. The Committee compromised on
this point by requiring both Latin and Greek Conferences to
be held at the same place, the University of Michigan.[2] It was
felt that in the liberal climate of Ann Arbor the Conference
members could coordinate their efforts in determining the role
of the classics in the schools. English was accepted as a full part-
ner, and the various sciences comprised one-third of the Committee's conferences. On the other hand, the social sciences
were all encompassed by one committee. Notably omitted for
consideration were such subjects as drawing, music, bookkeeping and other commercial subjects, pedagogy and psychology,
manual training, and philosophy. The Committee limited its
attention to subjects it felt were best suited to give substantial
mental training.

It was decided that each of the nine Conferences should have
ten members who—as the NEA had charged—were to be representative of schools and colleges and of the various geographical
regions of the country. Over one hundred names were selected,
some as alternates. Twenty alternates finally did attend, causing the neat school-college and regional representation to break
down somewhat.[3]

Not surprisingly, the Committee of Ten picked its own kind;
they drew in influential scholars, men who had been involved
in various associations that were working in school-college articulation, and highly respected school teachers.[4]

The roll of influential scholars was truly impressive. The
Latin Conference had Charles E. Bennett of Cornell, James H.
Dillard, Jesse's old colleague at Tulane, and Chicago's Wil-
liam Gardner Hale. The Greek Conference was chaired by
Michigan's Martin D'Ooge and included Abby Leach, one of

2. O. D. Robinson, "The Work of the Committee of Ten," *School Review*, 2 (1894), 366.
3. *Report of the Committee on Secondary School Studies*, p. 7.
4. C. W. Eliot, "Secondary School Programs, and the Conferences of
December 1892," *Proceedings* of the New England Association of Colleges
and Preparatory Schools (1893), p. 21. For a complete list of conference
members, see pp. 215–20.

Harvard's first female students, a Vassar professor in 1892, and Benjamin Ide Wheeler of Cornell. George Lyman Kittredge of Harvard was secretary of the English Conference. Johns Hopkins' Simon Newcomb chaired the Mathematics Conference, with William E. Byerly of Harvard, Florian Cajori of Colorado College, and Truman H. Safford of Williams as members. Ira Remsen, also from Johns Hopkins, chaired the Physics Conference. Indiana's President J. M. Coulter worked on Natural History, and Wisconsin's President Charles K. Adams, Pennsylvania's James Harvey Robinson, Princeton's Woodrow Wilson, and Albert Bushnell Hart from Harvard served on the History Conference. The most notable geographers were W. M. Davis of Harvard and Mark W. Harrington of the U.S. Weather Bureau.

Three schoolmen closely associated with the work of professional associations on college entrance requirements were included: Roxbury Latin's William C. Collar, a first-rate classicist; Cincinnati's E. W. Coy, who was very active in the NEA; and New Bedford's Ray Greene Huling. There were many well-known teachers. New York's extraordinary Julius Sachs attended the Latin Conference; Ashley Hunt, of the Tulane High School, represented the college preparatory departments; and Andover's Clifford Moore participated at the Greek Conference. Two famous schoolmen attended the English Conference: Brooklyn's School Superintendent William H. Maxwell, who with Nicholas Murray Butler shortly afterward became collaborating editor of *Educational Review,* and the outspoken and liberal Samuel Thurber of Girls' High School, Boston. William T. Peck of Providence was included. James L. Patterson of Lawrenceville, who in 1935 was considered "perhaps the greatest teacher the School has had," attended the Mathematics Conference.[5] Colonel Francis W. Parker of Quincy and Chicago was a member for Geography.

The membership of the Conferences, then, had characteristics similar to those of the Committee of Ten. The Ninety were drawn from colleges—presidents and professors—and from sec-

5. Mulford, *History of Lawrenceville School,* p. 95 n.

ondary schools. The most prestigeful of the universities that had been swept up by sciences were represented in considerable numbers. Almost half of the total of 100 persons involved came from the Northeastern states; the South and West could muster only twenty, but this imbalance corresponded roughly to school enrollment. The only states that could claim under-representation were those in the North Central area of the United States. Most striking is the fact that only seven of the Conference members were members of the NEA in 1892.

Those groups excluded in the selection of the Committee of Ten were again almost excluded from the Conferences. Only two school superintendents were included: Powell of Washington, a notable reformer, and Brooklyn's Maxwell. The few teachers who were chosen were mostly principals who also taught. The women school teachers were completely ignored; the only female asked to participate was Vassar's Abby Leach. And the men who would in a quarter of a century dominate the schools—the professors of education—were almost entirely absent. Several normal schoolmen were present, but their institutions were essentially secondary schools. More important was the omission of Michigan's Burke Hinsdale and Harvard's Paul H. Hanus, both of whom were professors of pedagogy. And the small rural high school had not one spokesman.[6]

The selection of the Ten and then the Ninety caused some stir, with various critics complaining about imbalances and omissions. Butler was provoked to counterattack vigorously:

> A curiously stupid effort is being made by a small clique of persons, whose interest in education is not entirely scientific or philanthropic, to convey the impression that the college men, who are now taking a greater part than ever before in educational discus-

6. Also apparently excluded were men from Yale. Eliot explained to Mackenzie: "Both the Yale professors who were invited to serve on our conferences declined. I expected nothing else, for it has been my uniform experience that Yale does not wish to take part in any cooperative movements." Eliot was being charitable in these remarks. C. W. Eliot to J. C. Mackenzie, December 14, 1892, Mackenzie Papers, Lawrenceville School.

sions—to the immense improvement of these discussions, by the way—know nothing about the details of
common school work or the limitations under which
it is carried on. President Eliot, in particular, has been
subjected to treatment that is simply outrageous. Because he has said some things about high school and
grammar school work that individuals directly responsible for that work do not like, he has been vilified
and abused by the representatives of the dominant,
optimistic, self-glorifying philistinism in a way that
would do credit to Billingsgate. As a matter of fact,
President Eliot's knowledge of what the elementary
and secondary schools are accomplishing, both here
and abroad, is both extensive and accurate. . . . No
one person has accomplished and suggested half as
much.[7]

A. B. Hart also testified to the prejudice against the university
men: "It is well known that college professors are not included within the popular definition of the word 'educator.' "[8]

Actually, the university men on the Committee and the Conferences had had considerable experience in the lower schools.[9]
Most of the Ten, it will be recalled, had either extensively
visited or taught at secondary schools. Baker, labeled by the
critics as a "college man,"[10] had spent his entire career up to
1892 in the lower institutions. Further, it is of considerable interest to see how much movement there was between the vari-

7. N. M. Butler, editorial in *Educational Review, 4* (1892), p. 206.
8. A. B. Hart, in discussion of F. Cogswell, "The Cambridge Experiment," NEA *Proceedings* (1894), p. 338. Hart's observation holds just as
true today.
9. Of the 100, 53 were in tertiary institutions, 45 in secondary, and two
in the service of the federal government at the time the *Report* was published. It is also of interest that the editors of the two leading journals in
the field of education, *Educational Review* and *School Review*, were "college" men, Butler of Columbia and Jacob Schurman, the president of Cornell.
10. See E. P. Cubberley, *Public Education in the United States* (rev. ed.
Boston, 1934), pp. 542-44.

ous levels of education in this period, something that largely died out in the twentieth century. Thomas C. Chamberlin of the Geography Conference, for example, had been a high school principal before entering the faculty at Chicago. Wheeler of Cornell, soon to become president of the University of California, had taught at the Providence High School for four years. Simon Newcomb had kept school in rural Maryland in his youth. Smith of Vanderbilt, Dillard of Tulane, D'Ooge of Michigan, and Gummere of Haverford all had had secondary school teaching experience. College men sometimes even returned to the schools, although this was not common. Robert Porter Keep taught Greek at West Point and Yale before starting on a school career that ended at Norwich Free Academy. Charles H. Grandgent tutored at Harvard in modern foreign languages, moved to the Boston school system from 1889 to 1896, and then returned to Cambridge as a professor. Other college men were active in school affairs. Safford of Williams published an article on "Modern Teaching of Arithmetic" in the *Atlantic Monthly* in 1891. A. B. Hart was very active in the Cambridge school system and published a variety of articles on the lower schools. Harvard's W. M. Davis gave lectures on map reading for local teachers. Clearly, the spheres of college teaching and school teaching were not rigorously separated. Most of the college men on the Committee of Ten and at the Conferences were well acquainted with the secondary schools, often at first hand, and certainly were competent to consider their curricula and college entrance requirements.

Many of the participants at the Conferences were nationally influential educators. Kittredge, Wilson, Sachs, Parker, Remsen, Newcomb, Maxwell, Powell, D'Ooge, Adams, Davis: the roster reads like a list of the scholarly and pedagogical giants of America in the '90s. Because these men were the oracles of culture, their words would be read.[11] Eliot was fully aware of

11. One interesting index of the importance of the 100 persons who worked on the *Report* is the number to date enshrined in the *Dictionary of American Biography*. Thirty-nine are now listed. Of these, 31 had had experience in college teaching and 23 in school teaching. Fully 15 had studied in Germany.

this: "The best hope of exerting an influence throughout the nation over school and college programmes is through the voluntary action of a few experts in each subject of instruction, who can command the cooperation of institutions which have obtained an acknowledged preeminence, and can act under the sanction of an association having a national organization."[12]

To give direction to the Conferences, the Committee of Ten drew up an elaborate list of questions:

1. In the school course of study extending approximately from the age of six years to eighteen years—a course including the periods of both elementary and secondary instruction—at what age should the study which is the subject of the Conference be first introduced?

2. After it is introduced, how many hours a week for how many years should be devoted to it?

3. How many hours a week for how many years should be devoted to it during the last four years of the complete course; that is, during the ordinary high school period?

4. What topics, or parts, of the subject may reasonably be covered during the whole course?

5. What topics, or parts, of the subject may best be reserved for the last four years?

6. In what form and to what extent should the subject enter into college requirements for admission? Such questions as the sufficiency of translation at sight as a test of knowledge of a language, or the superiority of a laboratory examination in a scientific subject to a written examination on a textbook, are intended to be suggested under this head by the phrase, "in what form."

7. Should the subject be treated differently for pupils who are going to college, for those going to a sci-

12. C. W. Eliot, "Undesirable and Desirable Uniformity in Schools," NEA *Proceedings* (1892), p. 94.

entific school, and for those who presumably are going to neither?

8. At what stage should this differentiation begin,
if any be recommended?

9. Can any description be given of the best method
of teaching this subject throughout the school course?

10. Can any description be given of the best mode
of testing attainments in this subject at college admission examinations?

11. For those cases in which colleges and universities permit a division of the admission examination
into a preliminary and final examination, separated
by at least a year, can the best limit between the preliminary and final examinations be approximately defined?[13]

These questions are striking as they clearly indicate the path
the Committee of Ten was taking. The NCE had asked each
Conference "to consider the proper limits of its subject"; this
appears to have meant the limit of each subject in terms of its
mechanical inclusion in the school program rather than its
limit in terms of the aims and scope of the subject itself. Limit
to the Committee meant hours per year, not knowledge, skills,
and values. The Committee expected no answers as to the place
of history, or physics, or English literature, or Greek within the
broad scheme of education, and no philosophical rationale
for the teaching of certain aspects of each; these answers were
briskly assumed when the Conference subjects were assigned.
The questions they asked were mechanical—how long, when,
how—never what and why. The objectives of the subjects were
completely subordinated to the mechanics of presenting them.

Several other items are of significance. The Ten clearly took
into consideration the curriculum of the elementary schools
with the first and second questions, a not unexpected move.
College admissions problems got a full share of consideration.
One question, Number 6, was clearly loaded in favor of the

13. *Report on Secondary School Studies,* pp. 6–7.

liberal outlook—and the noncollege preparatory curricula proportionally less so. Question 7 was crucial in this regard. Robinson, the high school delegate, thought it useless, asserting that "no teacher in the United States has been heard from who could answer it in the affirmative."[14] Presumably the other nine members did not necessarily agree with Robinson's conclusion; in any event, the question was both legitimate and timely.

The eleven questions meant to guide the Conferences reveal the highly pragmatic and narrowly administrative slant the Committee of Ten was assuming. The National Council of Education charge had indicated such a slant, and the Committee was if anything strengthening it. There was no indication that the Committee sensed that the NCE had overlooked any of the crucial factors affecting secondary education in America or that the Committee was going to take a broad, fresh look at the institutions it was charged to improve. Led by a practical administrator, the Ten stayed close to concrete curricular problems.

One precedent the Committee of Ten established was its financial support by the NEA. The sponsoring body put up $2,500 to meet the Committee's expenses and, while this grant covered barely half of the cost of the *Report,* it did constitute the first outlay for research in the Association's history.[15] The NEA too wanted to join the ranks of science worshipers. Actually the Committee of Ten did not provide the impetus for the Association's decision to underwrite research. This had come earlier, largely, one suspects, through the efforts of Nicholas Murray Butler. In 1891 the NEA set up a Committee on Expenditure of Money for Pedagogical Research. The members were N. M. Butler, J. H. Baker, and W. T. Harris. It is not surprising to find that this Committee's first report in 1892 strongly supported a request by the National Council of Education to the NEA Directors for $2,500 for the Committee of Ten. Butler, Baker, and Harris indeed made no other recom-

14. Robinson, "The Work of the Committee of Ten," p. 367.
15. C. W. Eliot, "Secondary School Programs," p. 19.

mendations.[16] The Directors probably balked at the size of the sum. One vice-president, W. R. Garrett of Tennessee, wanted the grant cut to $1,000.[17] There must have been more controversy than was reflected by the stiff published *Proceedings;* Harris wrote Butler after the convention that his "timely action in the meeting of the Board of Directors . . . saved the ship."[18]

Eliot thought the grant liberal, but hoped to hold expenditures to a minimum by getting free passes or at least half-fares from the railroads for members' travel. He also hoped to hold the Conferences in cities where members could be lodged in private homes.[19] However, by December of 1892, Butler, still fully involved with the Committee's work, sent out form letters saying that "the investigations into the curriculum of the Secondary Schools being undertaken by the Committee of Ten . . . may have to be abandoned unless additional funds are provided to carry them forward. The $2,500 appropriated by the National Educational Association, will not suffice to pay the expenses. An additional $1,500 is necessary, and it must be raised within a week if possible." He went on to ask for funds but asserted that Eliot would raise $1,000 in Boston.[20] Funds were received—$50 from Seth Low, $30 from Julius Sachs, and so forth—and sent by Butler to Eliot, but money troubles were still hampering the Committee in March of the following year.[21] The final cost of the *Report,* including printing charges, must have been about $5,000. Small royalties from the Ameri-

16. "Report of the Committee on Expenditure of Money for Pedagogical Research," NEA *Proceedings* (1892), p. 250.

17. NEA *Proceedings* (1892), p. 31.

18. W. T. Harris to N. M. Butler, August 13, 1892, Butler Papers, Columbia University.

19. C. W. Eliot to J. C. Mackenzie, July 19, 1892. Mackenzie Papers, Lawrenceville School. Eliot had poor results in his efforts to win over the railroad companies; "the reductions obtainable were less numerous and considerable than hoped for." *Report of the Committee on Secondary School Studies,* p. 8.

20. N. M. Butler to J. C. Mackenzie, December 7, 1892, Mackenzie Papers, Lawrenceville School.

21. C. W. Eliot to John Tetlow, March 6, 1893, Tetlow Papers, Harvard University.

can Book Company edition of the document repaid some of this to the NEA over the years.

The Conferences met simultaneously at places widely separated across the country on the 28th, 29th, and 30th of December, 1892. Latin and Greek met at the same place, Ann Arbor; three Science Conferences, on Physics, Astronomy, and Chemistry, on Natural History, and on Geography, met in close proximity at various places near Chicago. English was at Vassar, Mathematics at Harvard, History at the University of Wisconsin, and Modern Languages at the Bureau of Education in Washington. Each Conference elected its own chairman and secretary and often invited local experts to participate. Frederick Jackson Turner and Charles H. Haskins, for example, joined in the deliberations of the History Conference. This latter Conference kept minutes that were sent as a preliminary report to Eliot.[22] Woodrow Wilson seems to have been the key mover; the detailed recommendations for the curriculum finally accepted by the Conference were essentially his. Hart and Wilson tangled over whether European or American history should be emphasized in the senior year course; Huling, the schoolman, effected a compromise. Viewed as a whole, these minutes bring to light the central weakness of all the Conferences: namely, that each could do little of practical importance in the short span of three days. The important issues were often dodged, and, encouraged by the Committee's questions, mechanical course-title shuffling resulted. While the members were able and concerned, they produced no documents of lasting and significant value.

This is not to say that the Conference reports were useless; they are full of much hard-headed, practical advice, most of it not new or imaginative, but some of it phrased felicitously and forcefully. The miserably prepared and barely competent teachers of the day could learn much from them.

22. Eliot Papers, Harvard University.

What these groups of experts reported to the Committee of Ten was to Eliot surprising. "In every Conference," he wrote, "an extraordinary unity of opinion was arrived at. The nine reports are characterized by an amount of agreement which quite surpasses the most sanguine anticipations. . . . When one considers the different localities, institutions, professional experiences, and personalities represented in each of the Conferences, the unanimity developed is very striking, and should carry great weight."[23]

The areas of agreement of the various Conferences were large, but, considering the background of the ninety members, not altogether surprising. Eight groups considered the elementary school curriculum as well as the secondary—the result of the Committee's first question. All groups favored the "shortening and enriching" thesis expounded by Eliot in 1888. The Latin Conference wanted its subject "begun not later than at the age of fourteen." The English group devoted a whole section entitled "The Study of English in Schools Below the High School Grade," spelling out in detail the composition, grammar, and reading work desired. The Modern Languages conferees were specific too: "We believe that children should, if possible, begin their study of German and French by the time they are ten years old. At that age their perceptions are acute, their vocal organs are still flexible, and they are comparatively free from that morbid fear of ridicule which impedes their progress in later years." The physicists wanted "the study of simple natural phenomena" introduced to the elementary grades; the natural historians urged nature study and botany and spelled out their wishes in detail. The History Conference recommended and outlined an ideal eight-year course from grades four to twelve. Geography had similar plans. Only the Greek scholars felt that their subject should not be taught in the elementary grades.[24]

Eliot considered "noteworthy" the restraint of the Conferences in not recommending the expansion of their subjects.

23. *Report of the Committee on Secondary School Studies*, pp. 11–12.
24. Ibid., pp. 61, 87–90, 96, 117, 142–58, 163.

Latin urged "no increase in the *quantity* of the preparation," but at the same time asserted that "through the careful choice of teachers, and the employment of better methods, a gain in the *quality* of the preparation can be secured without the expenditure of more time than is now generally given in the better schools." The Geography Conference—with the exception of one member, who submitted a minority report—went further stating that "too much time is given to the subject *in proportion to the results secured."* The geographers wanted the time actually spent to be more efficiently used. The History Conference demanded three forty-minute periods a week for eight years, in spite of Eliot's recommendation for "moderation." This amounted to one eighth of the school child's time. This—as the Conference avowed—was "radical"; but considering the Committee of Ten's belief in the righteousness of the new subject's cause, this demand did not seem inordinate.[25]

The Herbartians would be pleased to see the unanimity over "correlation," the tying together of subjects so that they were mutually contributory. Eliot summarized this forcefully:

> If the nine Conferences had sat all together as a single body, instead of sitting as detached and even isolated bodies, they could have not more forcibly expressed their conviction that every subject recommended for introduction into elementary and secondary schools should help every other; and that the teacher of each single subject should feel responsible for the advancement of the pupils in all subjects, and should distinctly contribute to this advancement.

The Latin and Greek Conferences agreed that instruction of their subjects should be coordinated. History, an obviously central subject, should overlap with Greek, English, and geography. All the languages should be tied together, the inflected tongues supporting English instruction.[26]

The Committee found another area of unanimity in claim-

25. Ibid., pp. 14, 60, 172–73. Italics in the original.
26. Ibid., pp. 16, 77, 80, 164, 199, 92.

ing that "every reader of this report and of the reports of the nine Conferences will be satisfied that to carry out the improvements proposed more highly trained teachers will be needed than are now ordinarily to be found for the service of the elementary and secondary schools." The Conferences were vehement on this subject. The historians pleaded for persons trained in the field and having "a knowledge of illuminating methods of teaching history." The Modern Language Conference recommended oral French and German instruction, but only "if the instructor has a practical command" of the language. What remark could have been more telling in describing the existing standards of teachers? The Physics group suggested a remedy— the use of a roving team of "special science-teachers or superintendents . . . to instruct the teachers of elementary schools in methods of teaching natural phenomena." One historian's remedy was more drastic: he felt that unless adequate teachers were available, his subject should be dropped from the curriculum entirely, as the damage done by incompetent instruction was worse than ignorance of history itself. The chaos in the schools resulting from the incompetence of teachers was generally recognized.[27]

There was also agreement over methods of teaching. The textbook-recitation-drill tradition was deplored, and the "scientific method" recommended. While the two classical language Conferences expressed some doubt about the effectiveness of the "inductive method" of teaching their subjects, the English scholars were less conservative, asserting that formal grammar could be justified only as a means of improving reading and composition and not as an end in itself. The Mathematics Conference wanted concrete examples and real situations used as often as possible. Laboratory work was to take fully one-half of the time recommended for physics and chemistry study, and laboratory efficiency was to be tested as a part of the college entrance requirements. The Conference on Natural History went even further; while agreeing that laboratory work should be-

27. Ibid., pp. 53, 187, 101, 117, 185.

come a part of the college entrance examinations, it asserted that such work should take a full three-fifths of the students' class time. The historians, desiring their students' notebooks to be "systematic and scientific," wanted the final high school year devoted to the intensive study of one small segment of history —"American Political Leaders from 1783–1830," for example— in the tradition of German historical scholarship. The History Conference went on to deplore the present pedagogical practice, scoring the prevalent text-rote memory system. All Conferences, with that on the Classics the least so, wanted a liberalized pedagogy in line with the "research" ideal prevalent in the society. The only subject that resisted experimental laboratory methods was the section of Natural History dealing with human physiology; in three painfully self-conscious pages, the Conference dutifully explained why textbooks alone were here desirable.[28]

The Committee's controversial seventh question was "answered in the negative by the Conferences." Eliot saw great importance in this:

> The Committee of Ten unanimously agree with the Conferences. Ninety-eight teachers [two Conference members had failed to join their groups], intimately concerned either with the actual work of American secondary schools, or with the results of that work as they appear in students who come to college, unanimously declare that every subject which is taught at all in a secondary school should be taught in the same way and to the same extent to every pupil so long as he pursues it, no matter what the probable destination of the pupil may be, or at what point his education is to cease. . . . Not that all pupils should pursue every subject for the same number of years; but so long as they do pursue it, they should all be treated alike.

28. Ibid., pp. 75, 82, 88–89, 117–18, 139, 141, 184, 177, 185, 158–61.

The English Conference extended this to say that all students should receive the same kind and quantity of instruction and that whatever this instruction was, it should be accepted for college admission. The History Conference spelled this out:

> The Conference believes that such a distinction [between different groups of pupils], especially in schools provided for the children by public taxation, is bad for all classes of pupils. It is the duty of the schools to furnish a well grounded and complete education for the child; it is the duty of higher institutions to accept a well grounded and complete education as a suitable preparation for entrance upon their courses.

The obvious implication here is that special preparatory courses for college entrance would no longer be supplied.[29]

Several aspects of unanimity in the Conference reports that Eliot did not consider worthy of notice stand out for a later reader. It was apparent that the Committee considered mental training a goal—if not the only goal—of education. The mathematicians asserted that "the method of teaching should be throughout objective, and such as to call into exercise the pupil's mental activity." In discussing the problem of unrealistic arithmetic exercises, the Conference felt it necessary to say:

> The opinion is widely prevalent that even if the [unrealistic] subjects are totally forgotten, a valuable mental discipline is acquired by the efforts made to master them. While the Conference admits that, considered in itself, this discipline has a certain value, it feels that such a discipline is greatly inferior to that which may be gained by a different class of exercises, and bears the same relation to a really improving discipline that lifting exercises in an ill-ventilated room bear to games in the open air.

29. Ibid., pp. 17, 93, 173–74.

Mental muscles were expected here, flexed in the most efficient way. In a section titled "Training of the Mind," the historians set down the claims for their discipline:

> The principal end of all education is training. In this respect history has a value different from, but in no way inferior to, that of language, mathematics, and science. The mind is chiefly developed in three ways: by cultivating the powers of discriminating observation; by strengthening the logical faculty of following an argument from point to point; and by improving the process of comparison, that is, the judgment . . . history and its allied branches are better adapted than any other studies to promote the invaluable mental power which we call the judgment.

The choice of words is truly revealing; similar terms are found in the Geography report. The consensus of the Committee and the Conferences on this point is important, for if the goal for all subjects was mental discipline rather than professional skill or vocational efficiency, history and geography became more or less interchangeable tools. Both trained the power of reasoning; thus it made no difference which one studied. Harris' five windows associated certain academic areas with various psychological aspects that needed to be cultivated—observation, judgment, and so forth—and the beliefs expressed by the various Conferences showed how each fit into this scheme. In addition, the new subjects in seeking equality with the old, argued for status on the basis not of content, but rather of their disciplinary value. The doctrine of mental discipline also explains the Conference's unanimity on Question 7. All children should be taught in the same way; there was only one way to teach a subject for its disciplinary value. Latin was taught not for its own sake but for the sake of mental training, something that all persons needed whether they were to become mechanics or classics scholars. Students had the right to select their own disciplinary studies, but having made their choice, they were all to be trained "to think" and therefore all trained in the same way.[30]

Another unfortunate aspect of similarity in the various Conference reports was their failure to grapple with some of the key questions for their disciplines. Happily, some of the groups went beyond the pure mechanism of the Committee of Ten's question and stated specific aims for their subjects. The English Conference was succinct: "The main objects of the teaching of English in schools seem to be two: (1) to enable the pupil to understand the expressed thoughts of others and to give expression to thoughts of his own; and (2) to cultivate a taste for reading, to give the pupil some acquaintance with good literature, and to furnish him with the means of extending that acquaintance." The Conference on Natural History phrased its aims for the elementary grades in terms of the "Result of Six Years' Work. Pupils are self-reliant and independent; they can observe, reason, and express; and they have a fair knowledge of the whole plant and its life history." The History Conference asserted that history's "chief object is the training of the judgment." These various aims, along with mental training, are unimpeachable, but what the Conferences did not do is demonstrate how the programs they proposed would meet these aims. Will the study of French history necessarily teach judgment? How does the required English syllabus cultivate a taste for reading? At no time did any Conference start by questioning even the few aims it expressed. The History Conference, whose report was by far the most lucid and useful of the nine, never examined the gap between its aims and classroom practice. How does one train others to use logical argument? The historians blithely assumed that chronological history would do so and never bothered to provide any evidence. Moreover, they simply titled their courses "Greek and Roman History," "American History," and so forth, and never specified the scope of the phrases. If the purpose of historical study is to acquire judgment, what aspects of American history should be studied? A few turning points? A chronological summary? The Conference

30. Ibid., pp. 105, 108, 168, 214.

never answered these questions and, by this omission, badly weakened its programs. All the Conferences suffered from a naive faith in the disciplinary value of their various subjects.[31]

This naiveté, coupled with the Committee's questions, led to an ill-considered mechanical course-juggling. The Latin scholars asserted that Latin should receive one-fifth of each school day for four years, never stating the logic that led them to this precise figure. The Greek Conference put forth similar demands. The three Science Conferences held a joint session and resolved that together they should be assigned one-quarter of the high school course; their rationale for this proportion was not stated. The English Conference, neglecting some crucial areas, felt obliged to specify the minimum number of examples of "bad English" to be used on the college entrance tests ("not less than a page of the examination book"). Several Conferences described in detail how notebooks were to be kept, and the Physics Conference appended ten pages listing references in half a dozen texts for chemistry experiments. While important points were often overlooked, then, trivial detail or unreasoned prescription found a place in the reports.[32]

The Conferences agreed on a number of minor items that Eliot felt were of importance, particularly when he considered the practices of the secondary schools of his day. All the Conferences felt that their subjects should be pursued for a period long enough to allow for "thoroughness"; he cited their conclusion that six-weeks' courses in world history or physics, for example, were a total waste. Eliot summed up this conclusion in a significant phrase: each subject should be taught long enough "to win from it the kind of mental training it is fitted to supply." The Conferences felt there should be no "short information courses." This conviction led them to reduce the large number of subjects offered by secondary schools in 1892—conservatively estimated as forty—and by this action they greatly altered the appearance of the curriculum.[33]

31. Ibid., pp. 86, 150, 170.
32. Ibid., pp. 61, 77, 123, 94.
33. Ibid., p. 44.

Several observations should be made on the individual reports, as each varied markedly in style from every other. The Physics, Chemistry, and Astronomy report was the shortest, filling only four and a half pages (excluding the appended experiment references). The History report, on the other hand, contained thirty-six readable pages, and that of Geography thirty-two pages, though these were confused and turgid. This Geography report dealt "with more novelties" than any of the others, Eliot felt; the Conference conceived its subject matter to include not simply cities, mountains, and oceans, but rather "the elements of botany, zoology, astronomy, and meteorology, as well as many considerations pertaining to commerce, government, and ethnology." This conception was more inclusive than that held by most practicing teachers, a factor that may have explained why the Conference had difficulty agreeing and why an important minority report was submitted. Only one other Conference, that on Physics, had a minority opinion expressed.[34]

The Mathematics Conference was quite blunt on the subject of arithmetic, claiming that "a radical change" was necessary. Eliot must have been pleased with this; the Conference met at Harvard, and in his capacity as a former mathematics tutor, he may have had a hand in shaping the statement. The Mathematics Conference was the only one to offer a slight differentiation of program for those not going to college; it provided for a few weeks of optional commercial arithmetic and bookkeeping for terminal students.[35]

The Conference reports reflected ideas that were congenial with those of the Ten. This is not surprising: the Ten did not disagree radically among themselves; the members they chose for the Conferences mirrored the Committee's own biases; and demands for the "new" or "English" subjects, including the sciences, plus a rather practical, even mechanical way of looking at the curriculum, were ideas seen in the reports of all the co-

34. Ibid., pp. 31–32.
35. Ibid., pp. 105, 107.

operating scholars and teachers. While the Committee's eleven questions and the resulting Conference reports had many flaws, the use made of them by Eliot and his nine colleagues would determine the extent to which they would fill the gap.

VII · THE REPORT

President Eliot requested the Conference chairmen to send him their reports by April 1, 1893. He hoped that the Committee of Ten could draw up its own summary in time for the 1893 NEA Convention, which was to be held in Chicago at the end of July. This Convention was to be part of the World's Columbian Exposition, and many international scholars and teachers would be in attendance. Unfortunately two Conference chairmen failed to meet the President's deadline, and Eliot was not able to start work until August.

As the Conference reports came to him, Eliot read them and had them set in type. On September 19, the first draft of the Committee's report, prepared by Eliot, together with the nine Conference reports, all in printed form, were sent off to the Committee members. With these Eliot sent a letter pointing out that the Natural History report was to be further revised by its author and asking, "Would it be advantageous for the Committee to consult certain pedagogical experts concerning the programme for secondary schools before they [the Committee] make up their own report, or would it be expedient to consult such experts on the whole body of recommendations which proceed from the nine Conferences . . . ? Would such a proceeding be good policy? Would it add to the weight of the report? As examples of the kind of expert I have in mind, I will name President G. Stanley Hall of Clark University, and Professor Nicholas Murray Butler of Columbia College." Apparently the Committee opposed this plan; if they had not, G. Stanley Hall's biting attacks on the *Report* might not have taken place.[1] Another intriguing aspect of the letter is a reference to a "Board of Inspectors" that had presumably been discussed at the November 1892 meeting or in correspondence. Eliot wrote that such a board was not appropriate, and the matter was apparently laid to rest.[2]

The nine men replied to Eliot's letter—the *Report* draft was printed on wide galley sheets that provided considerable margin space for their comments—and the President drew up a second draft over which the Committee would work at their second and final meeting at Columbia in early November 1893.[3]

Between November 1892 and November 1893 the Committee members' opinions were hardening, and in different directions. Eliot, thoroughly gloomy,[4] wrote to Robinson: "It is clear that the Committee of Ten are going to have great difficulty in agreeing to any general report."[5] Members apparently corresponded among themselves on the subject of their study. Harris, for example, sent Mackenzie a copy of his essay, "The Function of the Study of Latin and Greek," along with a copy of the St. Louis School Report for 1873, which he explained showed "how the 'five windows of the soul' have been remembered in making up the programme."[6] These two classicists, though their views were moderate enough, were digging in, probably as a result of the 1892 fight over whether there would be a single Conference for Latin and Greek or separate ones.

1. See below, pp. 195-96. If the "pedagogical experts" were left off the Committee, it is interesting that Eliot missed them, and that he exhibited the value he placed on the wisdom of the so-called "professional educator."

2. C. W. Eliot to J. C. Mackenzie et al., September 19, 1893, Mackenzie Papers, Lawrenceville School.

3. Chicago had been considered as the second place of meeting to accommodate Messrs. Baker, Jesse, and King; but New York won out. C. W. Eliot to J. Tetlow, March 6, 9, 1893, Tetlow Papers, Harvard University.

4. J. C. Mackenzie, "The Course for Academies and High Schools Recommended by the Committee of Ten," *Independent, 46* (1894), 984.

5. C. W. Eliot to O. D. Robinson, October 24, 1893, quoted in O. D. Robinson, "The Work of the Committee of Ten," *School Review, 2* (1894), 368.

6. W. T. Harris to J. C. Mackenzie, November 26, 1892, Mackenzie Papers, Lawrenceville School.

The Committee, with Eliot's second draft in hand, met from November 8 to November 11, 1893, at Columbia College. Eight meetings were held, each of three hours' duration,[7] and "the discussions at the prolonged meeting were vigorous and comprehensive, and resulted in a thorough revision of the preliminary report."[8] Eliot polished this third draft, resubmitted it by mail to his colleagues, and incorporated their resulting suggestions into a final copy. James Baker, though he signed the final draft, decided to submit a minority report as well. The *Report* in toto was dated December 4, 1893.

The *Report of the Committee on Secondary School Studies* is a document 249 pages in length, 59 of them dealing with the Ten's report and 190 presenting the separate Conference reports. Eliot, in his spare, direct style, opened the report with the administrative details of the Committee's formation, the NCE charge, the meetings held, and the names of those involved. He even felt it necessary to note in a stern schoolmasterly tone the two absentees from the Conferences and the tardiness in submission of two Conference reports. Not before the thirteenth page was he content to start discussing the Conference reports. After general comments on their striking unanimity, he presented a summary of each, noting points he felt were unusual and significant. The conclusions of the Committee of Ten itself fill only 21 of the 259 pages.

Eliot, in preparing the first draft of the *Report,* made a chart on which all the recommendations of the Conferences were recorded, subject by subject, from grade one of the elementary school to grade twelve of the secondary school. This he called Table I. Table II was a refinement showing the curricula for each of the four secondary school years as the Conferences had recommended, including the number of periods per week each subject would be offered. Eliot found that freshmen would be in class 22 periods a week, sophomores $37\frac{1}{2}$, juniors 35, and seniors $37\frac{1}{2}$, and he properly concluded that this class load, considering that a period was 40 to 45 minutes in length, was

7. N. M. Butler, editorial in *Educational Review, 6* (1893), 514–15.
8. *Report of the Committee on Secondary School Studies,* p. 12.

excessive. In other words, the strict recommendations of the nine Conferences, in terms of what should be taught, in which of the school years, and for how many periods per week, could not be carried out.

Clearly Eliot was attempting to form a curriculum simply by combining the nine Conference suggestions and, in attempting this, he was assuming that all nine subject areas studied were of equal value. The Conferences by no means argued for equal time for their subjects; but the Committee of Ten, by deciding not to construct a strict hierarchy of priorities between subjects, plainly implied equal status for all nine, English with Latin and history with Greek, for example. This fact is of fundamental importance, and, while it is no surprise in view of the opinions held by the ten Committee men, it was important indeed for the time—a time in which many conservative educators questioned the disciplinary value of English and history and the natural sciences. The Committee of Ten had given a decided bias to its report in 1892 by selecting those nine subject areas for study, and in 1893 its application of the Conferences' recommendations to teaching those areas showed that the bias had not changed.

As Table II yielded no reasonable course of study, the Committee had the job of developing one by compromise. To Oscar Robinson, Eliot wrote of his doubts about the prospects: "I am more and more led to believe that the Committee of Ten will have to confine themselves to interpreting the results of the Conferences. I do not believe that any two members of the Committee would agree on the details of a specific programme for a secondary school."[9] But Eliot was revealing his gloom to the one member who probably was most out of sympathy with him—gloom that was unrealistic. Compromise would come; and to that end, one route Eliot chose was to juggle Table II.

Several of the traditional subjects had been given five periods a week by their appropriate Conferences—Latin, algebra, Greek, chemistry, and physics among them. The lesser subjects,

9. C. W. Eliot to O. D. Robinson, October 27, 1893, quoted in Robinson, "The Work of the Committee of Ten," p. 370.

primarily history and the modern languages, requested less. Eliot arbitrarily changed the five periods to four (except for the first-year courses in each foreign language) and added science to the first-year course, but changed none of the time schedules of the lesser subjects. The result was a four-year curriculum that still required the students to be in class from twenty-five to thirty-four periods a week, a number considered excessive; Table III, then, was a useless exercise. Eliot, however, kept the Table prominently in his *Report,* a somewhat surprising but very important decision and one that upset several Committee members. Harris wrote to Eliot after the November 1893 meeting:

> The program, Table three, which was scarcely discussed at all in the conference at New York, makes altogether the most prominent figure in the whole Report, as now presented. It will give the impression to all teachers that the Committee of Ten laid most stress on digesting and reconciling the several reports of the special conferences. While, as I understand it, the Committee spent most of its time in constructing an ideal program, in the *light of the discussions* of the several committees, not hesitating to depart from the recommendations of the special conferences, when it became necessary, in the opinions of the members of the Committee of Ten. The question arose at one of the meetings in New York whether this program, No. 3, should be retained. I now seem to see that it was a mistake that we retained it, because the program, Table No. 3, which we scarcely even considered seriously, now seems the chief product of our Committee.[10]

As a result of this pressure, Eliot softened the language explaining the table, asserting that it intended "no judgment or rec-

10. W. T. Harris to C. W. Eliot, November 22, 1893, Mackenzie Papers, Lawrenceville School. Italics in the original. Mackenzie, Angell, and Robinson also objected to the prominence given Table III.

ommendations of the Committee."[11] Still, he left it in, believing it was the best model from which individual schools could develop their own curricula, or, as he saw in the report, "the possible source of a great variety of secondary school programmes." In the *Report* Eliot also significantly pointed out that "Table III reduces somewhat the proportional time devoted to Latin, English, and mathematics, and increases the proportional time devoted to natural science."[12] Such a realignment was one with which he was clearly in sympathy; he may have observed that the Committee was not moving in that direction as fast as he had hoped, for at the New York meetings "the lion's share of attention"[13] was given to discussion of an "ideal" classical course—a predominantly linguistic one.

Table IV, described by Eliot as only a sample of the kind of program that could be developed from Table III, was the result of the Committee's compromises. This was difficult to achieve, for the ten men were writing a course of study in great detail, right down to the number of hours to be spent on each subject each week. At this level the disagreements between classicists and scientists, mental trainers and practical men, became enlarged. "There was danger . . . in that the Committee of Ten did not represent in its members all branches of the course of study, the traditional and the newly proposed, with equal ability. The net results of the work of the Committee of Ten as found in the classical programme of Table No. 4 are therefore by no means authoritative or conclusive even to its own members."[14] Yet results there were, and these followed a not unexpected pattern.

Table IV set out four "courses": Classical, Latin-Scientific, Modern Languages, and English. All had a basic core, however,

11. *Report of the Committee on Secondary School Studies,* p. 40. See also C. W. Eliot to J. C. Mackenzie, December 1, 1893. Mackenzie Papers, Lawrenceville School.

12. *Report of the Committee on Secondary School Studies,* p. 42.

13. W. T. Harris, "The Committee of Ten on Secondary Schools," *Educational Review,* 7 (1894), 3.

14. Harris, "The Committee of Ten on Secondary Schools," p. 4.

and could have been described as a single course with electives. The classical course required four years of Latin, two of Greek, and three of either French or German. In those schools where tradition or "local public opinion" deemed it wise, Greek was allotted three years and the modern languages two. Geography was taught in the first year, physics in the second, and chemistry in the fourth, for fewer periods per week than the languages. English was given a few hours a week each year, but history was to be taught only in the first two years and in the final one as an elective option with mathematics. The Committee had decided that twenty periods a week was desirable; of these, over the four-year span, the classical languages dominated over one-third. All linguistic studies together encompassed two-thirds of a student's time, and the sciences and mathematics together comprised but a fourth. Eliot, in the *Report* itself, asserts that "History and English suffer serious contraction."[15]

The Latin-Scientific course also had a distinct linguistic bias. While Latin and science alone each claimed about a quarter of the student's time, the languages together—Latin, English, and the modern tongues—took over a half of the periods. Mathematics remained as in the Classical course, but history suffered even further loss. The Modern Language course was identical with the Latin-Scientific save for the introduction of either French or German for Latin. The English course was a clear departure from the preceding pattern, however: it provided equal time for one foreign language, English, and science and divided the remaining one-third of the time between history and mathematics, giving each more periods than were allowed in the other courses.

The contents of these four courses raised a host of issues; indeed, the very method of arriving at them is worthy of comment. At no place in the Committee's *Report* is there argument spelling out a hierarchy of subjects, but in assigning a number of hours of class time in Table IV, a clear hierarchy emerges: linguistic studies are favored, with mathematics, the sciences,

15. *Report of the Committee on Secondary School Studies,* pp. 46, 44.

and history following, the last at a considerable distance. The assignment of hours per week represented far more to Eliot than merely an administrative detail:

> The details of the time-allotment for the several studies which enter into the secondary school programme may seem to some persons mechanical, or even trivial —a technical matter to be deal with by each superintendent of schools, or by each principal of a secondary school, acting on his own individual experience and judgment; but such is not the opinion of the Committee of Ten. The Committee believe that to establish just proportions between the several subjects, or groups of allied subjects, on which the Conferences were held, it is essential that each principal subject shall be taught thoroughly and extensively, and therefore for an adequate number of periods a week on the school programme. If twice as much time is given in a school to Latin as is given to mathematics, the attainments of the pupils in Latin ought to be twice as great as they are in mathematics, provided that equally good work is done in the two subjects; and Latin will have twice the educational value of mathematics. . . . If every subject is to provide a substantial mental training, it must have a time-allotment sufficient to produce that fruit.[16]

In this way Eliot justified the elaborate juggling of hours represented in Tables II and III and the detail with which Table IV is constructed. But he fails to be convincing. What are pupils' attainments? How can one measure relative attainments, for instance those of a single history class and a single physics class? Eliot not only fails to define his terms; he also provides no proof for his assertion that learning a subject is a direct function of the time spent at it. The experience of teachers, not to mention the empirical studies of psychologists, tends to cast

16. Ibid., p. 43, see also p. 38.

doubt on the validity of Eliot's argument. Minutes of teaching are not identical pennies placed in a bank.

The linguistic emphasis of the Committee's recommended curriculum has already been demonstrated, as well as Eliot's implicit rejoinder to it—Table III. The convinced classicists among the Ten obviously put up a strong fight; as Harris himself had said, the classical course of Table IV took the "lion's share" of the Committee's time. Harris, long known as a defender of the ancient languages as educational tools, teamed up with Mackenzie to promote their cause. The heat they generated is revealed in a letter sent by Harris to Lawrenceville: "It seems to me that there should be a consensus on the part of the advocates of Latin and Greek and that the strongest grounds for these studies should be set forward and made as plain as possible to the Philistines."[17] There is little mystery as to who at least one Philistine was. It is also amusing to note, in the light of the criticism that the *Report* eventually drew for reflecting the "college professor's, traditional bias," that the two most vehement supporters of the ancient languages were schoolmen.

Yet, although Latin was fully upheld by the *Report*, Greek received—as in Eliot's Chelsea High School curriculum—only two years of secondary school work (the Greek Conference had recommended three). As Eliot wrote in the *Report* itself, "one member of the Committee is firmly of the opinion that Greek comes too late"—that is, in the third year.[18] This single point was to be the rallying ground of the conservative opponents of the *Report* once it was published.

It is interesting to note, in view of the linguistic bias of the Committee's recommendations, that the *Report* was considered radical in its day, for it contained a number of important liberal recommendations.

17. W. T. Harris to J. C. Mackenzie, January 6, 1893, Mackenzie Papers, Lawrenceville School.
18. *Report of the Committee on Secondary School Studies*, p. 45. The one member probably was either Harris or Robinson, surprising to say. See below, p. 179.

First of all, the four courses recommended by the Committee contained a common core of subjects to be taken by all students. In the first year each student took English, algebra, history, and physical geography, plus one language—Latin or, in two courses, possibly French or German. Geometry and physics were common courses in the second year; English was taken by all, but for varying periods per week. Mathematics continued as a common subject in the last two years, as did English; and chemistry was required for all in the senior year. As Eliot wrote, the four courses all "make sufficiently continuous the instruction in each of the main lines, namely, language, science, history, and mathematics."[19] While this was not exactly true, it was true enough to be radical: the four elements, like Harris' similar five windows of the soul, were all rated equal, languages and mathematics with science and history. The Committee of Ten clearly dignified the new disciplines, raising them to a status that was well established even by the next generation.

More liberal for its day was the recommendation that all colleges accept students who had reached a satisfactory standard in any one of the suggested courses. As Eliot dramatized:

> A College might say,—We will accept for admission any groups of studies taken from the secondary school programme, provided that the sum of the studies in each of the four years amounts to sixteen, or eighteen, or twenty periods a week,—as may be thought best. . . . On the theory that all the subjects are to be considered equivalent in educational rank for the purpose of admission to college, it would make no difference which subject [a student] had chosen from the programme—he would have had four years of strong and effective mental training.[20]

This recommendation of the Committee of Ten to recognize sound work in any of the courses that led to mental discipline constituted a radical move in the eyes of conservative colleges

19. *Report of the Committee on Secondary School Studies*, pp. 44–45.
20. Ibid., pp. 52–53.

—Yale, for instance. However, the Committee's resolution was no real departure from the Midwestern practice of accreditation.

The Committee bluntly lectured the colleges on their responsibilities not only to liberalize their admission requirements, but also on their duty to education in general:

> In regard to preparing young men and women for the business of teaching, the country has a right to expect much more than it has yet obtained from the colleges and normal schools. The common expectation of attainment for pupils of the normal schools has been altogether too low the country over. . . . As to the colleges, it is quite as much an enlargement of sympathies as an improvement of apparatus or of teaching that they need. They ought to take more interest than they have heretofore done, not only in the secondary, but in the elementary schools, and they ought to take pains to fit men well for the duties of a school superintendent. They already train a considerable number of the best principals of high schools and academies; but this is not sufficient. They should take an active interest, through their presidents, professors, and other teachers, in improving the schools in their respective localities, and in contributing to the thorough discussion of all questions affecting the welfare of both the elementary and the secondary schools.[21]

Little did the Committee know that its efforts represented a high water mark of college and university cooperation with the lower schools.

The Committee did not justify its liberal college admission recommendations upon the claims of the new disciplines alone. It more importantly stressed the nature of the American secondary school, and its rationale was made explicit:

> The secondary schools of the United States, taken as a whole, do not exist for the purpose of preparing boys

21. Ibid., pp. 54–55.

and girls for colleges. Only an insignificant percentage of the graduates of these schools go to colleges or scientific schools. Their main function is to prepare for the duties of life that small proportion of all the children in the country—a proportion small in number, but very important to the welfare of the nation—who show themselves able to profit by an education prolonged to the eighteenth year, and whose parents are able to support them while they remain so long in school. . . . A secondary school programme intended for national use must therefore be made for those children whose education is not to be pursued beyond the secondary school. The preparation of a few pupils for college or scientific school should in the ordinary school be the incidental, and not the principal object. At the same time, it is obviously desirable that the colleges and scientific schools should be accessible to all boys or girls who have completed creditably the secondary school course. Their parents often do not decide for them, four years before the college age, that they shall go to college, and they themselves may not, perhaps, feel the desire to continue their education until near the end of their school course. In order that any successful graduate of a good secondary school should be free to present himself at the gates of the college or scientific school of his choice, it is necessary that the colleges and scientific schools of the country should accept for admission to appropriate courses of their instruction the attainments of any youth who has passed creditably through a good secondary school course, no matter to what group of subjects he may have mainly devoted himself in the secondary school.[22]

The logic of this argument was indeed liberal for the 1890s, particularly in the East, but it had been expressed by members

22. Ibid., pp. 51–52.

of the Committee of Ten before. "I believe," wrote Harris in 1883, "that the best course of study for any one pupil is the best of [sic] all others so far as fundamental disciplines are concerned."[23] Baker told the NCE in 1887, "President Eliot has expressed the opinion that in the future it will be found that the high school course, which is best to fit pupils for life, is also best to fit them for college. This is my own opinion."[24] This view solved one aspect of the "education for life" versus "education for college" dilemma: there was to be no difference between them. Life and college were both best prepared for by a mental discipline developed through the study of the academic subjects. What the colleges required and what life demanded were not, in the Committee's view, different or contradictory.

Attention should be called, however, to a particular phrase in Eliot's previously quoted argument: the high schools were to train that small proportion of the youths "whose parents are able to support them while they remain so long in school." Eliot and his Committee did not visualize universal public secondary education, much less a national economy that would make possible the removal of all children under sixteen from the labor force. The Committee's view on this matter can be called aristocratic; it argued that it supported higher education only for those who could afford it. This point of view is in all probability erroneous; the Committee and Eliot did not in this instance—or in many other instances—foresee a time when more children could attend school. They argued their point from the viewpoint of the realities of 1892, when the overwhelming proportion of children could not and did not spend their teen-age, income-producing years in schoolrooms.

The Committee felt that the difference between the Classical and Latin-Scientific courses was an important one in that

23. W. T. Harris, "On the Relation of the College to the Common School," *Proceedings* of the American Institute of Instruction (1883), p. 166.

24. J. H. Baker, discussion of the Report of the Committee on Secondary Education, NEA *Proceedings* (1887), p. 288.

each course led the student into a different path of life: the Classical with Greek into a career in letters via the A.B. degree, the Latin-Scientific into technology via the S.B. Accordingly, the Committee tried to delay the date when the student had to make his choice until as late as the third year of high school. Eliot explained the Committee's reasoning:

> In the first place they [the Ten] endeavored to postpone until the third year the grave choice between the Classical course and the Latin-Scientific. They believed that this bifurcation should occur as late as possible, since the choice between these two roads often determines for life the youth's career. Moreover, they believed that it is possible to make this important decision for a boy on good grounds, only when he has had opportunity to exhibit his quality and discover his tastes by making excursions into all the principal fields of knowledge.

He further asserted that, even if a student left school at the tenth-grade level, the first two years of high school, with their general, unspecialized, common course, would "be highly profitable by themselves."[25] Accordingly, physics was to be taken by all, and was pushed down to the second high school year, while Greek was considered more properly an elective and accordingly was started only in the third year. By making the first two years of secondary school general for all, the Committee felt that it protected both the interests of those leaving early—who would receive a balanced education—and the interests of those college bound—who could sample both the humanities and the sciences before starting their specialized training.

It is interesting to note, parenthetically, that the Committee of Ten has been credited with inventing that American phenomenon, the junior high school. Mention has been made above of the Committee's and Conferences' interest in improving the standard of the elementary school and of their

25. *Report of the Committee on Secondary School Studies*, pp. 45–46, 48.

133

recommendations for "dipping down," for teaching subjects normally begun in the secondary school in the elementary grades. Eliot explained: "In the opinion of the Committee, several subjects now reserved for high schools, such as
algebra, geometry, natural science, and foreign languages—
should be begun earlier than now, and therefore within the
schools classified as elementary; or as an alternative, the secondary school period should be made to begin two years
earlier than at present, leaving six years instead of eight for
the elementary school period."[26] It is doubtful that the Committee seriously considered the merits of these eight-four and
six-six systems, but Harris for one was upset by Eliot's notions.
"I had hoped," he wrote to Eliot,

> that the position would have been made a little
> clearer that it is the course of study which makes the
> the secondary school. Put Latin and algebra back
> into the elementary course means [sic] that the elemen-
> tary course shall be shortened and the secondary
> course lengthened. In one place in this Report the
> words of the Committee might be taken to imply
> that secondary studies may be introduced into the
> elementary course.[27]

Harris, it will be recalled, favored the one-room schoolhouse
type of elementary education. Departmental instruction, virtually required if the Committee's recommendations for dipping down were carried out, would change the character of
the lower school. Eliot, on the other hand, surely looked at
this problem of standards in the same way as he had viewed
Harvard's similar problems: requiring the elementary schools
to cover more ground would enable the secondary schools to
raise their standards, just as Harvard raised the value of its
own A.B. by demanding sounder preparation by the high

26. Ibid., p. 45.
27. W. T. Harris to C. W. Eliot, November 22, 1893, Mackenzie Papers,
Lawrenceville School.

schools. But to call Eliot the father of the junior high school is reading far too much into the *Report*.

President Eliot was well known for his espousal of the elective system at Harvard. The so-called "equivalence of studies" was one of its aspects, and exposed him to the most abuse. Those who upheld this theory asserted that certain academic subjects—Latin, mathematics, history, physics—all provided mental discipline and therefore it mattered little in the long run which of them a student took. While Eliot never went to this extreme, his terse explanations of the rationale behind his elective reforms conveyed the impression that he did, and his many critics expected "equivalence" to appear in the *Report* of the Committee of Ten.

Eliot himself was frankly uncertain about the value of any subject. "I am fundamentally a complete skeptic as to the necessity of any subject whatever as an element in the education of a gentleman and a scholar."[28] He developed this idea further:

> I cannot agree with you [he wrote W. H. Smiley in October 1894] that every maker of a practical programme ought to be able to answer with confidence the question—are all subjects equivalent for general education? Theoretical views on that subject certainly need to be supported by practical experience, and the fact seems to me to be that the educational world does not supply the needed experience. We know a little something by experience concerning the educational value of Latin, Greek, and Mathematics; but what do we know with certainty about the educational value of History, the Modern Languages, Ethics, or Natural History? Where have these subjects been taught long enough, and with intelligent methods enough, to demonstrate their value? I have heard of two or three

28. C. W. Eliot to S. M. MacVane, June 18, 1897, Eliot Papers, Harvard University.

schools in this country where History has really been taught as seriously as Latin, and with good results; but there are thousands of schools in which History is taught by a method which can hardly produce any good result so far as mental discipline is concerned. Moreover, it is taught to a very small extent—not enough to bring out its disciplinary value. The same thing is true so far as I can see of most of the new subjects. We may therefore *believe* that it is possible to develop a child's mind as well through the study of History, or Natural History, or Modern Languages as through the study of Latin, Greek, Geometry and Algebra, and we may believe this firmly enough to wish to try judicious experiments; but can we say that we have confident convictions?[29]

Ray Greene Huling, writing in 1894, cast disbelief on Eliot's view: "It is a somewhat open secret that the main report [of the Committee of Ten], when originally written, had as the scarlet cord running through it the idea of the practical equivalence of the principal subjects of secondary study for the purposes of general education. In the discussion which ensued upon the first reading, so much opposition to this idea was manifested that in the revision this theory received scant illustration."[30] Unfortunately none of the original drafts of the *Report* have come to light to evaluate the truth of Huling's assertion, but it makes one skeptical to read Harris' view —Harris being no lover of the equivalence theory. "I think the Report as it stands now," Harris wrote Eliot in November 1893, "is better than the first draft of it, and the first draft, as I have already stated to you, seemed good enough to surpass any reasonable expectations. Hence I cordially indorse the Report."[31] Harris made his ideas on the subject even more

29. C. W. Eliot to W. H. Smiley, October 31, 1894, Eliot Papers, Harvard University.

30. R. G. Huling, "The Reports on Secondary School Studies," *School Review*, 2 (1894), 271.

31. W. T. Harris to C. W. Eliot, November 22, 1893, Mackenzie Papers, Lawrenceville School.

explicit in a letter to Professor H. N. Gardiner of Smith College. "I would say," he wrote,

> that I am one of the most emphatic "dissenters" from the doctrine of equivalence of studies as opposed by President Baker [in his minority report]. I say "opposed by President Baker" rather than "proposed by the Report of the Committee of Ten" because it was the understanding of the majority of the Committee of Ten that such equivalence was not set forward in that Report on a distinct doctrine. It was our belief that such a doctrine is held by President Eliot with more or less of confidence, but we did not suppose that President Eliot was quite prepared to utter it as his final opinion, and we did not find it in the Report as we read it and discussed it.[32]

President Baker, on the contrary, expressed in his minority report the opinion that equivalence had found its way into the *Report*. He cited various sentences to support his view:

> I cannot endorse expressions that appear to sanction the idea that the choice of subjects in secondary schools may be a matter of comparative indifference. I note especially the following sentences, referring the reader to their context for accurate interpretation. . . .
> If twice as much time is given in a school to Latin as is given to mathematics, the attainments of the pupils in Latin ought to be twice as great as they are in mathematics, provided that equally good work is done in the two subjects; and Latin will have twice the educational value of mathematics. . . .
> The schedule of studies contained in Table III permits flexibility and variety in three respects. First, it is not necessary that any school should teach all the

32. W. T. Harris to H. N. Gardiner, March 2, 1895, Bureau of Education Records, U.S. Archives.

subjects which it contains, or any particular set of subjects. . . .

Every youth who entered college would have spent
four years in studying a few subjects thoroughly; and
on the theory that all subjects are to be considered
equivalent in educational rank for the purpose of admission to college, it would make no difference
which subjects he had chosen from the programme—
he would have had four years of strong and effective
mental training. . . .

All such statements are based upon the theory that,
for the purposes of general education, one study is as
good as another,—a theory which appears to me to ignore Philosophy, Psychology and Science of Education. It is a theory which makes education formal
and does not consider the nature and value of content. . . . Secondary school programmes can not well
omit mathematics, or science, or history, or literature,
or the culture of the ancient classics. An education
which gives a view in all directions is the work of the
elementary and secondary schools.[33]

Baker read far too much into his selected quotations. In the
first of them, Eliot did not suggest that either subject should
not be studied; he was merely demonstrating the value of
each for mental discipline—a concept with which Baker was
in total agreement. The quotation concerning Table III does
not suggest that the subjects taught in a school are "a matter
of comparative indifference"; it merely says that some schools
may not want to offer every subject suggested by the nine
Conferences. Boston Latin, for example, might not offer intensive history in the twelfth grade, while a small rural high
school might not offer Greek. The third quotation on college
entrance assumes that schools would have viable courses—
Classical, English, and so forth—and students who had completed them should be admitted for advanced work regard-

33. *Report of the Committee on Secondary School Studies*, pp. 56–57.

less of which course they had pursued. Nowhere does Eliot say that a boy who has studied only science, or only Latin, should be admitted into Harvard or any other institution. Baker, in a word, misread the *Report;* he found notions in it that were not there. He wrote, "the majority of the Committee rejected the theory of equivalence of studies," and this was true; but he should have included Eliot with the majority. For Eliot's elective system, seen in the *Report* as four parallel courses of equal worth, was not a radical scheme that equated Egyptian hieroglyphics with physics, and Choctaw with Latin, as Baker vividly suggested. Baker missed the fact that the Committee—Eliot included—recommended a general core of subjects that all students had to take—a core comprised the main lines, language, science, history, and mathematics. The core was considered of such importance that electives were pushed up into the third and fourth secondary school years. The equivalence charges against the committee and against Eliot were red herrings. John Tetlow made this clear in a speech before the New England Association of Colleges and Preparatory Schools:

> It has been charged that the report asserts the doctrine of equivalent values,—the doctrine, I mean, that one subject is as good as another for the training of the mind. This . . . is an unwarranted allegation. The report merely says that subjects having the same time allotment and pursued with the same seriousness should be accorded equal rank for purposes of admission to college, which is quite another thing. I grant that even this mild form of the doctrine of equivalent values may be open to question . . . [but] no one, I think, will be disposed to condemn the conservative application of it by the committee in the programmes they have recommended. The doctrine, as there embodied, is practically non-existent.[34]

34. J. Tetlow, in discussion of resolutions pertaining to the Report of the Committee of Ten, *Proceedings* of the New England Association of Colleges and Preparatory Schools, Second Special Meeting (1894), pp. 6–7.

While the *Report* set down a core of work required for all, it expressed a desire for much flexibility within it. Strict uniformity was not a goal. Eliot wrote: "In my opinion the right aims in any room of a primary or grammar school are to recognize at the beginning of the year, as promptly as possible, the different capacities and powers of the children; to carry them forward throughout the year, each at his own gait and speed; and to turn them out at the end very much more different in capacity and attainments than they were at the beginning."[35] He wanted uniformity of standard; but there were to be individual variations in how that standard was met. In the *Report* Eliot suggests individual guidance: "Each pupil, under the supervision of the teachers, and with the advice of parents or friends, may make choice between several different four-years' courses arranged by the school; or, if the school authorities prefer, the pupil may be allowed to make year by year a carefully guided choice among a limited number of subjects; or these two methods may be combined."[36] This is not radical equivalence; it is conservative provision for individual likes and dislikes, strengths and weaknesses.

A liberal touch that gave even more ammunition to the critics who found the *Report* radical was something close to Eliot's heart: teaching by scientific inquiry. The laboratory method in chemistry was practiced widely as a result of his efforts, and in one of the first drafts of the *Report* he included the following sentence: "The scientific method of inquiry is the same for all subjects of human knowledge, however widely the several fields in which the method is applied may seem to differ." Harris balked at this: "I am afraid," he wrote, "that this is too strong a statement and that the differences between the sciences of nature and the sciences of man are not allowed for."[37] Harris' objection, backed probably by Mackenzie and

35. C. W. Eliot, "Undesirable and Desirable Uniformity in Schools," NEA *Proceedings* (1892), p. 83.

36. *Report of the Committee in Secondary School Studies*, p. 40.

37. W. T. Harris to C. W. Eliot, November 22, 1893, Mackenzie Papers, Lawrenceville School.

Angell, led to the deletion of the sentence. Consequently the *Report* says little about pedagogy except to suggest field trips and laboratory periods for the sciences. The *Report* mentioned, too, that elementary school methods were employed in teaching the higher subjects: the Committee deplored this practice.[38]

In some respects, then, the *Report* of the Committee of Ten was indeed liberal, and so received considerable abuse from those in American education who held fast to the conservative position.

The *Report on Secondary School Studies* as literature is uninspiring. Its author, Eliot, never a master of the felicitous phrase, reveals throughout his penchant for spare, colorless language. His belief in the importance of administrative detail makes the document even less interesting; the first twelve pages, filled with the details of the various meetings, must have put off many a reader. Equally disappointing is the excessive emphasis on such pedestrian matters as the number of hours a week each subject would be taught. Eliot's justification for this detail is lamentably weak, and the reader is hard put to identify a unifying philosophy in the assignment of subjects to the curriculum. One gets the impression that the Committee, having decided upon the scope of the nine Conferences, spent its remaining energies trying to fit the curricular pieces they produced into a single unified program. This would be misleading, though, because the *Report* was more than an assembled jigsaw puzzle; it brings into the open the conflicting forces of tradition and change.

The element of tradition was demonstrated by the adherence of the Committee and its Conferences to the tenets of mental discipline, or, as Eliot called it, "strong and effective mental training."[39] The mind was to be strengthened by in-

---

38. *Report of the Committee on Secondary School Studies*, p. 45.

39. Ibid., p. 53. In this connection, see also B. A. Hinsdale, "The Dogma of Formal Discipline," NEA *Proceedings* (1894), pp. 625-35. This paper, read as part of the discussion of the *Report* of the Committee of Ten,

tellectual calisthenics not unlike those favored by the Yale faculty in 1828. The Committee's acceptance of this doctrine is actually no surprise, in spite of the fact that many of its members, and the members of the Conferences too, were well known scientists, for the science of learning and behavior was still in its infancy and posed no serious question for traditional theory. The Committee and the Conferences automatically assumed that there was no argument on their psychological position, and they did not even bother to spell out their rationale.

Tradition was also well represented in the curriculum. The classical program, considered by many the most important one, consisted largely of Latin and Greek. Linguistic studies dominated. Mathematics suffered no retreat. The staples of the Latin School were still well represented.

But the forces of change were represented too. The new disciplines—history, English, French, German, the natural sciences—gained a secure place in the secondary school. Table III demonstrated this clearly; and the emphasis placed on it, Harris' objections notwithstanding, was an indication of things to come. It is true that these subjects were presented to only a limited degree in Table IV; but even there, the general studies program for all students lasted only for two years; and the relative demotion, if not elimination, of Greek is significant.

The ideas of the scientific method and its application to the psychology of learning were apparent. Time and again the Conference members asked for the use of laboratories so that the students could learn the means of seeking truth. The demand from the History Conference for close study of a restricted topic in the last year of school best demonstrates how thoroughly the idea of teaching the method of a discipline had won over scholars in fields even outside the natural sciences. Research was to be taught; indeed the Committee of Ten itself had been called upon to conduct research and was justified by the NEA on that ground. Objective appraisal of relevant

---

may well be considered the opening gun in the attack on the "faculty psychology" beliefs about learning.

data was expected of the Ten—and they in turn expected such habits to be fostered in the schools. Science thus found its way into their recommendations for pedagogy in the schools.

Thus the *Report* of the Committee of Ten was plainly a compromise between traditions in American secondary education and pressing changes in the intellectual climate; and these were largely the result of the rise of science. The aim of the schools remained implicit and unchallenged: mental discipline—whether the student intended to enter college or enter directly into life. The curriculum retained the traditional massive linguistic base, but added to it were other studies, which, while not wholly vocational and still disciplinary (and justified on that ground), were new. History, science, mathematics, and language all gained equal status; they were Eliot's "main lines" for all students to traverse and represented a skillful compromise between traditional practices and the demands for change. The compromise was not only a balanced one; it was realistic as well, for the final curriculum presented in Table IV varied little from that actually found in many large urban school systems.[40]

The expectation that all students in the schools would study for mental discipline obviated the need for vocational studies, for these would be informational, not disciplinary. The school's main function was to discipline the mind so that it could absorb information. Practical knowledge would follow later, on the job in "life." Oscar Robinson, the public high school principal, argued vigorously for subjects like penmanship, stenography, manual training, and mental science, but the most he received was optional bookkeeping and commercial arithmetic for a few weeks in the second and third year algebra course, together with the statement that "if it were desired to provide more amply for subjects thought to have practical importance in trade or the useful arts, it would be easy

40. See B. Mehl, "The High School at the Turn of the Century," unpublished dissertation, University of Illinois (1954), p. 212. Also above, pp. 61 ff., and *Fortieth Annual Report of the* (Chicago) *Board of Education* (1894), p. 45.

to provide options in such subjects for some of the science contained in the third and fourth years of the 'English' programme."[41] Eliot summed up the majority view in a letter to Robinson: "I believe it to be absolutely impossible to make a course valuable for training to which these various and numerous subjects are admitted."[42] Eighteen-ninety-three agreed with Eliot; 1913 would be far less certain.

The *Report* of the Committee of Ten, then, presented a compromise quite in tune with the educational thought of its day. At the same time, however, it dodged the key educational questions. Most important, it lacked foresight: it failed to deal with the crucial issues that affected the schools and would continue to affect them for decades. Most of the blame probably lies with the National Council of Education as they had spelled out the scope of the *Report*. The Ten, however, could have broadened their study by asserting that the task assigned them required a close look at the society of which the schools were a part. It was obvious that the Committee and the Conferences felt no compulsion to remain strictly within the limits of the NCE's immediate demands because they took into account such issues as the serious problem of unqualified and incompetent teachers. Why, then, did they not consider the questions of control of schools and accommodation of the rising number of students?

Because they did not examine the schools in the context of society at large, Eliot and his associates failed to evaluate the direct role of laymen and politicians in the schools; and they did not plan ahead for the schools in light of the rising enrollments. They limited their remarks to problems involved in

41. *Report of the Committee on Secondary School Studies*, p. 50.

42. C. W. Eliot to O. D. Robinson, October 24, 1893, in Robinson, "The Work of the Committee of Ten," p. 368. In the above article, Robinson, quoting from his correspondence with Eliot, shows how Harvard's president must have worked. Six letters passed between the men in a period of as many weeks. Adding to this the correspondence Eliot surely had with the other eight men, the Conference chairman, Butler, N. A. Calkins of the NEA, printers, and donors of money, and the drafting of the *Report* itself, and all this in a day before vast clerical staffs, one sees the extent of the contribution of himself that Eliot made.

mechanics of the curriculum and college entrance requirements, problems which, while important, should have had
low priority on the educational scene. Eliot felt, quite correctly, that entrance requirements were a useful lever for the
reform of academic standards; but academic standards of any
kind were unobtainable until certain basic roadblocks in the
structure of American schools were eliminated.

The first of these was political control. As long as school
budgets and teacher appointments were tools of the politicians, no major reform was possible. Teaching certificates were
granted almost at whim; in 1893 no state protected its children
from obvious incompetents or political hacks.[43] The Committee of Ten, however, blithely ignored the entire issue. It
preached to colleges and to teachers, but failed to address the
real force behind most American schools: the politicians.

The Committee also overlooked the vast differences among
secondary schools in America. Its recommendations were intended only for a particular kind of school—the urban high
school—and the small, rural institutions were hardly considered. The pontifical statements about all the main lines being
covered thoroughly, and for a sufficient length of time, gave
little comfort to the one- or two-man staffs of many secondary
schools. The Committee must have deplored such schools; it
could at least have tried to provide some kind of modus vivendi
for them, some formula to follow. The Committee's *Report*
offered direct help to only a few urban high schools and private institutions, and these, ironically, were schools that
needed help the least.

The overwhelming concern of school administrators simply
to house their rapidly increasing student body and to provide
it with teachers was ignored by the Committee. No suggestions came from the Conferences or the Ten for the most efficient use of the best teachers or of buildings. The Committee assumed that the classroom with thirty to fifty students
and one teacher was sacred. No consideration was given to

43. See W. S. Elsbree, *The American Teacher* (New York, 1939), pp.
336–58.

any other kind of arrangement: a Lancastrian system, large lectures, independent study, split school sessions, to mention some possibilities. The problems arising from a rapidly growing school population were totally ignored.

Other realities of school organization were also overlooked. It was easy for the *Report* to assert that every subject taught in a secondary school at all should be taught in the same way and to the same extent to every pupil so long as he pursues it; but this approach did not take into account the problem of the dull student. Would he carry on with his age group, or would he stay back indefinitely? The Committee was naive in thinking that the "unanimous opinion" of ninety-eight teachers solved the problem of providing for students of varied ability. While it was reasonable to maintain that all students taking the same subject should be required to meet a common standard, what became of those who either greatly exceeded or fell short of that standard? The Ten simply did not consider the problem of the student who was not academically inclined. Although few such students were attending secondary schools at all in 1894, the figures available to the Ten suggested that an increasing number would be doing so. In the fifteen years after 1893 the composition of American secondary schools changed radically, as the enrollment consisted of both larger numbers of students and a larger percentage of the appropriate age group.[44] This trend should have been clear to the Committee, scholars that they were and equipped with the best statistical sources. But they ignored the future and prescribed for the schools of the present, even though these were changing before their very eyes.

On the other hand, the Committee did face up to the problem of poor teachers. The Conferences had made it clear that their various subjects depended on good instruction, and the Committee made concrete suggestions how better teaching might be secured. It suggested making full use of summer schools and institutes, and proposed that colleges and univer-

44. See U.S. Bureau of the Census, *Historical Statistics of the United States, Colonial Times to 1957* (Washington, 1960), p. 214.

sities should provide training for the elementary and secondary school teachers from surrounding regions. An additional recommendation was that principals and experienced teachers in each school system should aid and supervise their staffs. The Committee felt that the traditional subjects were taught best in the schools of the day, and felt obliged to state "their unanimous opinion that, under existing conditions in the United States as to the training of teachers and the provision of necessary means of instruction, the two programmes called respectively Modern Languages and English must in practice be distinctly inferior to the other two."[45]

The *Report,* then, limited itself exclusively to the internal problems of the schools, to curricula and entrance requirements, to teachers and teaching. The limitation was imposed by the NCE, the Ten, and the Conferences because they saw the school as an institution isolated from the society of which it was a part. Nevertheless, the *Report,* in its narrow framework, presented a reasonable compromise and gave direction to many schoolmen of the day. With all its limitations, it made a marked impression on the American educational scene.

The document was completed and signed—by mail, not in person—on December 4, 1893. Eliot sent the completed draft to the Committee's secretary, John Tetlow, on the following day. "This stage of our undertaking approaches completion," Eliot wrote. "What vistas of debate open."[46]

45. *Report of the Committee on Secondary School Studies,* p. 48.
46. C. W. Eliot to J. Tetlow, December 5, 1893, Tetlow Papers, Harvard University.

"An event of capital importance to educators": This is how the Committee of Ten's *Report* was described in the lead article of the *Dial* in January 1894, the month in which the Bureau of Education issued the document.[1] In May of 1894, *Harper's Weekly* reported that the "enthusiastic popular reception of [the Committee's] report is ample evidence that the time was ripe for reform."[2] By August over thirty magazine articles had been written on the subject.[3] Clearly the *Report* of the Committee of Ten was not ignored in the manner usually experienced by NEA documents. For better or worse, the work of Eliot and his colleagues was studied and discussed.

The interest in the document did not, of course, happen by chance. The *Report* had to be propagandized, and Nicholas Murray Butler undertook the job with alacrity. Butler, of course, was hardly objective on the subject of the *Report*, and the energy he displayed in spreading the Committee's word is evidence enough of this. He had played a major role in appointing the Committee and providing it with funds; he had held meetings of the Ten in his home; and he had been in close touch at least with Eliot and Harris during 1893.

Butler's principal advertising weapon was his *Educational Review*, the most respected journal of its kind in America.

1. "The Report on Secondary Education," *Dial*, *16* (1894), 35.

2. "The Royal Commission on Secondary Education," *Harper's Weekly*, *38* (1894), 435.

3. J. C. Mackenzie, "The Course for Academies and High Schools Recommended by the Committee of Ten," *Independent*, *46* (1894), 983.

Starting in September 1892, he kept his readers constantly informed of the Committee's work. The Ten were mentioned—always in a favorable light—in December 1892; in January, February, June, November, and December 1893; and in January 1894, just before the *Report* was issued. Butler persuaded Harris to write the "kick-off" piece in this last issue; the Commissioner, as dispassionate an observer as the *Review* editor, wrote: "The good to be expected from these conferences, special and general, will be found in the fact that this report will turn the attention of the best thinkers among our teachers to the question of the comparative educational value of the several branches of study. It will thus mark an era in educational progress."[4] A February editorial painted glowing pictures—present and future: "The demand for the report is very large, and already requests for it are being received from leading students of education in Europe. Several faculties of colleges and secondary schools have begun the systematic study and discussion of the committee's recommendations, and before another year rolls round they will be found in force at various points throughout the country." Butler also felt obliged to deal with the minority report, asserting that "the *Educational Review* and, we suspect, the Committee of Ten themselves cordially agree" with Baker. " 'Equivalence,' he said, "is not raised directly in the *Report,* though President Baker does not propose to allow it to drop out of sight."[5] February's issue was highlighted by the second article on the *Report,* this one by President Eliot, whose views were hardly unfavorable. In March, C. F. P. Bancroft, Principal of Phillips Academy, Andover, wrote on "The Report of the Committee of Ten, from the Point of View of the College Preparatory School," a thin but laudatory article. In the same issue Butler printed a far better piece, by Charles DeGarmo, entitled "The Report of the Committee of Ten, from the Point of View of Educational Theory." DeGarmo suggested that the members of the Com-

4. W. T. Harris, "The Committee of Ten on Secondary Schools," *Educational Review,* 7 (1894), 4.

5. Ibid., p. 202.

mittee, in implying "equivalence" as criticized by Baker in his minority report, really meant it in a "Pickwickian sense, for they nowhere suggest in the programmes they offer that the humanities are so valuable that the sciences may be forgotten, or that a pupil can know so much of the physical world that he needs to know nothing of himself or of what the race has done." DeGarmo also saw in the Conference reports a departure from strict mental discipline: "The special reports bring out in a light, which to some will be startling, the fact of the substantial abandonment of the well-worn theory of *formal discipline,* or the idea that the mind can store up mechanical force in a few subjects, like grammar and mathematics, which can be used with efficiency in any department of life."[6] De-Garmo's arguments explained away "equivalence," a fact Butler must have appreciated. In its April issue *Educational Review* continued to print articles on the *Report:* J. E. Bradley wrote on the view of the document taken by the smaller colleges, and J. S. Clark wrote on "Art in Secondary Education: an Omission of the Committee of Ten." Clark echoed Baker: the Committee took "too little account of imagination and feeling [and] lay comparatively too much emphasis in facts and too little on ideals." Clark wanted the "poetic element" to find expression in the secondary schools, but his criticism of the *Report* as a whole was temperate and sprinkled with praise for its "admirably scientific" qualities.[7] In May the *Review* included articles by two Conference members. Colonel Francis W. Parker wrote on "The Report of the Committee of Ten —Its Use for the Improvement of Teachers Now at Work in the Schools," in which he suggested that the *Report* be indexed and made into syllabi for the use of practicing teachers. Julius Sachs, writing from the point of view of a college preparatory schoolman, felt that the Conference reports were the most valuable part of the document, and prophesied that liberal teachers with open minds would welcome the Committee's suggestions. The June issue provided a bibliography of state-

6. Ibid., pp. 278, 277. Italics in original.
7. Ibid., pp. 375, 376.

ments about the *Report;* it mentioned almost without exception articles and editorials that were either laudatory or only
moderately critical.[8]

Butler did not limit his advertising campaign to his own
Review, with its specialized audience. After the Ten's final
meetings, he wrote a short piece for the November 1893
Harper's Weekly entitled "An Important Educational Conference" and a full-scale article, "The Reform of High-School
Education," for the same journal's January 13, 1894, issue. The
latter must have been written before the general publication
of the *Report*—evidence in itself of the close contact between
Butler and members of the Committee. The article praised
the work of Eliot and concluded that the *Report* was the "most
important" single document in American educational history,
a document that "would affect Europe as well as the United
States."[9] Butler wrote a three-and-a-half column editorial for
The Nation's January 18 issue describing—if not lavishly prais-
ing—the Committee's work.[10] In March, he published an article in *The Atlantic,* "The Reform of Secondary Education
in the United States," proclaiming the *Report* "sound to the
core." He commented favorably on the linguistic slant to the
Report: "No scheme can be called radical that proposes to
give 52.5 per cent of all secondary education to language
study, or, adding history, 62.8 per cent to the humanities."
This conservative attitude would appeal to *Atlantic* readers.[11]
To *Century* magazine, a journal published not only in this
country but in England, Butler addressed an "Open Letter"
that filled two pages of the June 1894 issue. The movement
for the reform of secondary education, he reported, "seems
destined to accomplish even more than its most enthusiastic

8. Ibid., *8,* 103–04.
9. *Harper's Weekly, 38* (1894), 42.
10. *Nation, 58* (1894), 44–45. There was no byline on the piece, but it
is in Butler's style. *Poole's Index* credits him with it; and the editorial is
contained in the *Educational Review* bibliography for the Committee of
Ten.
11. *Atlantic, 73* (1894), 376, 380. Part of this article was reprinted in
Critic, 21 (1894), 147.

promoters dared to hope for," and this resulted from the Committee's *Report*. The suggested programs (Table IV) were printed in full.[12] And Butler received additional support when the *Review of Reviews* devoted an entire page in its April 1894 issue to quotations from articles on the *Report* originally printed in *Educational Review*.[13] It was obvious that Professor Butler was trying to spread the Committee of Ten's message not only to educators but also to literate laymen. The zeal he displayed in pursuing this objective was considerable, and one must grant that while he was not an announced member of the Committee of Ten, he was beyond doubt its most effective advocate.

Reviews of the *Report*, however, were not unanimous in praise—a fact that led Butler to engage in angry name-calling. In a March editorial in *Educational Review*, he wrote:

> It is as much of a compliment to the report that it is sneered at by some persons as that it is well received by others. The small, but noisy class of persons who conspire to produce what have been capitally described as the "fly-by-night educational papers," and those worthies who regard a college as a blot on the face of the earth and a college professor as *ipso facto* an ignoramus, are beating the tom-toms and rallying the faithful against the report, apparently because President Eliot had a hand in framing it. This sort of thing is very puerile and contemptible and vulgar; but the individuals referred to take themselves so seriously and are taken so seriously by some of those who ought to know better, that a word of warning is sometimes necessary. It is a disgrace to the country, and a severe reflection upon the intelligence of many of our teachers, that these "fly-by-night" papers have the circulation they do.[14]

12. *Century, 48* (1894), 314–16.
13. *Review of Reviews, 9* (1894), 467.
14. 7 (1894), 308.

One fly-by-night paper, the *Journal of Education,* struck back in its March 22 issue. After quoting Butler, the editor, A. E. Winship, solemnly asked: "Seriously, where is there any one engaged in educational work who regards a college as a blot on the face of the earth and a college professor as an ignoramus?" He went out of his way to praise Eliot, but concluded by summing up the *Report:* "There is nothing sacred about it. . . . There is no evidence of genius, no indication of greatness, nothing classic about it. It is simply a departure. It is on a new line. It is on a good line. It is so good that the wonder is that it is not better."[15] In spite of Winship's straight-faced denials, however, his journal damned the *Report* by innuendo. In a February issue, for example, sections of all the Conference reports were printed, and the paragraphs introducing them questioned the college professors' abilities in a hardly complimentary fashion and suggested that the $2500 granted the Ten by the NEA had been misspent.[16]

Other journals that Butler may have considered fly-by-nights were equally critical. Frank H. Kasson's *Education* had reservations; in March 1894 the editor asserted that

> the revelations of the report are indeed "most important" since they prove that so many of the leading educational thinkers of the country are still largely out of sympathy with the steady movement of the American Educational Public. It is hardly too much to say that this report represents the attempt of its authors and such as that agree with them to capture the common school system of the country in the vital region of its upper grammar and high school [sic] and reconstruct it, in the interest of the university methods and aims of the present time.[17]

Kasson not only saw a conspiracy on the part of the colleges. In an April editorial, he criticized the *Report* as being far too conservative:

15. A. E. Winship, editorial in *Journal of Education, 39* (1894), 185.
16. Ibid., p. 83.
17. *14* (1893–94), 432–33.

Our best public high and normal schools, with their broad instruction in English, history, the sciences, industrial training, music and drawing; with an important rising class of institutions like the Mass. Institute of Technology, Drexel, Pratt, Woodward, Armour and other similar foundations, are believed by large numbers of the wisest, best and most influential people of the country to offer a better preparation, not only for the practical but the higher realms of American life, than the ordinary college of the past or present.

Kasson pointed out that women had been ignored for positions on the Committee; "the educational public," he averred, "would be glad to hear from a similar council of eminent women teachers; from another conference of wise parents of children." Even the advice of the children should be solicited, Kasson concluded.[18]

Popular Educator reflected somewhat the same point of view. Its "Critic" saw "a rapidly approaching trial of strength" between American and European educational systems and feared that the colleges might nurture an elite.[19] The June editorial, however, paid the *Report* an indirect compliment by tacitly assuming that all subscribers had read it. The *Boston Journal* agreed with this threat of college domination ("it is time to sound a new note of alarm"), and its editorial on the subject was immediately reprinted by Winship's *Journal*.[20] And *The Dial*, editorially favorable to the *Report*, printed in its February 16th issue, a caustically hostile letter from Caskie Harrison, attacking the colleges, any comparison with Europe,

18. Ibid., pp. 497, 498.
19. *11* (1893–94), 295. The Committee of Ten had made no comparison of U.S. and European education in its *Report*, but Butler in his many articles had. The fears of several observers about the "foreign" influence of the *Report* were inspired by the editor of *Educational Review*, then, rather than by Eliot and his colleagues.
20. *39* (1894), 36.

and even James Mackenzie, the man who wanted state supervision of private schools.[21]

A steadier voice was that of Jacob Schurman, President of Cornell University and editor of *School Review*. He felt the Committee should have weighed the relative merits of the various subjects of its curriculum before assigning them time allotments—that a clear priority should have been determined. In addition he felt the nine Conferences had not embraced all the subjects that should be taught; ethics, for example, had been overlooked. Schurman had more to say about the mental discipline argument in the *Report* than had DeGarmo: "The Committee of Ten, and some of the conferences as well, have fallen victims to that popular psychology which defines education merely as the training of the mental faculties. As though the materials of instruction were a matter of indifference! This preposterous doctrine would destroy the value of the Committee's report. . . . No, education is not merely a training of mental powers. It is a process of nutrition. Mind grows by what it feeds on."[22]

A California journal which had opened its editorial by calling the *Report* "one of the most important educational papers ever published in this country,—perhaps the most important," took up the "equivalence" question and, influenced by Eliot's reputation, the editor went on to say that

> a section of more doubtful usefulness follows—written unmistakably by President Eliot, the very phraseology being that in which he has before clothed the same views . . . When one notes further that this talk of "democracy of studies" is coupled with irresponsibly phrased suggestions as to what might be done, and that even in this very section, whenever a distinct recommendation of the committee is made, a very different proposition replaces it, viz: that any one *of the*

21. *Dial, 16* (1894), 102–03.
22. J. C. Schurman, "The Report on Secondary School Studies," *School Review*, 2 (1894), 93.

four groups offered should admit to *corresponding courses,*—and sees that nine tenths of the readers will take the chairman's mere suggestion as the recommendation of the committee,—the section assumes an aspect even disingenuous. The committee undoubtedly passed on this section, wording and all, and but one of the ten protested; yet it certainly seems at this distance as if they made a grave error in allowing the chairman's well known hobby to be interpolated, as a sort of suggestion, into the midst of their formal, and quite different recommendations.[23]

Eliot found better treatment at the hands of J. M. Greenwood in the *Western School Journal*. Greenwood, who felt the Committee had made too many compromises, was sure that if Eliot and Harris had been given the job alone the results would have been much better.[24]

Such was the immediate reaction to the *Report*. Butler praised it effusively in both professional and lay publications. Others opposed it, principally on the ground of its "college domination" and on the matter of "equivalence"; at the same time, they agreed that the document was important and was actually being read. But except for Butler's articles, the principal popular publications of the day were silent. While the details of the *Report* were finding many readers and critics within the educational field, they evoked little interest among the American people—a not especially surprising fact. The public was interested in secondary schools, but it was not prepared to wade through the 249 pages of heavy prose. This they left to the professionals.

Certain members of the Committee of Ten, particularly Harris and Eliot, had a clear strategy for the *Report,* to ensure its wide reception. Butler certainly was a party to this plan. First of all, Harris prevailed upon the Secretary of the

23. *Overland Monthly, 23* (1894), 327–28. Italics in the original.
24. J. M. Greenwood, "The Report of the Conferences," *Western School Journal, 10* (1894), 77.

Interior, Hoke Smith, to print 30,000 copies of the *Report* and to distribute them gratis to key school and college men across the country. This assured that the *Report* would be found at least at the desks of important men in education and not remain buried in the NEA *Proceedings*. The printer's plates were then transferred to the American Book Company, which published a new edition, with an index, selling for thirty cents. As most of the publisher's records have been destroyed, it is impossible to determine how many copies were sold; but one can estimate from existing correspondence that the number may have reached fifteen thousand.[25] In any event, the *Report,* when not free, was available at very modest cost.

A second part of the strategy was the publication of articles. Butler naturally published pieces by Harris and Eliot in *Educational Review*. Commissioner Harris published a variety of materials on the Ten in his *Report* for 1892–93. Other members, particularly Mackenzie, also went to work. The Lawrenceville headmaster wrote a descriptive article for the *Independent*[26] and a more vigorous analysis for Schurman's *School Review*. In the latter article, Mackenzie supported the idea of starting secondary school studies in the seventh grade. Classicist that he was, he felt obliged to emphasize that "the programmes in Table IV, designated 'Modern Languages' and 'English,' were not contemplated by a majority of the Committee as suitable material for collegiate preparation," and that if this had been made clearer by Eliot, Baker would not have submitted a minority report. The two courses in question, Mackenzie felt, were for students who were not going on to college —a view clearly at odds with Eliot's. The best part of the *Report,* he felt, was "in its *inspirational* character"; "may we not confidently expect," he concluded, "that the Report of the

25. See T. H. Briggs, "The Committee of Ten," *Junior-Senior High School Clearing House, 6* (1931), 136. By 1901 American Book Company sales had reached 10,538. NEA *Proceedings* (1901), p. 45. The publisher's records do show an additional 7,000 copies printed after 1905. Manck Brammer to the present writer, May 26, 1960.

26. "The Course for Academies and High Schools Recommended by the Committee of Ten," *46* (1894), 983–84.

Committee of Ten is to mark an higher era in American education?"[27] Eliot applauded Mackenzie's promotional efforts: "I have heard excellent accounts of your services in various directions on behalf of the Committee of Ten," Eliot wrote in August 1894. "I am well content with the progress made in the discussion of that Report, and I notice already many good results from it. There will be a good many effects which will not be attributed to the Report; but that is no matter. What we want is to get good done."[28]

President Taylor published his views in the April issue of *School Review.* He isolated a number of principles set down by the *Report:* "The need for continuity in study, the need for 'quality' in teaching, the recognition of the fact that many students leave after the second year of secondary school and that any curriculum must be designed with these pupils in mind, and the need for improving and expanding elementary school work." Taylor, like Mackenzie, felt he had to deal explicitly with the question of equivalence, probably because of the strong opinion on this matter that the first critics of the document had expressed: "The Committee of Ten numbered among its members some who are able advocates of the theory that all studies are equal in educational value, but as a committee it deliberately refused to sanction the opinion, after much discussion, and confined the expressions of 'equivalence' to the lower range of practical rank in relation to college requirements. The thought of the committee was surely equivalence of results, in this aspect, rather than equivalence of value, intrinsically considered." About Eliot, Taylor concluded: "It was not the least appreciated of his great services to the committee that he held [his views] in check, however cherished, for the sake of the general truth in which we all could agree."[29]

A third part of the strategy adopted by the Committee of Ten

27. J. C. Mackenzie, "The Report of the Committee of Ten," *School Review*, 2 (1894), 149–55. Italics in original.

28. C. W. Eliot to J. C. Mackenzie, August 25, 1894, Mackenzie Papers, Lawrenceville School.

29. J. M. Taylor, "The Report of the Committee of Ten," *School Review*, 2 (1894), 196, 199.

was an effort to bring colleges to accept its recommendations for admission requirements. Eliot was very active in this endeavor. His particular plan was set forth in a letter sent to an official of the Michigan Schoolmaster's Club:

> In the first place, it seems to me that the most helpful method [to achieve unification of college admission requirements] is to adopt a temporary outline of desirable groups of studies for secondary schools, the four programmes recommended by the Committee of Ten. . . . I think that colleges and scientific schools should, if possible, be induced to accept any one of these four years' courses of study as qualifying satisfactorily for admission to corresponding courses in the colleges and scientific schools, and furthermore to raise, gradually and with adequate notice, their own standards of admission to the level of these programmes, subject by subject. . . . The practical mode of doing this seems to me to be as follows: let a group—the larger the better—of American universities maintain admission examinations in all the subjects which enter into those four programmes. . . . Let every institution belonging to the group, and as many other institutions as can be brought to act with them, declare each for itself how many and what examinations it will absolutely require for admission, and how many and what choices among the remaining subjects it will permit, taking care, however, not to demand more in the sum of prescribed and optional subjects than the total represented in any one of the four programmes of the Committee of Ten. Each university or college might make its own arrangements as to the use it would make of the complete set of examinations; but all would maintain the same standard in each subject, and would permit any and every subject in the list to count towards admission in some way or other. By means of large options taken from a uniform and

ample list of studies the individuality of different colleges can be preserved.

Eliot saw the principal difficulty of this plan in the new disciplines, and asserted: "I believe that accepted substitutes for
the traditional subjects should never be made easier for the
pupil than the traditional subjects. That is not the way to win
respect for the new subjects, or to prove their equivalence to
the old subjects. ... We should not aim to open easy ways into
the colleges and scientific schools; but we should try to open
various new roads all of which require as much energy and
judgment to travel them successfully as the old roads require."[30]
Eliot presented this same program to the Association of Colleges in New England at their November 1894 meeting; the
Association set up a committee to study the problem.[31] He
wrote William H. Smiley of the Secondary Department of the
NEA in October 1894, urging him to have his department consider school-college acceptance of the *Report* at its 1895 meeting.[32] Apparently, he also wrote directly to college presidents.[33]
To Columbia's Seth Low, a year and a half after the *Report*
was published, he wrote a letter specifying his aim in promot-
ing the new disciplines:

> As you may have read between the lines of the Re-
> port of the Committee of Ten, I am very much in-
> terested in promoting a great widening of the require-
> ments for admission to our colleges. I want to see sub-
> stantial requirements arranged in History, Chemistry,
> and Physics, and Natural History, so that the colleges
> can safely accept these subjects for admission on a

30. C. W. Eliot to W. H. Butts, November 24, 1894, Eliot Papers, Harvard University. Parts of this letter were quoted by John Tetlow at the
1894 special meeting of the New England Association of Colleges and
Preparatory Schools.

31. Draft of Minutes, Association of Colleges in New England, Eliot Papers, Harvard University.

32. C. W. Eliot to W. H. Smiley, October 31, 1894, Eliot Papers, Harvard
University.

33. C. K. Adams, "Impressions of the Report," New York Regents, *Bulletin, 28* (1894), 318.

level with the traditional subjects. I believe that this change would greatly improve the public secondary schools, and greatly broaden the foundations of our colleges in the schools below them.[34]

Eliot, of course, had his own college to deal with. While Harvard's faculty had both broadened and raised the standard of its admission requirements during the '80s,[35] it had not done so without severe conflict; members of various departments were openly hostile to Eliot. The President had to move slowly,[36] and it was not until December 1894 that his faculty acted. It passed a resolution on the 11th of that month, ordering "that the several departments prepare and report to their division committees, which shall in turn report to this Faculty . . . plans of study in the subjects of their respective departments used in the programmes of the Committee of Ten for Secondary Schools."[37] Study and discussion went on for several years, much of it under the aegis of Professor Albert Bushnell Hart, who had been a member of the History Conference. A principal problem was that Harvard's existing standards were higher than any of those of the four programs, the Classical included,[38] and the faculty could hardly be expected to lower them.

To disseminate the influence of the *Report* more widely, James Baker of Colorado suggested either that the Ten continue their deliberations and publications or that the NCE set

34. C. W. Eliot to S. Low, October 26, 1895, Eliot Papers, Harvard University.

35. See above, p. 57.

36. See C. W. Eliot to J. B. Angell, November 18, 1893, Eliot Papers, Harvard University.

37. Harvard Faculty of Arts and Sciences, *Record*, 2 (1894), 58–59; University Archives, Harvard University. Eliot proposed a general study; the complicated system of levels of reporting—from department to division to general faculty—come as amendments. Even with this administrative device to protect itself from any radical move, the faculty approved the resolution by only a 26–13 vote, a demonstration of the resistance to Eliot within his own staff.

38. A. B. Hart to C. W. Eliot, April 6, 1896, Eliot Papers, Harvard University.

up a new committee for this purpose.[39] Eliot and Angell were clearly opposed to this strategy. They felt that although the Ten's suggestions were "tentative," the most useful and productive move after their publication was discussion by the educational world at large rather than further deliberation by the Committee. Eliot felt that Baker was trying to reach an unattainable ideal. He wrote Angell:

> I saw in my first intercourse with [Baker], nearly two years ago, that he believed it possible to invent a uniform high school programme for the entire country. That idea he still clings to—indeed, he thinks he can write that programme himself, and that it would clearly resemble his programme in the Denver High School. That is the real reason why he advocates a continuation of the work of our Committee, or of some committee. I need not say that I agree with you in thinking that the National Council had better not continue our Committee. Public discussion of our work is the next thing in order, and I should think two or three years a short time to allow for that discussion.[40]

Eliot believed that if the Committee's recommendations for elementary schools were followed, within ten years the standard of the students entering high school would be so much improved that the programs recommended in the *Report* would have to be discarded as too easy.[41] Continued refinement of Table IV as Baker recommended, then, was to Eliot a waste of time. Argument, discussion, and, hopefully, some general changes were what Eliot desired. Baker's suggestion was not put into effect.

The final part of the strategy to spread the *Report*'s recom-

39. *Report of the Committee on Secondary School Studies*, p. 59.
40. C. W. Eliot to J. B. Angell, December 9, 1893, Eliot Papers, Harvard University. Eliot reveals in this letter that Angell had written to Baker, asking him not to submit his minority report.
41. C. W. Eliot to W. H. Butts, November 24, 1894, Eliot Papers, Harvard University.

mendations was for the Ten to attend teachers' meetings and association gatherings and promote wide discussion of their proposals among teachers. The NEA and its several departments quite naturally planned to consider the *Report* fully; other smaller and regional associations also discussed it at their meetings.

The first meeting of an NEA group was that of the Department of Superintendence, held at Richmond, Virginia, from February 20 to 22, 1894, only a month after the release of the *Report*. Two of the thirteen papers presented at that conference were devoted exclusively to the Committee of Ten, while others mentioned it in connection with other topics. One, by Colonel Francis Parker, dealt with the application of the *Report* by practicing teachers (this was later published as an article in *Educational Review*); the other, by Commissioner Harris, was entitled "The Curriculum for Secondary Schools."

Parker's piece stimulated much discussion about in-service teacher training. Only one man, Superintendent J. M. Greenwood of Kansas City, appeared to question the *Report's* findings. He felt the Committee criticized teachers far too harshly:

> In behalf of the city teachers who constitute the silent majority of this report, I will say that in New York, in Richmond, in San Francisco, in Boston, in Cleveland, in Toronto, in St. Louis, in Chicago, or in any of the best schools of the country, the teachers are doing excellent work that these men [the Ten and the Conferences] say they are not doing; better than the gentlemen themselves can do, and yet they are presenting for us, as they claim, and not for themselves. Let them take their own medicine first.[42]

Harris' views, as he presented them in his paper, received sharper criticism. He emphasized several points of particular interest to him: that the *Report* was a compromise, that the

42. J. M. Greenwood, in discussion of F. W. Parker, "The Report of the Committee of Ten—Its Use for the Improvement of Teachers Now at Work in the Schools," NEA *Proceedings* (1894), p. 454.

classical course of Table IV represented the heart of the recommendations rather than Table III, that the classical languages were a central aspect of education, and that the five windows of the soul all needed attention in the school. The speech was formally reviewed by Superintendent Maxwell of Brooklyn, himself a member of the English Conference. He denounced, among other things, the requirement of classical languages for the boy who would not go to college; such a boy should read translations, Maxwell asserted, citing the English Bible as an exemplary kind of translation. He concluded his remarks with a truly Butler-like utterance:

> If the superintendents will unite in their efforts to put into execution the propositions set forth by the Committee of Ten, they will take a long step forward in the reform of elementary as well as of secondary education. This report may not unfitly be regarded as the cloud by day and the pillar of fire by night that is to lead us into the promised land. This report will be the superintendents' armor, offensive and defensive. Clothed with this authority, he need not fear to resist attacks or to demolish abuses. It is the noblest monument of their work ever erected by the teachers of America through their National Educational Association.[43]

Charles DeGarmo, President of Swarthmore College, asked Harris why "the economic phase in education"—manual training—had been omitted; Harris replied that carpentry and metal work were elementary studies, but that "natural philosophy or physics and chemistry are secondary studies, and these give to the worker in wood and iron a training in directive power which enables him to lay out work for others." J. M. Greenwood criticized the amount of work required of students

---

43. W. H. Maxwell, in discussion of W. T. Harris, "The Curriculum for Secondary Schools," NEA *Proceedings* (1894), p. 512.

by the *Report*. "The specialists" on the Conference, he argued, "lacked loading sense."[44]

But there was far stronger criticism—criticism so sharp that it does not appear at all in the *Proceedings* of the meeting. We are aware it exists only because Nicholas Murray Butler, who was present, felt compelled to call attention to it in an editorial in *Educational Review*:

> Mr. Nightingale of Chicago took the floor, and in a blizzard-like voice proceeded to make an ignorant and indecent attack upon the Committee of Ten. It was evident that the vast audience was much upset by Mr. Nightingale's remarks, and every serious-minded man in the hall was shocked and ashamed at the exhibition. Unfortunately a group of noisy sensationalists encouraged the speaker by their laughter and shouts of approval, and, continuing their demonstrations for an hour, they managed to interrupt and degrade the interesting colloquy that had developed between Dr. Harris, Superintendent Maxwell, and Colonel Parker. In the evening, however, President MacAlister, in a passage of great refinement and delicacy, administered a stinging rebuke to Mr. Nightingale [also not published].[45]

With a striking difference of tone, Butler wrote Eliot this summation of the meeting:

> I have just returned from the annual meeting of the Department of Superintendence, where the Report of the Committee of Ten was a prominent feature in the intellectual landscape, and I am sure you will be glad to hear that it was received with almost unqualified admiration and with substantial approval by the large body of serious-minded public school men. One

44. NEA *Proceedings* (1894), pp. 513, 514.
45. N. M. Butler, editorial in *Educational Review*, 7 (1894), p. 405.

or two, notably Superintendent Greenwood of Kansas City, showed a disposition to find fault with matters of minute detail; and one or two others, notably Mr. Nightingale of Chicago, apparently unacquainted with the courtesies of life, endeavored to substitute a malicious attack upon the members of the Committee for criticism of their report. Both of these tendencies, however, were strongly reprehended by the leading men present, and on the whole you would have been very well satisfied at seeing and hearing the impression that the Report had made.[46]

Eliot replied:

I am more than content with the reception of the Report of the Committee of Ten. It is having a very thorough and useful discussion in this part of the country.

I have never had any dealings with Mr. Nightingale of Chicago, and I know nothing about him. If he had any malice against the members of the Committee, I think it must be of some impersonal nature.[47]

It is evident, then, that the *Report* met sharp criticism at Richmond, on the grounds of its literary bias, its failure to include manual training and other economic subjects, and its heavy course demands. And the membership of the Ten and the Conference apparently was once again the subject of derogatory remarks, this time by superintendents, who had been virtually excluded from the deliberations. The superintendents passed a resolution on the *Report*, but phrased it in measured terms: "We hereby emphasize our estimate of the able and valuable report of the Committee of Ten, and urge its careful study by all the teachers and school officials of the land."[48]

46. N. M. Butler to C. W. Eliot, February 26, 1894, Eliot Papers, Harvard University.

47. C. W. Eliot to N. M. Butler, March 1, 1894, Eliot Papers, Harvard University.

48. NEA *Proceedings* (1894), 417.

The National Council of Education met at Asbury Park, New Jersey, from July 6 to 10, 1894. E. W. Coy, President of the Council, urged Eliot to attend, but he could not do so because of a schedule conflict (he had planned to attend the convention of the American Institute of Instruction, which met during the same period). Instead, he sent a letter of transmission for the *Report*. This was presented on the morning of July 9th and was followed by a long paper by President Baker entitled "Review of the Report of the Committee of Ten." Baker described many of the Ten's proposals, lacing them with his personal views and concluding with a summary of his objections to them: "The lack of a bold and clear analysis of the value of subjects before correlating the recommendations of the conferences; the implications that the committee favored an extreme theory of equivalence of study; practical details in the organization of the model courses."[49] He suggested that the Council consider further study of these matters as well as the whole question of the elementary school curriculum. His final sentences expressed praise for Eliot.

Discussion of Baker's speech occupied the rest of the morning session and the entire afternoon. Fragments of the comments are preserved in the NEA *Proceedings*. Again there was much criticism, and again Professor Butler felt the need to speak out, this time to the gathering itself. "In listening to the discussion of the report of the Committee of Ten," he remarked to the NCE, "not only as it has taken place in this Council but in other educational bodies as well, I am reminded a little of the traditional attitude of the English peasant toward a new idea. It is said that when a new idea crosses the path of an English peasant, his first impulse is to "eave 'arf a brick at it.' There has been something of this disposition on the part of some participants in these discussions."[50]

Butler's "English peasants" on the NCE precipitated objections that had already been heard again and again. Superintendent Woodward of St. Louis once more expressed dis-

49. Ibid., p. 657.
50. Ibid., p. 666.

satisfaction over the Ten's exclusion of manual training and art. Joseph Baldwin of Huntsville, Texas, wanted "mental economy" to be added. Emerson White of Columbus, Ohio, and William Mowry of Salem, Massachusetts, found fault with the *Report*'s prescriptions for elementary schools. G. Stanley Hall spoke out against "equivalence" and against Eliot personally, and was supported by Providence's Superintendent Tarbell. Baker added his own objections to the discussions, asserting that his reservations were the same as those expressed at teachers' meetings from New York to California. Other members of the Committee spoke in defense of the *Report*. Harris again emphasized the importance of Table IV; Mackenzie and, surprisingly, Robinson stressed the important areas in which the Ten had found agreement; Benjamin Wheeler of Cornell, a member of the Greek Conference, eloquently seconded these views.

What emerges clearly is that the objections to the *Report* were falling into predictable categories: the omission of certain practical subjects, the omission of certain imaginative subjects like art, the proposals for elementary schools, the notion of "equivalence," the amount of work expected of pupils. Butler's *Review* and the editors of the *Proceedings* could not hide these sharp and, in the case of G. Stanley Hall, even bitter criticisms.

Baker tried to persuade the Council to retain the Committee, but was apparently talked out of it, for the Ten were discharged and their *Report* was accepted by a unanimous vote. On the following day the NCE passed a formal resolution: "The Council desires, in discharging the Committee of Ten, to express its high appreciation of the spirit with which they and their conferences entered upon their work, the devotion that marked their long labors and the great value of their report to the cause of education."[51]

It is significant that, earlier at this same convention, Pro-

51. Ibid., p. 605.

fessor Burke Hinsdale of the University of Michigan had presented a paper, "The Dogma of Formal Discipline," which implicitly challenged several of the psychological assumptions of the Committee of Ten. Drawing from examples of the changing rationale in school curricula, he reached several conclusions, two of which are of interest: "No one kind of mental exercise—no few kinds—can develop the whole mind. That end can be gained only through many and varied activities"; and "No study—no single group of studies—contains within itself the possibilities of a whole education. That balance of development which we should call a liberal education can be gained only through a measurably expanded curriculum." Hinsdale called mental discipline, valued so highly by the Committee of Ten, an untenable relic of scholasticism.[52] Learning was not "transferred" (to use a term shortly afterward popularized by the followers of Edward Lee Thorndike) from a single disciplinary study—say, the classical languages—to other fields in general. Hinsdale's paper thus provided the weapons used by later critics to attack the mental discipline arguments found in the *Report* of the Committee of Ten.

The convention of the National Educational Association was held from July 10th to July 13th at Asbury Park, following the NCE meeting. Unfortunately the country was in the grip of a railroad strike that limited attendance, but even so 6,000 teachers participated. Part of the third day was devoted specifically to the *Report* of the Committee of Ten and, as Butler reported to Eliot, the discussion was "earnest, intelligent, and sympathetic."[53]

Although Commissioner Harris addressed the Association on the subject of "The Influence of the Higher Education of a Country upon its Elementary Schools"—one of a series of speeches on teacher training—the Committee's best spokesman

52. Ibid., p. 634. See also B. Hinsdale, "President Eliot on Popular Education," *Intelligence, 13* (1893), 52 ff.

53. N. M. Butler to C. W. Eliot, July 25, 1894, Eliot Papers, Harvard University.

was James C. Mackenzie. In a speech with an unwieldy title—
"The Feasibility of Modifying the Programs of the Elementary and Secondary Schools to Meet the Suggestions in the Report of the Committee of Ten"—he provided by far the most
powerful and cogent description and evaluation of the *Report*
heard or read in the 1890s. He started realistically: "Doubtless
it [the *Report*] has defects and shortcomings—it is not offered
to our intelligent teachers as a Nebuchadnessar golden image
—but . . . it is offered as a good working hypothesis for the
teachers of our high and other secondary schools." Mackenzie
spoke forcibly of the surprising extent of agreement achieved
by the Committee and the Conferences, and described graphi-
cally the chaotic conditions in the schools that the Committee
was trying to remedy. He spoke of the favorable reception of
the *Report,* noting that of the twenty-five articles he had
seen, only two were unfavorable. Turning to the various criticisms made of the *Report,* he dealt with each in turn. To the
objection that manual training and other similar subjects were
omitted, he replied that "we were . . . confronted with the
stern necessity of choosing between the information studies
and courses and those that possess training character" and that
the Committee had chosen the latter. To the charge that the
Committee was "college dominated," he asserted that at least
seventy per cent of the participants in the Committee and Conferences had experience in secondary schools. "It is only
through ignorance of the facts, or something worse, that criticism can be made that the report is the work of college men. It
is, first and last, the schoolmasters' performance, in execution
as well as in conception." The Committee, he also stressed,
was prescribing for a student body the large majority of
which would not attend college at all. To the charge of
"equivalence" he said bluntly that "if the chairman is known
to have a marked conviction to the effect that Choctaw or road-
making have as much educational value as Latin, there is
nothing done or said by the committee in its official capacity,
so far as I can recall, to give the slightest warrant or authority

to such an opinion." He did, however, "deplore" the use of words in the *Report* that could mislead the "suspicious or unwary." To the charges that the suggested programs were uncorrelated and not precise, he claimed that teachers, not a Committee, should cope with these matters in the light of their own schools' situations. Mackenzie ended with a plea for a "trial" of the *Report*'s suggestions, calling the document "the first classic in American pedagogical literature."[54] Discussion followed, but was restricted to three of the Conference reports, those on Latin, English, and History. John T. Buchanan, principal of the Kansas City High School, agreed with most of the findings of the Latin report, but not with the suggestion to introduce the language in the elementary grades. Four rigorous years of Latin and three of Greek were to Buchanan the best policy. The English Conference was reviewed by no other than A. F. Nightingale, the man with the "blizzard-like voice" who had so irked Butler at Richmond earlier in the year; but Nightingale at Asbury Park gave a colorful and laudatory speech that received the accolades of even Butler in the September issue of *Educational Review*. Nightingale's speech, dotted with references to the *Report* as a "New Testament" and "an educational encyclical,"[55] was too flattering; while the speaker paid reasonably serious attention to the text of the English Conference report, he applied to the *Report* as a whole a thinly veiled and savage sarcasm. It is hard to see how Butler missed this. Frank McMurry praised the historians, though attacking them on two points, first claiming that they were "not up with the times" in thinking that history "taught right judgment" and second deploring the absence of a rationale for selecting which historical facts were to be taught.[56]

The NEA's Committee on Resolutions in 1894 consisted of five men and included both Superintendent Maxwell as chairman (a pro-*Report* man) and President Baker. Not surprisingly,

54. NEA *Proceedings* (1894), pp. 143–44, 149.
55. Ibid., pp. 163–64.
56. Ibid.

the resolutions that emerged reflect a series of compromises between these two men. Of the ten approved, three dealt with the
Report:

> 7. With the appointment of the Committee of Ten,
> the Association entered upon a legitimate field of edu-
> cational investigation and research. Through this ac-
> tion, the Association stands committed to a policy of
> action, as well as of discussion; a policy from which
> may be expected results of great fruitfulness and im-
> portance. To the distinguished Chairman and his as-
> sociates of the committee are due our sincere and
> hearty thanks for the labor, patience and ability
> which they devoted to the important questions they
> were called to consider. Their remarkable report will
> stand for years to come as a monument of American
> scholarship and a source of inspiration to American
> teachers.
>
> 8. We desire to emphasize the essential importance
> of including, either formally or incidentally, art and
> ethics in courses of study for all grades. We believe no
> analysis of the divisions of human knowledge is ade-
> quate, which does not distinctly recognize these lines
> of work.
>
> 9. We proclaim our belief in the view of education
> which attaches importance to content, as well as to
> formal training; and we commend to all teachers the
> study of the relative values of different kinds of
> knowledge, as well as the study of the correlation of
> all knowledge.[57]

Baker simply could not let the issue lie.

While the NEA was the most important and influential
teachers' association, other groups were also discussing the
Report of the Committee of Ten; and this aided the members

57. Ibid., p. 35.

of the Committee in their strategy to stir up discussion of the secondary curriculum.

President Eliot, for example, attended the annual meeting of the American Institute of Instruction at Bethlehem, New Hampshire, in early July 1894; the Ten spread their efforts over the various educational gatherings. There, he read a paper significantly entitled "The Unity of Educational Reform," which outlined the Committee's views and at the same time sharply rebuked those who insisted that college men could not and should not suggest curricula for the elementary and secondary schools. Frank A. Hill, Secretary of the Massachusetts Board of Education (the American Institute was essentially a northeastern group), followed Eliot with a paper called "The Report of the Committee of Ten," in which he criticized the *Report* for recommending courses too difficult for children and for ignoring the normal schools. Hill thought most highly of the Latin-Scientific program. The discussion of Hill's address was opened by A. E. Winship of the *Journal of Education,* who labeled the *Report* "the most disappointing educational document that has been issued with promise of usefulness in many a day." He felt that the $2500 had been spread too thin, and that the Committee had tried to do too much. Winship caustically quoted Eliot: "Is it too much to ask for the mastery of one subject?"[58] The Institute, however, decided to favor Hill over Winship and passed a resolution praising the *Report,* urging the improvement of Latin-Scientific and English courses in the schools, and recommending that colleges admit graduates from such improved courses.[59]

Early July was also the occasion for the University Convocation of the State of New York. Butler, Baker, Robinson, G. Stanley Hall, and Benjamin T. Wheeler, among others, were present. The key speech on the *Report* by Superintendent Kennedy of Batavia was laudatory. Hall, as usual, was critical:

58. *Proceedings* of the American Institute of Instruction (1894), pp. 188, 190.
59. Ibid., p. xv.

"The report of the Committee of Ten seems to me to be a sort of stirring of the waters, a sort of new-fashioned egg-beater which stirs better than most old-fashioned ones."[60] Baker agreed in remarks similar to those he was to make the following week at the NEA convention. Robinson, oddly enough, criticized the *Report* for allowing only two years of Greek and was supported by other public school principals, demonstrating once again that the classics' defenders were not always college or private school men. There was much discussion of the recommendations made by the individual Conferences, and Butler reported that "the Committee's report was not very much injured."[61]

Further west, the Michigan Schoolmasters' Club was active. They had heard Baker on the subject of the Committee in November 1892; and in March 1894, further discussion of the *Report* took place. Burke Hinsdale spoke in terms that anticipated his speech to the NCE later in the year on the "dogma of formal discipline." Angell and Eliot sent letters of explanation to be read at the meeting. Martin D'Ooge and other Conference members attended discussions. The entire meeting was reported in a supplement to the June number of the *Inlander*, a student publication.[62]

There were many other meetings. The Iowa State Teachers Association heard Miss Minnie Moore assert that practical work should be offered in the schools, and Miss Julia J. Sweet attacked the collegiate, linguistic bias of the *Report*. Miss Sweet termed Baker "the best balanced man on the committee."[63] The Missouri State Teachers Association passed a resolution favorable to the *Report*.[64] The Nebraska Association of

60. New York Regents, *Bulletin, 28* (1894), 303–04.

61. N. M. Butler, editorial in *Educational Review, 8* (1894), 306.

62. See above, p. 159; and Leslie A. Butler, *The Michigan Schoolmasters' Club* (Ann Arbor, 1957), 116–22.

63. C. R. Aurner, *History of Education in Iowa* (Iowa City, 1915), *3*, 249–50, and J. J. Sweet, "The Report of the Committee of Ten," *Proceedings* of the Iowa State Teachers Association (1894), pp. 123–24.

64. *Forty-Fifth Report of the Public Schools of the State of Missouri* (1894), p. 48.

Superintendents and Principals of Graded Schools discussed the document in May 1894; as early as December 1893, President Jesse was spreading the Committee's word to the Southwest Teachers' Association. The *Report* was also considered by various teachers' groups in Indiana, Pennsylvania, North Carolina, Connecticut, Minnesota, New Hampshire, and New York.[65] Eliot spoke to several groups meeting near Boston: to the Harvard Teachers' Association, to the Massachusetts High and Classical Association, to the Boston Schoolmasters. The Association of Colleges and Preparatory Schools in the Middle States and Maryland discussed aspects of the *Report* for several years following its publication. Taylor was its president in 1894, Butler in 1895, Mackenzie in 1896. Eliot, Julius Sachs, Ira Remsen, Herbert Baxter Adams, and James H. Robinson also presented their views to the Association. Clearly the message of the *Report* was widely discussed at teachers' meetings.

The meetings of two associations, the New England Association of Colleges and Preparatory Schools and the American Philological Association, developed in ways markedly different from those of the other meetings.

The New England Association had John Tetlow for its President, and in 1893 had heard President Eliot describe the direction the deliberations of the Ten were taking.[66] At the 1894 meeting, held in October, it was expected that a resolution favorable to the *Report* would be passed. Ray Greene Huling began the discussion with a long and favorable paper. Eliot answered questions, and eventually Tetlow surrendered the chair to L. Clark Seelye in order to present four resolutions which, in essence, called upon secondary schools to offer the four courses recommended by the Committee and upon colleges to accept graduates from any one of these courses for

65. See weekly issues of the *Journal of Education* (1894) and the monthly issues of *School Review* (1894) for the announcements and summaries of teachers' meetings.

66. C. W. Eliot, "Secondary School Programs, and the Conferences of December, 1892," *Proceedings* of the New England Association of Colleges and Preparatory Schools (1894), pp. 19–34.

admission. Tetlow, who had expected his resolutions to be adopted almost immediately, was surprised to find one member arguing for delay. This was William C. Collar of the Roxbury Latin School and of the Committee's Latin Conference. Discussion continued; then President Hyde of Bowdoin made a speech on the *Report* urging increased emphasis on Latin teaching. The following day a new resolution was introduced, recommending that any high school graduate be accepted for admission to college who had completed any one of the Committee's courses *which included Latin*. Still Collar, along with others, urged delay. Finally, the Association decided to hold a special meeting on Tetlow's proposals, as amended, in December.

John Tetlow opened this special meeting with a long plea for accepting the *Report* and for the resolutions put forward. J. E. Goodwin of Newton agreed. A. L. Goodrich of Salem brought up the old argument that the programs recommended were too difficult for children. President Taylor, from Vassar, favored the *Report* and asked that it be accepted forthwith. At that point, a young member of the Harvard Greek department, Professor H. H. Morgan, rose to read a telegram just received from the American Philological Association, which was then meeting in Philadelphia. The message asserted that that Association had "voted unanimously and enthusiastically, that in any programme for the classical course in schools preparing pupils for American colleges not less than three years instruction in Greek should be required." The telegram also took pains to state that "almost all New England colleges [were] represented, besides many others" at the APA convention. Morgan then read a letter from Professor T. D. Seymour of Yale stating that "we at Yale are ready to secure a 'closer articulation' [between colleges and schools], but we are not ready to cut down by a year the requirements in Greek." Morgan finished by offering an amendment to Tetlow's motion calling for a requirement of three years of Greek in the Classical program.[67]

67. *Proceedings* of the New England Association of Colleges and Preparatory Schools, Special Meeting (1894), pp. 24–27.

Even the dry minutes of the Association record Tetlow's surprise at this new development. There was more to come: letters from Greek professors W. W. Goodwin and J. W. White, and remarks by a young colleague of Morgan's, F. D. Allen. The classicists' attack was well organized and effective; as Professor Charles E. Fay admitted,

> I see no possibility of securing the passage of the original resolutions in the face of a protest of such authority and seemingly so justifiable. . . . Doubtless others like myself had come prepared to vote for the resolutions as drafted, and had not been moved by any of the considerations urged against them up to the moment of Professor Morgan's presentation of the protest against the classical course. This protest, so powerfully reinforced, cannot but carry great weight, and doubtless the conference is now irrevocably divided in opinion.[68]

Eliot, who had been given a few hours' warning by Morgan of the Greek scholars' move,[69] rose at this point, asserting: "It is perfectly well known that Greek is maintained with difficulty in the public secondary schools in the United States . . . [the Greek scholars' demand] is a rash demand, and the more imperative and uncompromising, the rasher it is. Indeed, it seems to me to illustrate the saying, 'Quem Deus vult perdere prius dementat.' " He then offered a compromise resolution that withheld approval of the four programs and, in essence, endorsed only the principle of school-college articulation. Tetlow and Morgan agreed to this, and the resolution was adopted, printed, and distributed to the various colleges and schools in New England.[70] Tetlow later wrote to Eliot of his deep disap-

68. Ibid., pp. 31–32.
69. C. W. Eliot to J. Tetlow, January 1, 1895, Tetlow Papers, Harvard University.
70. *Proceedings* of the New England Association of Colleges and Preparatory Schools, Special Meeting (1894), pp. 32–34.

pointment.[71] He continued in the next years to press a plan upon the New England Association for liberal college admission requirements, but to no significant avail.

The American Philological Association kept busy, too. It set up a Committee of Twelve under the chairmanship of William W. Goodwin, a Harvard Greek professor, which included William G. Hale of the Ten's Latin Conference, Abby Leach of the Greek Conference, George Kittredge of Harvard and of the English Conference, C. F. P. Bancroft of Andover, William Rainey Harper of Chicago, Andrew F. West of Princeton, and Thomas D. Seymour of Yale. This Committee prepared an address that was presented to the 1895 NEA convention and "To the Teachers of the Classics and To All Friends of Sound Learning in the United States." The document reported that the APA unanimously adopted the resolution read by Morgan at the New England Association and asserted that the Committee of Ten's proposals, if put into effect, would "lower standards." It cited the Ten's Greek Conference as having recommended a three-year Greek course and deplored the Committee's rejection of it. It concluded: "The undersigned believe that both colleges and schools have a common interest in opposing a scheme which threatens to degrade them both at the expense of good scholarship. They therefore appeal earnestly to all who have the interest of sound learning at heart to unite with them in opposing the introduction of the so-called "Classical Program" of the committee of ten into the schools of the United States."[72]

This sharp attack upset Butler. "It would appear that the philologists, eager to defend Greek," he wrote, "have failed to bear in mind the very practical aspects of the problems that confronted the Committee of Ten"—one problem being that only a tiny minority of secondary schools offered Greek.[73] On

71. J. Tetlow to C. W. Eliot, January 3, 1895, Eliot Papers, Harvard University.
72. NEA *Proceedings* (1895), p. 635.
73. N. M. Butler, editorial in *Educational Review, 10* (1895), 307.

the other hand, Winship of the *Journal of Education* was gleeful; the Committee of Twelve, he wrote, "has utterly demoralized the 'Report of the Ten' and makes it ridiculous in the extreme. The *Journal* never bowed the knee to that farce [the *Report*]."[74] Butler wrote to Eliot that "determined and organized opposition is to be offered" and asked if Eliot wanted to use the pages of *Educational Review* to counterattack. Eliot replied that he would remain quiet, as the Committee was officially disbanded and that further argument by him would be wasted. He explained that if the Committee of Ten had been constructing five- or six-year programs, Greek would have received three years, but, within the four-year limit placed on the Ten, only two years of Greek could be provided for.[75]

The Twelve kept up their attack. In June 1896 they published a report on Latin in which they again scored the *Report* of the Committee of Ten. This APA document was sent to the 1896 NEA convention signed by the Twelve and also by many others: Francis Child of Harvard; William C. Collar, William H. Smiley, and Oliver S. Westcott, who had participated in various of the Ten's Conferences; Oscar Robinson, himself a member of the Ten; college presidents Charles F. Thwing of Western Reserve, William DeWitt Hyde of Bowdoin, Julia J. Irvine of Wellesley, Francis Patton of Princeton, Austin Scott of Rutgers, and B. A. Hinsdale of Michigan; schoolmen A. F. Nightingale of Chicago, Joseph Coit of St. Paul's, Moses Merrill of Boston Latin, and William G. Thayer of St. Marks.[76] In 1897, 6,000 circulars were sent by the Twelve to Latin and Greek teachers and other schoolmen asking if Greek should be taught for three years in the secondary school. One thousand replies were received, the majority calling for the three-year

74. A. E. Winship, editorial in *Journal of Education*, *42* (1895), 196. Tetlow answered Winship with a sharp rebuke printed in the next issue. Winship, of course, was no lover of a strict, classical education; he welcomed the Twelve only as they were attacking the Ten.

75. N. M. Butler to C. W. Eliot, July 23, 1895, and C. W. Eliot to N. M. Butler, July 26, 1895, Eliot Papers, Harvard University.

76. NEA *Proceedings* (1896), pp. 560–61.

course. This was reported to the NEA and to the New England Association by T. D. Seymour of Yale.[77]

Thus the classicists' attack on the *Report,* or that tiny portion of the *Report* dealing with Greek, was a furious one. The Ten, it will be recalled, provided for two years of Greek in the Classical Course unless (a footnote stated) local tradition or facilities deemed three years more desirable. This one point, hedged though it was by the footnote, inspired a wrath that retained its heat for four years. Ironically the wrath was led by Eliot's own Greek department with the assistance of men from Yale.

Reaction to the *Report* of the Committee of Ten, then, was varied. Most important, though, is the fact that there *was* reaction: the document was widely read and discussed. This was the primary goal of Butler and the members of the Ten, and their specific strategy to spread the Committee's recommendations was clearly successful. While there was no great public debate of the issues of secondary education—this was too much to ask for—the profession of teachers and administrators was fully involved.

In favor of the *Report* were the Ten's leading members, Eliot, Harris, Tetlow, and Mackenzie, and the energetic editor of *Educational Review.* Butler spread his laudatory message far and wide and, in a sense, influenced his readers to consider the document favorably. Other supporters of the *Report* were several big-city schoolmen, among them Coy of Cincinnati, Maxwell of Brooklyn, and Seaver of Boston. Also active supporters were liberal college men like A. B. Hart. All felt that while the *Report* provided only tentative solutions, it did bring some order to a chaotic situation, and moreover that it gave proper emphasis to the new subjects and helped liberalize outdated college entrance requirements.

Those opposed to the *Report* fell into two camps. On one hand there were the college men and schoolmen—those sup-

77. *Proceedings* of the New England Association of Colleges and Preparatory Schools (1897), pp. 79–88.

porting the Committee of Twelve, for example—who were convinced that the classical languages held the central place of languages in any scheme of education, and so deplored the relative demotion of Greek and the idea of college admission without an ancient language. They were strongly opposed to any version of the "equivalence" theory. On the other hand were the radicals, school and college men who deplored the presence in the *Report* of precisely those linguistic studies the Twelve had felt were absent. Critics like Greenwood of Kansas City, Kasson and Winship of the educational press, and Minnie Moore of Iowa deplored the exclusion of practical or vocational studies. They objected to college men telling them how to run their schools, almost on principle. They felt that the programs suggested by the Ten were universally too difficult for secondary school children and considered that the Committee's recommendations for dipping down certain subjects into the elementary schools were ill advised.

It is plain that the critics of the *Report,* divided as they were, represented the opposite poles of the dilemma posed by American educational history. Were the schools to be Latin schools and train the mind for college? Or were they to be academies that trained the mind for "life"? The Seymours and Nightingales were for strong, Latin School, linguistic training; the Greenwoods and Minnie Moores were for common school subjects to prepare for active life. And the *Report* stood right in the middle.

Eliot and Harris were men who visualized a compromise between the two traditions in American secondary education, and their *Report* reflects this view. It retained the disciplinary subjects but included among them English, history, modern foreign languages, and science. This was a moderate compromise, one already well established in many large public school systems.

The *Report* received little explicit criticism on the ground that it failed to deal with some of the more important causes of the chaos in secondary education. This is not altogether surprising: most critics of the *Report* conceived of the school as an institution isolated from the society of which it was a part, in the same way as did the Ten. Moreover, the critics had more than enough to say in opposition to the Ten within the confines of the *Report*'s recommendations. Explicit attack on the *Report* for its neglect of the practical and realistic aspects of school conditions came with the next generation of educators.

IX · THE EFFECT

Discussion of the *Report* of the Committee of Ten was one thing; putting the proposed reforms into effect was another. Educators expended many words arguing over the Committee's findings—one participant said he thought there were far too many[1]—but the words alone had little meaning. What did have significance was the action taken by schoolmen and college men to make changes in the light of the *Report*. A critic writing in 1910 reported: "It may safely be said that there is not a high school in the United States today that is not affected by the Report of this great committee; its total influence is beyond estimate."[2] The perceptive president of Bowdoin, William De Witt Hyde, who had been critical of the *Report* when it was first published, in 1899 called it "the greatest impulse in the direction of efficiency, variety, serviceableness, and vitality [secondary education] has ever received and [it was] winning the grandest victory ever achieved in the field of American education."[3]

The *Report* indeed had profound effects, of two kinds: it influenced school programs and courses, and (a less tangible effect) it exerted a broad general influence on school policy and the thinking of educators. This second kind of influence was the more important of the two.

The annual reports of important school commissioners and

1. New York Regents, *Bulletin, 28* (1894), 319.

2. E. O. Sisson, "An Educational Emergency," *Atlantic Monthly, 106* (1910), 56.

3. W. D. Hyde, "President Eliot as an Educational Reformer," *Atlantic Monthly, 83* (1899), 354–55.

superintendents demonstrated the extent to which the Committee of Ten influenced school curricula. Significant indeed was the fact that the Bureau of Education altered the format for its charts of school curricula to conform with the Ten's four courses. Commissioner Harris stated flatly in 1904: "The scheme of studies recommended by the committee of ten on secondary school studies to the National Educational Association in 1893 has become the model for all secondary, or high schools, public and private."[4] The *Report* was summarized Conference by Conference in the June 1894 *Pennsylvania School Journal,* organ of the Superintendent of Public Instruction in that state.[5] The Maine School Report of 1895 recommended that the *Report* be consulted, and outlined two composite courses: an English course without any language and a college preparatory course that was heavily linguistic.[6] The Committee was quoted in the Report of the Massachusetts Board of Education, and in the Vermont and Wisconsin School Reports.[7] In these and other documents, however, it is significant that while the Committee of Ten figured prominently in many, the principal matters discussed by the state school officers were practical ones—buildings, teachers, and pupils. Indeed the sad condition of outhouses, mentioned earlier, received as much attention as the *Report* itself.

Some states followed the NEA lead and set up their own committees on the pattern of the Ten. The Michigan State Teachers' Association organized their own Committee of Ten in 1894, which eventually recommended a four-course curriculum—Classical, Latin-Scientific, Scientific, and English—for the graded schools of the state.[8] In July 1895 a Kentucky

4. *Report of the Commissioner of Education* (1904), 2, 1727.
5. *Pennsylvania School Journal, 42* (1894), 554–56.
6. *Report of the* (Maine) *State Superintendent of Common Schools* (1895), pp. 87–88.
7. *Annual Report of the* (Massachusetts) *Board of Education* (1894–95), pp. 128 ff.; *Thirty-Third Vermont School Report* (1894), pp. 97–98; *Biennial Report of the State Superintendent of the State of Wisconsin* (1894), p. 58.
8. D. Putnam, *The Development of Primary and Secondary Public Education in Michigan* (Ann Arbor, 1904), p. 104.

Committee of Ten started its work, acknowledging its debt to the NEA Committee. Three courses—Classical, Scientific, and Latin-English—were suggested, and the Committee recommended that schools using them be accredited by the state university and other Kentucky colleges.[9] Iowa had a Committee of Seven in 1895 and a Committee of Twelve in 1898; the former made various recommendations for high school courses of two, three, and four years; the last called for a Latin-Scientific course conforming to the pattern provided by the Ten.[10] The University of Mississippi faculty and trustees supported a committee that set up four courses, only one of which called for Latin and all of which excluded Greek.[11] Even if they found the *Report*'s specific recommendations impractical, then, many states were using the Committee's example in evolving their own curricula.

City school authorities also showed interest in the *Report*. Superintendent Seaver of Boston devoted virtually all of his 1894 school report to a detailed, laudatory analysis of the Committee of Ten's recommendations.[12] The reactions of various Rhode Island educators were printed together in a report published by the state. W. T. Peck of Providence, G. C. Fisher of Pawtucket, F. A. Spratt of Johnston, and the city school officers of Woonsocket and Smithfield all described how the *Report* had led to changes in their local curricula. One town ceased teaching political economy and put more emphasis on civil government. A superintendent happily reported that his own views on the teaching of natural history coincided with those of the Committee. Another town altered its mathematics and English curricula to conform with the Ten's suggestions and still another set up a curriculum committee for a

9. Document in Eliot Papers, Harvard University.

10. C. R. Aurner, *History of Education in Iowa* (Iowa City, 1915), *3*, 348–52.

11. *Biennial Report of the* (Mississippi) *State Superintendent* (1894–95), p. 571. See also W. C. Ryan et al., *Secondary Education in the South* (Chapel Hill, 1946), p. 117.

12. *Fourteenth Annual Report of the Superintendent of the City of Boston* (1894).

careful study of the whole problem.[13] The suggestions for dipping down into the elementary grades were put into practice in Leominster, Massachusetts, although the high school curriculum in that town was not altered to meet the Committee's specifications.[14] The principal of the Wilmington, Delaware, high school used the Committee's recommendations as a standard by which to measure his school's performance.[15] But again, as with the state reports, the practical issues of space, staff, and equipment filled most of the pages of city officials' reports. The schoolmen on the job were interested, but distracted by the enormous administrative demands that the Ten had totally ignored.

In 1906 Edwin Dexter made a close study of the curricula used by over eighty schools in 1895 and 1904 to reveal the extent to which the precise prescriptions of the Committee had been put into practice.[16] He found that the suggestions of the Latin Conference had had a fair reception: in 1894 only 46 per cent of the schools studied had a four-year Latin cycle, but by 1904, 80 per cent of them met this standard. There was a 10 per cent drop in the use of Vergil's *Bucolics,* as the Conference had recommended. A four-year, five-period-a-week course in English as contemplated by the Ten was seen in 52 per cent of the schools in 1894 and in 68 per cent in 1904. An additional 32 per cent in the latter year had at least three years of English—a sharp rise over 1894. The trend in the modern foreign languages, on the other hand, was away from the Committee's recommendations—possibly, Dexter suggested, a result of introducing elective systems. No real change was seen in the mathematics curriculum at the secondary school level. The trends in physics and chemistry seemed to follow the pattern suggested by Professor W. J. Waggener in his minority state-

13. *Twenty-Fifth Annual Report of the* (Rhode Island) *State Board of Education* (1894), pp. 119, 123, 135, 138, 142.

14. *Annual Report of the Leominster Public Schools* (1894), pp. 11, 21–22, 29–30.

15. *Report of the Principal of the* (Wilmington) *High School* (1895).

16. E. G. Dexter, "Ten Years' Influence of the Report of the Committee of Ten," *School Review, 14* (1906), 255 ff.

ment to the Conference report rather than the one offered in Remsen's Conference statement itself. Astronomy, recommended as an elective by the Conference, showed a 50-per-cent decline over the ten-year period. In natural history there was "a slight change for the better," but history itself remained largely neglected: American history, seen in 57 per cent of the schools in 1894, appeared in 86 per cent of them in 1904, to be sure, but the other historical areas showed no increase. There was a decrease in the teaching of the various subjects covered by the Conference on geography. Greek was taught too little in either year to show any trend one way or the other. Dexter's study of curricula concluded:

> The report of the Committee of Ten seems not to have influenced directly to a marked degree the curriculum of the public high schools. This does not mean that it has not fully justified itself through directing thought to the problems of the curriculum and making those problems, so to speak, conscious of themselves; but with the shaping of its details it has had little to do. In fact, more of the specific recommendations of the committee have been actually violated by the trend of high-school organization, or have proved inert, than have been followed.[17]

Clearly the recommendations of the Ten in their strictest sense were not followed; but the Committee, it will be remembered, had no desire for the schools to do so. One school, the Michigan Military Academy, incorporated Table IV to the letter but, the headmaster reported, had to alter it almost immediately because the curriculum was too difficult for the students.[18]

On the other hand, there were indications that schools were heeding the Committee's plea for curricula that followed the several main lines exclusively. The Missouri College Union,

17. Dexter, "Ten Years' Influence," p. 269.
18. W. H. Butts, "An Experiment in Schedule Making," *School Review*, 2 (1894), 412.

for example, adopted a modified form of Table IV that became "virtually the standard for high schools and academies in Missouri from that time [1894] to 1911."[19] In 1898 the North Central Association passed a resolution calling for secondary school studies to be offered in five areas of knowledge: language; mathematics; natural and physical science; history and literature; civics and economics. Students were to plan their courses in such a way as to cover all five, and the courses were "to be plastic as to permit alternative options."[20] These recommendations clearly showed the influence of the Committee of Ten.

Further evidence of the extent to which schools were narrowing their curricula to the main lines is available in the annual *Reports* of the United States Commissioner of Education. One scholar has compiled comparative percentages of public high school students in each of the broad academic areas.[21] Thirty-five per cent of these students were taking Latin in 1890, 51 per cent in 1900, and 49 per cent in 1910. If all foreign languages are lumped together, the percentages show an even greater increase. Mathematics showed a similar rise—67 per cent in 1890, 86 per cent in 1900, 90 per cent in 1910. The sciences almost tripled their percentage of students in the twenty-year period. Virtually all students studied English in 1910. By the same year roughly two-thirds of the students were taking some sort of history. At the same time, business subjects dropped adherents—only 11 per cent of the students elected them in 1910—and all nonacademic subjects together accounted for only a few students. The trend was clearly toward the

19. H. O. Severance, *Richard Henry Jesse* (mimeographed) (Columbia, Mo., 1937), p. 130.
20. *Proceedings* of the North Central Association (1898), p. viii.
21. J. F. Latimer, *What's Happened to Our High Schools?* (Washington, 1958), pp. 21–61. The percentages were arrived at by dividing the total number of public high school students taking courses in each field by the total public secondary school enrollments. As course titles varied, as the reporting by schools to the Commissioner was somewhat haphazard, and as many students took more than one course in the same field during a single year, the figures are somewhat misleading and should be used only to demonstrate the trend.

"main lines" advocated in the *Report* of the Committee of Ten. Particularly interesting is the rise in the percentage of Latin students—a 174-per-cent increase from 1890 to 1898, as one distinguished classicist happily pointed out, and the sharpest rise of any subject.[22] Latin remained until 1910 the symbol of culture and the most respected vehicle for imparting mental discipline; the Ten would have happily endorsed the latter proposition.

To summarize, then, the influence of the Committee's specific recommendations—that is, Table IV—was slight. "The effect of [the Committee's] Report," a critic wrote in 1934, "was to supersede a program of short courses in many subjects, of the old academy type, by one of relatively few subjects, and it soon led to considerable uniformity in secondary school courses throughout the United States."[23] These few subjects were the well established linguistic and mathematical areas as well as a number of the new subjects, including English, natural and physical sciences, and history. Vocational subjects such as manual training, although vigorously argued for, made proportionally little gain in the fifteen years following the publication of the *Report*—which, of course, had deliberately omitted them.

The indirect effect of the *Report* of the Committee of Ten upon general school policy, by contrast, was far greater than its influence upon specific curricula. It is difficult to assess this influence, but what evidence does exist is impressive.

First of all, the *Report* became a standard by which schools evaluated their own policies. This was the usage mentioned most often in school reports; principals and superintendents,

22. A. F. West, "A New Revival," *Educational Review*, *18* (1899), 256. History gained 152 per cent, Geometry 147 per cent, Algebra 141 per cent, Greek 94 per cent during the same period. The student body itself increased 86 per cent.

23. E. P. Cubberley, *Public Education in the United States* (rev. ed. Boston, 1934), p. 543. Bernard Mehl also finds "a uniform pattern based upon the spirit of the report of the Committee of Ten": "The High School at the Turn of the Century," unpublished dissertation, University of Illinois (1954), p. 268.

impressed by the prestige of the members of the Committee, inevitably accepted the *Report* as too important a statement of policy to dismiss lightly. *The Outlook* expressed this point of view editorially, four years after the *Report*. "The report on secondary education . . . is recognized today in all educational circles in the United States as an authoritative exposition of the principles upon which the greatest educators agree, and the methods by which secondary education, for its greatest efficiency, must be carried forward."[24] The authority enjoyed by the *Report* partially explains the trend toward the main lines apparent in the U.S. Commissioner's *Reports* up to 1910. Naturally, application of the document as a standard was precisely what President Eliot most favored. Mackenzie had called the *Report*'s greatest value "inspirational," and in many cases it probably was. Albert Bushnell Hart, a member of the American Historical Association's Committee of Seven in 1897, gave striking evidence of this in a letter to Eliot. "The western members of the Committee," he wrote, "speak in warm terms of the far-reaching effect of the Report of the Committee of Ten, throughout the West, in rousing teachers and inspiring schools."[25] Eliot must have been gratified by reports like this one, received well after the *Report* was published.

The Committee of Ten had sanctioned what amounted to a limited elective system in secondary schools. All four of its courses in Table IV had a central, common core to be taken by all students. Classicists, scientists, and English students branched off into their own fields during certain times of each year, particularly the final one. Table IV, as Eliot admitted, could easily have been written as one course with electives, much on the pattern of the Chelsea High School program he designed in 1885. The principle of election, not only for minor subjects like art of political economy, but also for the main line subjects, was established in the Committee's *Report*.

By 1910 "election of studies" was a feature of most high

24. 57 (1897), 561.
25. A. B. Hart to C. W. Eliot, April 17, 1897, Eliot Papers, Harvard University.

school programs. In 1900 Eliot himself told the NEA that "the introduction of freedom in choice of studies" was a key reform of the nineteenth century.[26] Meetings of various educational groups after 1894 heard frequent addresses on the subject of election. The teacher most closely associated with the movement was Boston's Samuel Thurber, of the Committee of Ten's English Conference, who had vigorously but vainly argued for a completely elective secondary school curriculum during the 1890s. He felt uniformity was unthinkable in the schools. "No thinker, or committee of thinkers, can prescribe [the school's] aims, methods, or proportions."[27] Thurber's views as presented and discussed at the 1894 meeting of the Harvard Teachers' Association were printed in *Educational Review* and filled almost an entire issue.[28] *School Review* and the *Journal of Education* also published articles on election, and the NEA and the American Institute of Instruction dealt with the matter. Eliot's plan for "flexibility and variety" in school and college curricula—first seen at Harvard—was fully established in secondary schools after the publication of the *Report* of the Committee of Ten.

The elective system had important effects on high school graduation and college entrance requirements. The Committee of Ten had asserted that any one of its four courses should be acceptable for graduation and college admission. They claimed—and justifiably—a true equivalence of subjects: the Latin-Scientific Course graduate was just as educated as the student who went through the Classical Course. The academic subjects were interchangeable, and in the years following the *Report* this view was fully accepted. Of the fourteen resolutions passed by the NEA Committee on College Entrance Requirements in 1899, the first recommended flatly "that the principle

26. C. W. Eliot, in discussion of N. M. Butler, "Status of Education at the Close of the Century," NEA *Proceedings* (1900), p. 196. See also P. H. Hanus, *Educational Aims and Educational Values* (New York, 1899), pp. 62 ff.

27. S. Thurber, "Freedom from Prescription: An Essential Condition of Success in our Secondary Education," *School Review*, 2 (1894), 512.

28. *15* (1898), 442 ff.

of election be recognized in secondary schools."[29] Thus, the Committee of Ten, by advocating election of studies and claiming equal value of all subjects making up the academic curriculum, inadvertently gave rise to a system that treats hours and semesters of school work as coins in some sort of educational bank. The credit-hour system, still in vogue today, is an extreme form of the plan that the Ten had in mind. This unexpected development from the *Report* has been much deplored and called "the worst enemy of quality, freedom, and an organic concept of learning in our high schools."[30]

The Committee of Ten was touted as a body formed for the purpose of educational research, the first such project financed by the NEA. Research was highly regarded at the turn of the century: the society was in love with science. More research by other committees of experts in the field of education followed on the heels of the Ten. The NEA sponsored a Committee of Fifteen on Elementary Education, which reported in 1895 on city school systems, correlation of subjects, and teacher training. William H. Maxwell was chairman of this committee, and Harris was a member. The Fifteen—significantly—focused their studies on two areas raised by the Ten. Their *Report* received wide circulation; in addition to being propagandized by Butler (Maxwell was his deputy at the *Educational Review*), it appeared in its entirety in Butler's *Review* and in the U.S. Commissioner's *Report*. This group's findings were subjected to the same type of discussion as the *Report* of the Ten, though Harris for his part felt the efforts of the Fifteen fell short of Eliot's Committee. To N. A. Calkins of the NEA he wrote, "I do not count the 'Report of the Committee of Fifteen' to be anything like so valuable a report as that of the Committee of Ten"; and to Eliot he wrote in a similar vein.[31] This report was followed in 1897 by a Committee of Twelve

29. *Report of the* (NEA) *Committee on College Entrance Requirements* (Chicago, 1899), p. 27.

30. R. Ulich, *Professional Education as a Humane Study* (New York, 1956), p. 15.

31. W. T. Harris to N. A. Calkins, March 25, 1895, and W. T. Harris to C .W. Eliot, March 27, 1895. Bureau of Education Records, U.S. Archives.

that studied rural schools; again Harris was a member. A committee for examining college entrance requirements published its report in 1899. The chairman was Superintendent Nightingale of Chicago,[32] who had been so hostile to the Ten's report; even so, the document they produced closely followed the main lines set forth in 1893, though Greek was allowed an extra year.[33]

James Baker felt a desire for a new committee, to undertake a study of the "culture element and the economy of time in education."[34] The precise nature of this proposal required clarification, and in 1904 the National Council of Education named a committee, headed by Eliot and having Baker as a member, to study the proposal. In time, Baker's suggestions were put into reasonable order (though not before Eliot put some harsh statements in letters to his committee[35]), and the result was the Report of the Committee on the Economy of Time. The NEA discussed the findings in 1912 and 1913.

There were other committees of the NEA and similar academic organizations. The American Historical Association,

32. The composition of this Committee of Thirteen is of interest. W. H. Smiley, Henry B. Fine, and Ray Greene Huling, formerly of the Ten's Conferences, were members. No college president was included, but there were four experts in "education": Paul H. Hanus of Harvard, Burke A. Hinsdale of Michigan, James E. Russell of Teachers' College, Columbia, and Charles H. Thurber of Chicago. Another member, George B. Aiton, was a Minnesota state inspector of high schools. The Committee drew on the advice of the American Philological Association's Committee of Twelve and committees of the Modern Language Association, the American Historical Association, and others.

33. The Ten may have inspired other committees as well. James Mackenzie gave the Committee of Ten the credit for serving as the example to the British Government which formed the Royal Commission on Secondary Education in 1894. Lord Bryce was Chairman of this Commission and corresponded much with Eliot and Angell on secondary school matters. Brian Hone pointed out to the present writer the interesting though probably insignificant fact that Bryce's biographer, who must have read the considerable Bryce-Eliot correspondence, was H. A. L. Fisher, in 1918 the author of the Fisher Act.

34. See J. H. Baker, "The Culture Element and the Economy of Time in Education," *Educational Review,* 27 (1904), 494–96.

35. C. W. Eliot to committee members, April 1, 1904, Eliot Papers, Harvard University.

perhaps depressed because the schools had failed to respond to the suggestions of the History Conference, set up its own Committee of Seven, which issued a report in 1899. In 1912 a Committee of Five took up the question, and others followed. It is clear that the Committee of Ten opened the floodgates for groups studying every nook and cranny of the curriculum. Research by committee became firmly entrenched once the precedent was established in 1893.

An important influence of the Committee of Ten on the American educational scene was its notable example of close school-college cooperation. Eliot and his colleagues had keenly felt the need for this, and Eliot spelled out the reasons in his speech "The Unity of Educational Reform." From 1892 to 1910 there was continuous cooperation between schoolteachers and professors. Although none of the various committees mentioned above had the stature of the Ten, their very existence was proof of this cooperation. Eliot was president of the NEA in 1904, and Harvard was opened to the delegates at the meeting. He was also active in the Harvard Teachers' Association, as was his successor President Lowell for a few years after him. Of equal significance was the Harvard Schools Examination Board set up by Eliot. This board (of which he was chairman, and which drew its membership from the University faculty) would examine any school requesting such a study and make a confidential report to its governors. Such was the form this cooperation took at Harvard.

Of more general concern were college entrance requirements. As we have already noted, these were tackled by groups of school and college men working together. The result of their efforts was the College Entrance Examination Board, organized by Butler[36] in the Association of Colleges and Preparatory Schools in the Middle States and Maryland. It gave its first examinations in 1901, and shortly thereafter other eastern colleges joined the group. In 1901 the North Central Association organized a Commission on Accredited Schools, a body com-

36. Possibly at the suggestion of Eliot. See H. James, *Charles W. Eliot* (Boston, 1930), *1*, 368.

posed half of college men and half of schoolteachers. The Commission was to inspect schools, and in this way relieve the colleges of wasteful duplication of effort. Thus the pattern of accreditation continued to function in that part of the country, as did the pattern of examinations in the East.

Evidence of the considerable effect of the *Report* was the continuing publication of arguments against it. The strenuous activities of the APA Committee of Twelve have already been described. One of the *Report*'s most vehement critics was President G. Stanley Hall of Clark University, who as late as 1904 still felt it necessary to take up the cudgel. In his massive two-volume work, *Adolescence,* he started by listing the beneficial effects of the Committees that began with the Ten:

> [They have made] many junctures between secondary and higher education; greatly increased the interest of faculties in high schools; given the former fruitful pedagogical themes for their own discussions; brought about a more friendly feeling and better mutual acquaintance; given slow colleges a wholesome stimulation; made school courses richer, given them better logical sequence; detected many weak points; closed many gaps, defined standards of what education means; brought great advantages from uniformity and cooperation, and no doubt, on the whole, have improved the conditions of college entrance examinations and aided in continuity.

From here he went into attack:

> One interesting result is the standardizing of high school knowledge, as hardware and even agricultural products. . . . Knowledge is no longer bullion from the mine, but is minted with a hall-mark of at least some numerical committee. Everything must count and so much, for herein lies its educational value. There is no more wild, free, vigorous growth of the forest, but everything is in pots or rows like a rococo garden.

Intellectual pabulum has lost all gamey flavor and is stall-fed or canned.

Then, for five closely-printed pages, Hall assaulted "three extraordinary fallacies" of the Committee of Ten. The first was the idea that all children should study the same subjects in the same way as long as they were in school, the second was the principle of equivalence, and the third was the idea that fitting for college was the same as fitting for life. Hall used psychological arguments in attacking these ideas, and did so with characteristic color and heat.[37]

Needless to say, this tirade disturbed Eliot. He had said earlier that he would not answer the critics of the *Report*, but in 1905 he wrote to Butler that he felt "inclined" to write an article "on the assumptions of the report of the Committee of Ten."[38] Accordingly "The Fundamental Assumptions of the Report of the Committee of Ten" appeared in the November *Educational Review* and answered Hall point for point. Eliot asserted that the "educational theory" propounded in the *Report* was "thoroly [sic] sound" and that the twelve years since the *Report*'s publication had borne this out. He quoted Hall's list of favorable effects of the various committees and ended his paper with the cutting remark that "from such an observer of the progress of education this judgment was high value."[39] On this point Eliot was wholly correct, for Hall's criticism—coming ten years after the *Report*—is compelling evidence of the profound effect the Committee of Ten's recommendations had exerted on school policy.

The reasons why the *Report* had such a profound effect are not difficult to perceive. First of all, the *Report* came at the very time when such an authoritative document was badly needed. Secondary schools, few and restricted in the first part of the nineteenth century, were mushrooming in the 1890s,

37. G. S. Hall, *Adolescence* (New York, 1904), 2, 508–14.
38. C. W. Eliot to N. M. Butler, May 6, 1905, Eliot Papers, Harvard University.
39. *30* (1905), 343. Eliot also read the paper at the July meeting of the American Institute of Instruction.

and in the chaos this expansion created the *Report* provided much-needed direction for teachers and administrators. As there were no other statements of school policy for it to compete with, it found a wide audience. Within the narrow field of the curriculum the *Report* served as a beacon.

A second explanation for the *Report*'s effect was the authority of its membership. Editors Winship and Kasson and others might thunder against the "college domination" of the Committee, but the fact remained that the words of Eliot, Angell, Harris and the rest carried tremendous prestige. The Committee had been wisely selected with just such an effect in mind. Teachers listened to this balanced group of nationally influential men, and many did what they suggested.

Next was the fact that the *Report* had a carefully planned distribution. Butler and his journal; the 30,000 free copies sent to key personnel by the U.S. Bureau of Education; the speeches by various members of the Ten; the inevitable and numerous discussions—all contributed to spread the recommendations of the Committee. This propaganda effort in a day when the advertising industry was still in its infancy was masterfully done.

Another explanation for the *Report*'s success, and a profound one, was the fact that the Committee accurately reflected the scholarly mood of the day. Its members adhered to the tradition of mental discipline, but saw that the new academic subjects might well provide this discipline just as adequately as the classics and mathematics did. The purpose of secondary schools was to train minds; few disagreed with this conclusion in 1893. The main lines were the proper vehicles for intellectual training, and this is amply demonstrated by the curricula as they stood fifteen years after 1893. Science and the scientific method were found not only in the methods of research of the Committee, but also in the programs and methods recommended in the *Report* itself.

One of the most important reasons for the wide acceptance of the *Report* was its moderate tone. It went to neither extreme —the old-time Latin School nor the manual training school—but it made concessions to each camp. Linguistic studies maintained their primacy, if in reduced form; the sciences and other English subjects were introduced and the colleges were asked to accept them for admission. The Committee's plans were moderate, too, in that they described what the best city schools were actually doing in 1893. Thus, the plans were easily put into effect in urban school systems and could not be dismissed as wholly visionary by anyone.

Ironically, another reason the schools accepted the *Report's* recommendations for improving their curricula was the fact that it carefully avoided mentioning many of the basic causes of the chaos in secondary education. As has been pointed out, the Ten failed to consider the central problems of the control of schools: crooked politics, outsized enrollment, changes in society. If they had prescribed remedies for these ills, they might well have generated considerable and powerful opposition. By staying close to the mechanics of the school curriculum, the Ten had only to convince the schoolmen; the politicians and the public in general were unconcerned. Accordingly, once the schoolmen were won over, the battle was won—that is, until the hard facts of a changing society, combined with an exploding school population, caused the inevitable upheaval in the decades after 1900.

It has been seen how the effect of the *Report* was national. At no time prior to the Ten had a group of such authority both in education and in the society at large sat down in order to prescribe for the schools, and at no time prior to 1893 was the dissemination of a document so easy or so carefully planned. The *Report* was timely in every sense, and it was assured a hearing in most parts of the country. Accordingly it changed the secondary schools in most states, and in an important sense it standardized the main line subjects in secondary school curriculum. It was the first such effective document in the history of American education, its only possible competitor being the report of the Yale faculty in 1828.[40]

40. One cannot but contrast the *Report* of the Committee of Ten with the similar report, *The American High School Today* (New York, 1959),

Beginning around 1910, however, the pattern of school policy charted by the Committee of Ten in 1893 was gradually discarded. Secondary education was changing rapidly, and the changes caused schoolmen to consider the *Report* obsolete. Accordingly, both the specific curricula and the general rationale for education expressed by the Committee were cast off.

There are several reasons for this change in attitude. The most important was the tremendous increase in the number of children attending secondary school. In 1890 there were about 360,000 of them, according to the U.S. Commissioner of Education—6.7 per cent of the fourteen-to-seventeen age group. These figures virtually doubled by 1900; and in 1910, 1,115,398 children were in secondary schools—15.4 per cent of the relevant age group. By 1920 the figures had again doubled, reaching 2,500,176, or 32.3 per cent.[41] The increase in numbers overwhelmed the school authorities, whose preoccupation with buildings and equipment, noted before, continued apace. More significant, however, was the percentage figure, for it showed that children from certain groups in the society were now attending secondary school who had not previously done so. When children of immigrants and other lower-class groups entered the secondary schools, they presented for the educators

prepared by another Harvard President, James B. Conant, in 1958. The so-called Conant Report has clearly had an effect in providing for schools a high standard (the "academic inventory") and in changing various curricular patterns, particularly in the foreign languages. The Conant Report has much in common with its 1893 forebear, and its success may be due in part to some of the same factors as those that operated for the Committee of Ten. The Conant Report was timely—the schools were under considerable attack and needed an authoritative blueprint—; it was backed by a nationally influential leader who was appealing to both college and school men; it was meticulously propagandized; it reflected a scholarly view, damning "frill" courses; it was moderate and practical and suggested no radical departures but rather what the best schools of the country were already doing; it avoided many of the same issues avoided by the Ten and for some of the same reasons. While the comparison is hardly perfect, it is close enough to suggest that James Conant, born in the year the *Report* of the Committee of Ten was published, may have learned much from the example of Charles Eliot.

41. U.S. Commissioner of Education, *Biennial Survey of Education in the United States* (1952–54), *1*, 26.

new kinds of pedagogical problems. To many of them, school was not a place to achieve mental discipline but rather a place to gain vocational training. The children were unruly, coming as many of them did from social groups where bookishness was considered anathema. They would not sit quietly and read and recite dutifully; they could see no purpose in it and, unlike their more respectful forebears, they openly rebelled against it. Eliot had spoken of the desirability of "interesting" the child in his work, and he believed it was possible to train a child to "want" the linguistic, abstract studies. But to interest the new type of student seen in the schools from 1910 onward presented to many teachers a wholly different problem from the one dealt with by Eliot in his day. It is not surprising that these teachers sought an answer in nonlinguistic studies, obviously closer to their students' desires.

With this vast change in the student body came a new rationale for the schools, and with it a new curriculum. As the reformers of politics, business, and the cities became prominent at the turn of the century, they spread the idea that something was wrong with American society, that the traditional cohesion and dignity were gone. To repair this lack, some reformers turned to the schools—and found them wholly detached from life in its broadest sense. The schools, devoted to mental discipline, were not dealing with the social problems the reformers had publicized. There was a gap between the schools and the society, and the reformers, seeking to repair their society through education, moved to bring the schools' curricula closer to society's needs.[42]

The schools were called upon to replace various agencies in the society that had previously had great responsibilities. As the hold of the Church loosened, the schools were asked to take up the responsibility for moral education. As the discipline of the family unit appeared to be not rigorous enough to train the child, the school was asked to teach him about manners, health, and adjustment to life. As industry became more

42. See O. Handlin, *John Dewey's Challenge to Education* (New York, 1959).

complex and centralized and the apprenticeship system further declined, the schools were asked to provide strict vocational training. In sum, society gave the schools full responsibility to train not only their students' intellects, but now also their social and vocational selves.

Coupled with this transformed rationale for the schools was a changed view of the child himself. Mental discipline, already scored as an untenable dogma by Burke Hinsdale in 1894, was sharply criticized after the turn of the century. Psychologists began to question seriously the principle of "transfer of training"—that is, the child's ability to transfer the mental skill achieved in one discipline to another.[43] A grasp of the intricacies of Latin grammar, they concluded, was of little help in grasping the intricacies of one's monthly budget. If this was so, and the pedagogues of the early 1900s accepted the doctrine, then it was necessary to teach children specifically about monthly budgets. Indeed Latin grammar, being less useful and applicable than budgeting, might well be scrapped from the curriculum altogether. As a leading reformer explained in 1909, "Reading, Writing, Arithmetic, Grammar, Geography, and History, the staples of the elementary curriculum, are really of little value except as they are closely related with the needs and problems of our social, civic, and industrial life."[44] How different is this philosophy from that of the Committee of Ten.

To deal with the massive influx of new students and with the vexing new pedagogical and psychological problems, a group of "professional" educators appeared, men whose full-time efforts were devoted to a study of the science of education.

43. "Improvement in any single mental function rarely brings about equal improvement in any other function, no matter how similar, for the working of every mental function-group is conditioned by the nature of the data in each particular case." Such was the conclusion of E. L. Thorndike and R. S. Woodworth, "The Influence of Improvement in One Mental Function upon the Efficiency of Other Functions," *Psychological Review, 8* (1901), 250. This and other studies, by Thorndike especially, had enormous impact.

44. E. P. Cubberley, *Changing Conceptions of Education* (Boston, 1909), p. 66.

It is true that men like Burke Hinsdale and Paul Hanus were already devoting their energies to the "art and science of teaching" in the nineteenth century, but after 1900 the number of professors of education rapidly grew in proportion to the very considerable demand. They were the men who largely carried out the investigations that led to the setback of the revered mental discipline theory—men like Edward Lee Thorndike, James Earl Russell, and, to an extent, John Dewey. These men soon became the new oracles for education, taking over the reins once held by Eliot and Angell and the others. The committees of the new day were manned by the new men, a trend already discernible in the membership of the NEA Committee on College Entrance Requirements of 1899. Butler, a man whose active career extended from the 1890s to the 1930s, deplored this change, and spoke of the '90s as "that great epoch" when "Harris ruled the educational philosophy of the United States and when Eliot was leading men on to strengthen and elevate the thought of the American people and to build sound and progressive policies not only for the schools but for the country."[45] The new leaders built their schools in the isolation of the new discipline of Education and accordingly carried little of the prestige that had attached to many of the members of the Committee of Ten.

Thus the so-called progressive movement ran its course, shaped by the pressures of rising school enrollments, new kinds of pupils, and new demands upon the schools, and by a new group of leaders who devoted their full scholarly energies to education as a separate discipline or science. The dimensions of this movement do not concern us here;[46] all that one need say is that the movement altered the policies suggested by the

45. N. M. Butler, *Across the Busy Years* (New York, 1935), *1*, 206.
46. See L. A. Cremin, *The Transformation of the School* (New York, 1961); H. M. Jones, F. Keppel, and R. Ulich, "On the Conflict between the 'Liberal Arts' and the 'Schools of Education,'" American Council of Learned Societies, *Newsletter, 5*, No. 2 (1954); J. B. Conant, *The Revolutionary Transformation of the American High School* (Cambridge, 1959); T. L. Smith, "Progressivism in American Education, 1880–1900," *Harvard Educational Review, 31* (1961).

Ten that had been followed in large measure until about 1910. Of course the shift from the philosophy of the Ten to that of the new group of educators was gradual and erratic, and many schools that put into effect the proposals of the *Report* retain them to this day. But in the broadest sense, the *Report* of the Committee of Ten was by 1920 no longer the standard by which schools measured their performance. The linguistically weighted, academic curriculum presented by the Ten for all children was largely discarded, as it was considered unteachable to many slow or unmotivated children and inappropriate in terms of the new psychology and philosophy of the time.

The demise of the predominant influence of the *Report* of the Committee of Ten was most clearly marked by the Commission on the Reorganization of Secondary Education, formed in 1911, which issued its report in 1918. In a document entitled the "Cardinal Principles of Secondary Education," published by the U.S. Bureau of Education, the Commission of eleven men set out goals for the secondary schools regarding "the following as the main objectives of education: 1. Health. 2. Command of fundamental processes. 3. Worthy home-membership. 4. Vocation. 5. Citizenship. 6. Worthy use of leisure. 7. Ethical character."[47] Increased scope for the schools was seen unmistakably here, the Commission readily asserting that vast social changes in the twentieth century had radically altered the role of the school.

The Commission was chaired by Clarence D. Kingsley, the Massachusetts State High School supervisor. P. P. Claxton, U.S. Commissioner of Education, was a member. One college president, Edward O. Sisson of Montana, was included, but he had spent most of his professional life in the schools. Three men were professors of Education, and the rest were persons involved in the administration of secondary schools. The very composition of the Commission demonstrated the change in educational leadership since 1892.

Like the Ten before it, the Commission called on other com-

47. "Cardinal Principles of Education," U.S. Bureau of Education, *Bulletin* 35 (Washington, 1918), 10–11.

mittees for help. The Ten saw need for only nine such groups, each representing a subject area and all together representing the full scope of the curriculum. The 1918 Commission had sixteen committees assisting it. The nine of 1892 were there: Latin and Greek were combined in a single committee; English, modern languages, and mathematics retained their identity. History and geography were dealt with by a single committee on social studies, and all the sciences were encompassed by one group. Thus the Ten's original nine Conferences were reduced to six. The remaining ten committees in 1918 were on a variety of subjects: "Organization and Administration of Secondary Education," agriculture, business education, household arts, industrial arts, music, physical education, vocational guidance, art education, and "Articulation of High School and College." Not one of the committees was chaired by a university scholar ranking with Ira Remsen or Charles Kendall Adams; most of the chairmen were educational specialists. The most prominent of these probably was Columbia's William Heard Kilpatrick, who headed the mathematics committee.

The new ideas proposed by these men had their effect even on the chairman of the Committee of Ten. Eliot, in his eighty-first year, read a paper to the Second Pan-American Scientific Congress in 1916, entitled "The Changes Needed in American Secondary Education." He asserted:

> The changes which ought to be made immediately in the programmes of American secondary schools, in order to correct the glaring deficiencies of the present programmes, are chiefly the introduction of more hand-, ear-, and eye-work, such as drawing, carpentry, turning, music, sewing, and cooking; and the giving of much more time to the sciences of observation—chemistry, physics, biology, and geography—not political, but geological and orthographical geography.

He wanted agriculture taught in rural schools and manual training in the city. In sum, he wanted training of "the senses of sight, hearing, taste, smell, and touch," and he scored the overemphasis on linguistic study.[48] Needless to say, the changes in American secondary schools and the doctrines of the new pedagogues were not lost on Charles W. Eliot. However, at the age of eighty-six, in a speech delivered to a Texas audience in 1921, Eliot recounted in detail the activities of the Committee of Ten—already ancient history. On this occasion, he held fast to the ideas he had proposed in 1893, and stated that the achievements of the Committee were great.[49]

The pattern set by the *Report* of the Committee of Ten was broken by 1920 because American society in the twentieth century demanded that its schools fill a wide variety of roles. The four programs recommended by the Ten still had great appeal for college-bound students, but for the vast majority, new curricula based on new goals were designed.

Had the Ten accurately predicted the changes in American society and education—changes clearly implied in the Commissioner of Education's statistics of 1892—the *Report* might have found a more permanent place in American school curricula. Obviously the *Report* alone could not have prescribed in detail for all aspects of the chaos evident in the secondary schools. It could, however, have met the issues squarely (as it did the issue of incompetent teachers), defined them, and given at least some direction to educators in coping with them. The Committee could well have recognized the difference between the linguistic curriculum it charted for the minority of the fourteen-to-seventeen-year-old age group and the demands of the overwhelming majority of teen-age children who were only too obviously seeking a place in secondary school. A Committee of the stature of the Ten could have begun the reforms that were to come later, and, one might suppose, could have checked some of the excesses seen in the progressive movement. But the Committee did not see the vast scope of the issues facing American secondary schools and thus did not prescribe for

48. C. W. Eliot, "The Changes Needed in American Secondary Education," printed in Eliot, *A Late Harvest* (Boston, 1924), pp. 100–01, 93.

49. C. W. Eliot, "American Education since the Civil War," in *A Late Harvest*, 129–41.

them in any way. As a result, the suggestions in the *Report* became obsolete within two decades.

And yet the *Report* remains important, both as a document typical of a period in American educational history and as a symbol of a certain kind of education. The split between the Latin School linguistic tradition and the academy-common school tradition is still with us, though in a form peculiar to this later day. The split can now be described as one between education as a solely intellectual process and education as a broad social process. School is for training the mind on the one hand and for training the mind plus the personality and vocational efficiency on the other. In the continuing argument between the proponents of each tradition, the *Report* has been raised by the "Latin School" group as the best statement of sound educational policy seen in American history. In 1958 a classicist published a book most of which was an explicit reaffirmation and, indeed, a positive deification of the Committee's principles.[50] An organization founded in 1956 and calling itself the Council for Basic Education has supported this view; in the introduction to one of its publications, *The Case for Basic Education,* the *Report* is called "one of the classic reports on American secondary schools."[51] The *Report,* then, a middle-of-the-road document in 1893, one criticized from both extremes, has become the Bible of the conservative group, a group cohesive enough by the 1950s to be called by a foreign educator the "new orthodoxy."[52]

Possibly this so-called new orthodoxy, which demands a return to the main lines of academic subjects and to mental discipline or intellectual training, is finding success; for, as in the period from 1894 to 1910, Latin enrollments are apparently rising,[53] and in the late 1950s there was much concern about im-

---

50. J. F. Latimer, *What's Happened to Our High Schools?* (Washington, 1958), see above, p. xi.

51. J. D. Koerner, ed., *The Case for Basic Education* (Boston, 1959), p. vii.

52. E. L. French of the University of Melbourne, in discussion with the writer.

53. Koerner, *The Case for Basic Education,* p. 123.

proving the intellectual side of the secondary schools, particularly in the sciences and mathematics. One can only speculate that, for the usual complex historical causes, the pendulum of school practice outlined by Harris in 1888[54] may be swinging back to the Latin School tradition, using as a symbol of excellence the *Report* of the Committee of Ten.

54. W. T. Harris, "The Pendulum of School Reform," *Education, 8* (1888), 347–50.

APPENDIX

*Report of the Committee of Ten
on Secondary School Studies,
With the Reports of the Conferences
Arranged By the Committee*[1]

TO THE NATIONAL COUNCIL OF EDUCATION:

The Committee of Ten appointed at the meeting of the National Educational Association at Saratoga on the 9th of July, 1892, have the honor to present the following report:—

At the meeting of the National Council of Education in 1891, a Committee appointed at a previous meeting made a valuable report through their Chairman, Mr. James H. Baker, then Principal of the Denver High School, on the general subject of uniformity in school programmes and in requirements for admission to college. The Committee was continued, and was authorized to procure a Conference on the subject of uniformity during the meeting of the National Council in 1892, the Conference to consist of representatives of leading colleges and secondary schools in different parts of the country. This Conference was duly summoned, and held meetings at Saratoga on July 7th, 8th, and 9th, 1892. There were present between twenty and thirty delegates. Their discussions took a wide range, but resulted in the following specific recommendations, which the Conference sent to the National Council of Education then in session.

1. That it is expedient to hold a conference of school and college teachers of each principal subject which enters into the programmes of secondary schools in the United States and into the requirements for admission to college—as, for example, of

1. *Report of the Committee on Secondary School Studies* (Washington, 1893), pp. 8–11.

Latin, of geometry, or of American history—each conference to consider the proper limits of its subject, the best methods of instruction, the most desirable allotment of time for the subject, and the best methods of testing the pupils' attainments therein, and each conference to represent fairly the different parts of the country.

2. That a Committeee be appointed with authority to select the members of these conferences and to arrange their meetings, the results of all the conferences to be reported to this Committee for such action as it may deem appropriate, and to form the basis of a report to be presented to the Council by this Committee.

3. That this Committee consists of the following gentlemen:

CHARLES W. ELIOT, President of Harvard University, Cambridge, Mass., *Chairman.*

WILLIAM T. HARRIS, Commissioner of Education, Washington, D.C.

JAMES B. ANGELL, President of the University of Michigan, Ann Arbor, Mich.

JOHN TETLOW, Head Master of the Girls' High School and the Girls' Latin School, Boston, Mass.

JAMES M. TAYLOR, President of Vassar College, Poughkeepsie, N.Y.

OSCAR D. ROBINSON, Principal of the High School, Albany, N.Y.

JAMES H. BAKER, President of the University of Colorado, Boulder, Colo.

RICHARD H. JESSE, President of the University of Missouri, Columbia, Mo.

JAMES C. MACKENZIE, Head Master of the Lawrenceville School, Lawrenceville, N.J.

HENRY C. KING, Professor in Oberlin College, Oberlin, Ohio.

These recommendations of the Conference were adopted by the National Council of Education on the 9th of July; and the Council communicated the recommendations to the Directors of the National Educational Association, with the further recommendation that an appropriation not exceeding $2500 be made by the Association towards the expenses of these conferences. On the 12th of July the Directors adopted a series of resolutions under which a sum not exceeding $2500 was made available for this undertaking during the academic year 1892–93.

Every gentleman named on the above Committee of Ten accepted his appointment; and the Committee met, with every member present, at Columbia College, New York City, from the 9th to the 11th of November, 1892, inclusive.

In preparation for this meeting, a table had been prepared by means of a prolonged correspondence with the principals of selected secondary schools in various parts of the country, which showed the subjects taught in forty leading secondary schools in the United States, and the total number of recitations, or exercises, allotted to each subject. Nearly two hundred schools were applied to for this information; but it did not prove practicable to obtain within three months verified statements from more than forty schools. This table proved conclusively, first, that the total number of subjects taught in these secondary schools was nearly forty, thirteen of which, however, were found in only a few schools; secondly, that many of these subjects were taught for such short periods that little training could be derived from them; and thirdly, that the time allotted to the same subject in the different schools varied widely. Even for the older subjects, like Latin and algebra, there appeared to be a wide diversity of practice with regard to the time allotted to them. Since this table was comparative in its nature,—that is, permitted comparisons to be made between different schools,— and could be easily misunderstood and misapplied by persons who had small acquaintance with school programmes, it was treated as a confidential document; and was issued at first only to the members of the Committee of Ten and the principals of the schools mentioned in the table. Later, it was sent—still as a confidential paper—to the members of the several conferences organized by the Committee of Ten.

The Committee of Ten, after a preliminary discussion on November 9th, decided on November 10th to organize conferences on the following subjects:—1. Latin; 2. Greek; 3. English; 4. Other Modern Languages; 5. Mathematics; 6. Physics, Astronomy, and Chemistry; 7. Natural History (Biology, including Botany, Zoölogy, and Physiology); 8. History, Civil Government, and Political Economy; 9. Geography (Physical Geography, Geology, and Meteorology). They also decided that each Conference should consist of ten members. They then proceeded to select the members of each of these Conferences, having regard in the selection to the scholarship and experience of the gentlemen named, to the fair division of the members between colleges on the one hand and schools on the other, and to the proper geographical distribution of the total membership. After selecting ninety members for the nine Conferences, the Committee decided on an additional number of names to be used as substitutes for persons originally chosen who should decline to serve, from two to four substitutes being selected for each Conference. In the selection of substitutes the Committee found it difficult to regard the geographical distribution of the persons selected with as much strictness as in the original selection; and, accordingly, when it became necessary to call on a considerable number of substitutes, the accurate geographical distribution of membership was somewhat impaired. The lists of the members of the several Conferences were finally adopted at a meeting of the Committee on November 11th; and the Chairman and Secretary of the Committee were then empowered to fill any vacancies which might occur.

The Committee next adopted the following list of questions as a guide for the discussions of all the Conferences, and directed that the Conferences be called together on the 28th of December:—

1. In the school course of study extending approximately from the age of six years to eighteen years—a course including the periods of both elementary and secondary instruction—at what age should the study

which is the subject of the Conference be first introduced?

2. After it is introduced, how many hours a week
for how many years should be devoted to it?

3. How many hours a week for how many years
should be devoted to it during the last four years of
the complete course; that is, during the ordinary high
school period?

4. What topics, or parts, of the subject may reasonably be covered during the whole course?

5. What topics, or parts, of the subject may best be
reserved for the last four years?

6. In what form and to what extent should the subject enter into college requirements for admission?
Such questions as the sufficiency of translation at sight
as a test of knowledge of a language, or the superiority
of a laboratory examination in a scientific subject to
a written examination on a text-book, are intended
to be suggested under this head by the phrase "in
what form."

7. Should the subject be treated differently for pupils who are going to college, for those who are going
to a scientific school, and for those who, presumably,
are going to neither?

8. At what stage should this differentiation begin,
if any be recommended?

9. Can any description be given of the best method
of teaching this subject throughout the school course?

10. Can any description be given of the best mode
of testing attainments in this subject at college admission examinations?

11. For those cases in which colleges and universities permit a division of the admission examination
into a preliminary and a final examination, separated
by at least a year, can the best limit between the preliminary and final examinations be approximately defined?

The Committee further voted that it was expedient that the Conferences on Latin and Greek meet at the same place. Finally, all further questions of detail with regard to the calling and the instruction of the Conferences were referred to the Chairman with full power.

During the ensuing six weeks, the composition of the nine Conferences was determined in accordance with the measures adopted by the Committee of Ten. Seventy persons originally selected by the Committee accepted the invitation of the Committee, and sixty-nine of these persons were present at the meetings of their respective Conferences on the 28th of December. Twenty substitutes accepted service, of whom twelve were persons selected by the Committee of Ten, and eight were selected under the authority granted to the Chairman and Secretary of the Committee in emergencies. One of these eight gentlemen was selected by a Conference at its first meeting. Two gentlemen who accepted service—one of the original members and one substitute—absented themselves from the meetings of their respective Conferences without giving any notice to the Chairman of the Committee of Ten, who was therefore unable to fill their places. With these two exceptions, all the Conferences met on December 28th with full membership.

The places of meeting were as follows:—for the Latin and Greek Conferences, the University of Michigan, Ann Arbor, Mich.; for the English Conference, Vassar College, Poughkeepsie, N.Y.; for the Conference on Other Modern Languages, the Bureau of Education, Washington, D.C.; for the Conference on Mathematics, Harvard University, Cambridge, Mass.; for the Conferences on Physics, Astronomy, and Chemistry, and on Natural History, the University of Chicago, Chicago, Ill.; for the Conference on History, Civil Government, and Political Economy, the University of Wisconsin, Madison, Wis.; for the Conference on Geography, the Cook County Normal School, Englewood, Ill. The Committee of Ten and all the Conferences enjoyed the hospitality of the several institutions at which they met, and the members were made welcome at private houses during the sessions. Through the exertions of Mr. N. A. Calkins, Chairman of the Trustees of the National Educational Association, important reductions of railroad fares were procured for some members of the Committee and of the Conferences; but the reductions obtainable were less numerous and considerable than the National Council of Education had hoped. In filling a few vacancies of which notice was received shortly before December 28th, it was necessary to regard as one qualification nearness of residence to the appointed places of meeting; but on the whole the weight and effectiveness of the several Conferences were not impaired by the necessary replacement of twenty of the members originally selected by the Committee of Ten. The list of the members of the Conferences on the 28th of December was as follows:—

1. *Latin.*

Professor CHARLES E. BENNETT, Cornell University, Ithaca, N.Y.

FREDERICK L. BLISS, Principal of the Detroit High School, Detroit, Mich.

JNO. T. BUCHANAN, Principal of the Kansas City High School, Kansas City, Mo.

WILLIAM C. COLLAR, Head Master of the Roxbury Latin School, Roxbury, Mass.

JOHN S. CROMBIE, Principal of the Adelphi Academy, Brooklyn, N.Y.

Professor JAMES H. DILLARD, Tulane University, New Orleans, La.

Rev. WILLIAM GALLAGHER, Principal of Williston Seminary, Easthampton, Mass.

Professor WILLIAM G. HALE, University of Chicago, Chicago, Ill.

Professor JOHN C. ROLFE, University of Michigan, Ann Arbor, Mich.

JULIUS SACHS, Principal of the Collegiate Institute for Boys, 38 West 59th Street, New York City.

2. *Greek.*

E. W. Coy, Principal of the Hughes High School, Cincinnati, O.

Professor Martin L. D'Ooge, University of Michigan, Ann Arbor, Mich.

A. F. Fleet, Superintendent of the Missouri Military Academy, Mexico, Mo.

Ashley D. Hurt, Head Master of the High School, Tulane University, New Orleans, La.

Robert D. Keep, Principal of the Free Academy, Norwich, Conn.

Professor Abby Leach, Vassar College, Poughkeepsie, N.Y.

Clifford H. Moore, Phillips Academy, Andover, Mass.

William H. Smiley, Principal of the High School, Denver, Colo.

Professor Charles F. Smith, Vanderbilt University, Nashville, Tenn.

Professor Benjamin I. Wheeler, Cornell University, Ithaca, N.Y.

3. *English.*

Professor Edward A. Allen, University of Missouri, Columbia, Mo.

F. A. Barbour, Michigan State Normal School, Ypsilanti, Mich.

Professor Frank A. Blackburn, University of Chicago, Chicago, Ill.

Professor Cornelius B. Bradley, University of California, Berkeley, Calif.

Professor Francis B. Gummere, Haverford College, Pa.

Professor Edward E. Hale, Jr., University of Iowa, Iowa City, Iowa.

Professor George L. Kittredge, Harvard University, Cambridge, Mass.

Charles L. Loos, Jr., High School, Dayton, Ohio.

216

W. H. MAXWELL, Superintendent of Schools, Brooklyn, N.Y.

SAMUEL THURBER, Master in the Girls' High School, Boston, Mass.

4. *Other Modern Languages.*

Professor JOSEPH L. ARMSTRONG, Trinity College, Durham, N.C.

THOMAS B. BRONSON, Lawrenceville School, Lawrenceville, N.J.

Professor ALPHONSE N. VAN DAELL, Massachusetts Institute of Technology, Boston, Mass.

CHARLES H. GRANDGENT, Director of Modern Language Instruction in the Public Schools, Boston, Mass.

Professor CHARLES HARRIS, Oberlin College, Oberlin, Ohio.

WILLIAM T. PECK, High School, Providence, R.I.

Professor SYLVESTER PRIMER, University of Texas, Austin, Texas.

JOHN J. SCHOBINGER, Principal of a Private School for Boys, Chicago, Ill.

ISIDORE H. B. SPIERS, William Penn Charter School, Philadelphia, Pa.

Professor WALTER D. TOY, University of North Carolina, Chapel Hill, N.C.

5. *Mathematics.*

Professor WILLIAM E. BYERLY, Harvard University, Cambridge, Mass.

Professor FLORIAN CAJORI, Colorado College, Colorado Springs, Colo.

ARTHUR H. CUTLER, Principal of a Private School for Boys, New York City.

Professor HENRY B. FINE, College of New Jersey, Princeton, N.J.

W. A. GREESON, Principal of the High School, Grand Rapids, Mich.

ANDREW INGRAHAM, Swain Free School, New Bedford, Mass.

Professor SIMON NEWCOMB, Johns Hopkins University, and Washington, D.C.

Professor GEORGE D. OLDS, Amherst College, Amherst, Mass.

JAMES L. PATTERSON, Lawrenceville School, Lawrenceville, N.J.

Professor T. H. SAFFORD, Williams College, Williamstown, Mass.

6. *Physics, Astronomy, and Chemistry.*

Professor BROWN AYERS, Tulane University, New Orleans, La.

IRVING W. FAY, The Belmont School, Belmont, Calif.

ALFRED P. GAGE, English High School, Boston, Mass.

GEORGE WARREN KRALL, Manual Training School, Washington University, St. Louis, Mo.

Professor WILLIAM W. PAYNE, Carleton College, Northfield, Minn.

WILLIAM McPHERSON, JR., 2901 Collinwood Avenue, Toledo, Ohio.

Professor IRA REMSEN, Johns Hopkins University, Baltimore, Md.

Professor JAMES H. SHEPARD, South Dakota Agricultural College, Brookings, So. Dak.

Professor WILLIAM J. WAGGENER, University of Colorado, Boulder, Colo.

GEORGE R. WHITE, Phillips Exeter Academy, Exeter, N.H.

7. *Natural History (Biology, including Botany, Zoölogy, and Physiology).*

Professor CHARLES E. BESSEY, University of Nebraska, Lincoln, Neb.

ARTHUR C. BOYDEN, Normal School, Bridgewater, Mass.

Professor SAMUEL F. CLARKE, Williams College, Williamstown, Mass.

Professor DOUGLAS H. CAMPBELL, Leland Stanford Jr. University, Palo Alto, Calif.

President JOHN M. COULTER, Indiana University, Bloomington, Ind.

Principal S. A. MERRITT, Helena, Montana.

W. B. POWELL, Superintendent of Schools, Washington, D.C.

CHARLES B. SCOTT, High School, St. Paul, Minn.

Professor ALBERT H. TUTTLE, University of Virginia, Charlottesville, Va.

O. S. WESTCOTT, Principal of the North Division High School, Chicago, Ill.

8. *History, Civil Government, and Political Economy.*

President CHARLES K. ADAMS, University of Wisconsin, Madison, Wis.

Professor EDWARD G. BOURNE, Adelbert College, Cleveland, Ohio.

ABRAM BROWN, Principal of the Central High School, Columbus, Ohio.

Professor A. B. HART, Harvard University, Cambridge, Mass.

RAY GREENE HULING, Principal of the High School, New Bedford, Mass.

Professor JESSE MACY, Iowa College, Grinnell, Iowa.

Professor JAMES HARVEY ROBINSON, University of Pennsylvania, Philadelphia, Pa.

Professor WILLIAM A. SCOTT, University of Wisconsin, Madison, Wis.

HENRY P. WARREN, Head Master of the Albany Academy, Albany, N.Y.

Professor WOODROW WILSON, College of New Jersey, Princeton, N.J.

9. *Geography (Physical Geography, Geology, and Meteorology).*

Professor THOMAS C. CHAMBERLIN, University of Chicago, Chicago, Ill.

Professor GEORGE L. COLLIE, Beloit College, Beloit, Wis.

Professor W. M. DAVIS, Harvard University, Cambridge, Mass.

DELWIN A. HAMLIN, Master of the Rice Training School, Boston, Mass.

Professor EDWIN J. HOUSTON, Central High School, Philadelphia, Pa.

Professor MARK W. HARRINGTON, The Weather Bureau, Washington, D.C.

CHARLES F. KING, Dearborn School, Boston, Mass.

FRANCIS W. PARKER, Principal of the Cook County Normal School, Englewood, Ill.

G. M. PHILIPS, Principal of the State Normal School, West Chester, Pa.

Professor ISRAEL C. RUSSELL, University of Michigan, Ann Arbor, Mich.

The ninety members of the Conferences were divided as follows,—forty-seven were in the service of colleges or universities, forty-two in the service of schools, and one was a government official formerly in the service of a university. A considerable number of the college men, however, had also had experience in schools. Each Conference, in accordance with a recommendation of the Committee of Ten, chose its own Chairman and Secretary; and these two officers prepared the report of each Conference. Six of the Chairmen were college men, and three were school men; while of the Secretaries, two were college men and seven school men. The Committee of Ten requested that the reports of the Conferences should be sent to their Chairman by the 1st of April, 1893—three months being thus allowed for the preparation of the reports. Seven Conferences substantially conformed to this request of the Committee; but the reports from the Conferences on Natural History and Geography were delayed until the second week in July. The Committee of Ten, being of course unable to prepare their own report until all the reports of the December Conferences had been received, were prevented from presenting their report, as they had intended, at the Education Congress which met at Chicago July 27th–29th.

All the Conferences sat for three days; their discussions were frank, earnest, and thorough; but in every Conference an extraordinary unity of opinion was arrived at. The nine reports are characterized by an amount of agreement which quite surpasses the most sanguine anticipations. Only two Conferences present minority reports, namely, the Conference on Physics, Astronomy, and Chemistry, and the Conference on Geography; and in the first case, the dissenting opinions touch only two points in the report of the majority, one of which is unimportant. In the great majority of matters brought before each Conference, the decision of the Conference was unanimous. When one considers the different localities, institutions, professional experiences, and personalities represented in each of the Conferences, the unanimity developed is very striking, and should carry great weight.

Before the 1st of October, 1893, the reports of the Conferences had all been printed, after revision in proof by the chairmen of the Conferences respectively, and had been distributed to the members of the Committee of Ten, together with a preliminary draft of a report for the Committee. With the aid of comments and suggestions received from members of the Committee a second draft of this report was made ready in print to serve as the ground-work of the deliberations of the Committee at their final meeting. This meeting was held at Columbia College from the 8th to the 11th of November, 1893, inclusive, every member being present except Professor King, who is spending the current academic year in Europe. The points of view and the fields of work of the different members of the Committee being fortunately various, the discussions at this prolonged meeting were vigorous and comprehensive, and resulted in a thorough revision of the preliminary report. This third revise having been submitted to the members of the Committee, a cordial agreement on both the form and the substance of the present report, with the exceptions stated in the minority report of President Baker, was arrived at after a correspondence which extended over three weeks. The report itself embodies the numerous votes and resolutions adopted by the Committee.

Professor King, having received in Europe the Conference reports, the two preliminary drafts of the Committee's report, and the third revise, desired to have his name signed to the final report.

The Council and the public will doubtless be impressed, at first sight, with the great number and variety of important changes urged by the Conferences; but on a careful reading of the appended reports it will appear that the spirit of the Conferences was distinctly conservative and moderate, although many of their recommendations are of a radical nature. The Conferences which found their tasks the most difficult were the Conferences on Physics, Astronomy, and Chemistry; Natural History; History, Civil Government, and Political Economy; and Geography; and these four Conferences make the longest and most elaborate reports, for the reason that these subjects are to-day more imperfectly dealt with in primary and secondary schools than are the subjects of the first five Conferences. The experts who met to confer together concerning the teaching of the last four subjects in the list of Conferences all felt the need of setting forth in an ample way what ought to be taught, in what order, and by what method. They ardently desired to have their respective subjects made equal to Latin, Greek, and Mathematics in weight and influence in the schools; but they knew that educational tradition was adverse to this desire, and that many teachers and directors of education felt no confidence in these subjects as disciplinary material. Hence the length and elaboration of these reports. In less degree, the Conferences on English and Other Modern Languages felt the same difficulties, these subjects being relatively new as substantial elements in school programmes.

The Committee of Ten requested the Conferences to make their reports and recommendations as specific as possible. This request was generally complied with; but, very naturally, the reports and recommendations are more specific concerning the selection of topics in each subject, the best methods of instruction, and the desirable appliances or apparatus, than concerning the allotment of time to each subject. The allotment of time is a very important matter of administrative detail; but it presents great difficulties, requires a comprehensive survey of the comparative claims of many subjects, and in different parts of the country is necessarily affected by the various local conditions and historical developments. Nevertheless, there will be found in the Conference reports recommendations of a fundamental and far-reaching character concerning the allotment of programme time to each subject.

It might have been expected that every Conference would have demanded for its subject a larger proportion of time than is now commonly assigned to it in primary and secondary schools; but, as a matter of fact, the reports are noteworthy for their moderation in this respect,—especially the reports on the old and well-established subjects. The Latin Conference declares that,—"In view of the just demand for more and better work in several other subjects of the preparatory course, it seemed clear to the Conference that no increase in the quantity of the preparation in Latin should be asked for." Among the votes passed by the Greek Conference will be noticed the following:—"That in making the following recommendations, this Conference desires that the average age at which pupils now enter college should be lowered rather than raised; and the Conference urges that no addition be made in the advanced requirements in Greek for admission to college." The Mathematical Conference recommends that the course in arithmetic in elementary schools should be abridged, and recommends only a moderate assignment of time to algebra and geometry. The Conference on Geography says of the present assignment of time to geography in primary and secondary schools that "it is the judgment of the Conference that too much time is given to the subject in proportion to the results secured. It is not their judgment that more time is given to the subject than it merits, but that either more should be accomplished, or less time taken to attain it."

Anyone who reads these nine reports consecutively will be struck with the fact that all these bodies of experts desire to have the elements of their several subjects taught earlier than they now are; and that the Conferences on all the subjects except the languages desire to have given in the elementary schools what may be called perspective views, or broad surveys, of their respective subjects—expecting that in later years of the school course parts of these same subjects will be taken up with more amplitude and detail. The Conferences on Latin, Greek, and the Modern Languages agree in desiring to have the study of foreign languages begin at a much earlier age than now,— the Latin Conference suggesting by a reference to European usage that Latin be begun from three to five years earlier than it commonly is now. The Conference on Mathematics wish to have given in elementary schools not only a general survey of arithmetic, but also the elements of algebra, and concrete geometry in connection with drawing. The Conference on Physics, Chemistry, and Astronomy urge that nature studies should constitute an important part of the elementary school course from the very beginning. The Conference on Natural History wish the elements of botany and zoölogy to be taught in the primary schools. The Conference on History wish the systematic study of history to begin as early as the tenth year of age, and the first two years of study to be devoted to mythology and to biography for the illustration of general history as well as of American history. Finally, the Conference on Geography recommend that the earlier course tread broadly of the earth, its environment and inhabitants, extending freely into fields which in later years of study are recognized as belonging to separate sciences.

In thus claiming entrance for their subjects into the earlier years of school attendance, the Conferences on the newer subjects are only seeking an advantage which the oldest subjects have long possessed. The elements of language, number, and geography have long been imparted to young children. As things now are, the high school teacher finds in the pupils fresh from the grammar schools no foundation of elementary mathematical conceptions outside of arithmetic; no acquaintance with algebraic language; and no accurate knowledge of geometrical forms. As to botany, zoölogy, chemistry, and physics, the minds of pupils entering the high school are ordinarily blank on these subjects. When college professors endeavor to teach chemistry, physics, botany, zoölogy, meteorology, or geology to persons of eighteen or twenty years of age, they discover that in most instances new habits of observing, reflecting, and recording have to be painfully acquired by the students,—habits which they should have acquired in early childhood. The college teacher of history finds in like manner that his subject has never taken any serious hold on the minds of pupils fresh from the secondary schools. He finds that they have devoted astonishingly little time to the subject; and that they have acquired no habit of historical investigation, or of the comparative examination of different historical narratives concerning the same periods or events. It is inevitable, therefore, that specialists in any one of the subjects which are pursued in the high schools or colleges should earnestly desire that the minds of young children be stored with some of the elementary facts and principles of their subject; and that all the mental habits, which the adult student will surely need, begin to be formed in the child's mind before the age of fourteen. It follows, as a matter of course, that all the Conferences except the Conference on Greek, make strong suggestions concerning the programmes of primary and grammar schools,—generally with some reference to the subsequent programmes of secondary schools. They desire important changes in the elementary grades; and the changes recommended are all in the direction of increasing simultaneously the interest and the substantial training quality of primary and grammar school studies.

If anyone feels dismayed at the number and variety of the subjects to be opened to children of tender age, let him observe that while these nine Conferences desire each their own subject to be brought into the courses of elementary schools, they all agree that these different subjects should be correlated and associated one with another by the programme and by the actual teaching. If the nine Conferences had sat all together as a single body, instead of sitting as detached and even isolated bodies, they could not have more forcibly expressed their conviction that every subject recommended for introduction into elementary and secondary schools should help every other; and that the teacher of each single subject should feel responsible for the advancement of the pupils in all subjects, and should distinctly contribute to this advancement.

On one very important question of general policy which affects profoundly the preparation of all school programmes, the Committee of Ten and all the Conferences are absolutely unanimous. Among the questions suggested for discussion in each Conference were the following:—

> 7. Should the subject be treated differently for pupils who are going to college, for those who are going to a scientific school, and for those who, presumably, are going to neither?
>
> 8. At what age should this differentiation begin, if any be recommended?

The 7th question is answereed unanimously in the negative by the Conferences, and the 8th therefore needs no answer. The Committee of Ten unanimously agree with the Conferences. Ninety-eight teachers, intimately concerned either with the actual work of American secondary schools, or with the results of that work as they appear in students who come to college, unanimously declare that every subject which is taught at all in a secondary school should be taught in the same way and to the same extent to every pupil so long as he pursues it, no matter what the probable destination of the pupil may be, or at what point his education is to cease. Thus, for all pupils who study Latin, or history, or algebra, for example, the allotment of time and the method of instruction in a given school should be the same year by year. Not that all the pupils should pursue every subject for the same number of years; but so long as they do pursue it, they should all be treated alike. It has been a very general custom in American high schools and academies to make up separate courses of study for pupils of supposed different destinations, the proportions of the several studies in the different courses being various. The principle laid down by the Conferences will, if logically carried out, make a great simplification in secondary school programmes. It will lead to each subject's being treated by the school in the same way by the year for all pupils, and this, whether the individual pupil be required to choose between courses which run through several years, or be allowed some choice among subjects year by year.

Persons who read all the appended reports will observe the frequent occurrence of the statement that, in order to introduce the changes recommended, teachers more highly trained will be needed in both the elementary and the secondary schools. There are frequent expressions to the effect that a higher grade of scholarship is needed in teachers of the lower classes, or that the general adoption of some method urged by a Conference must depend upon the better preparation of teachers in the high schools, model schools, normal schools, or colleges in which they are trained. The experienced principal or superintendent in reading the reports will be apt to say to himself,—"This recommendation is sound, but cannot be carried out without teachers who have received a training superior to that of the teachers now at my command." It must be remembered, in connection with these admissions, or expressions of anxiety, that the Conferences were urged by the Committee of Ten to advise the Committee concerning the best possible—almost the ideal—treatment of each subject taught in a secondary school course, without, however, losing sight of the actual condition of American schools, or pushing their recommendations beyond what might reasonably be considered attainable in a moderate number of years. The Committee believe that the Conferences have carried out wisely the desire of the Committee, in that they have recommended improvements, which, though great and seldom to be made at once and simultaneously, are by no means unattainable. The existing agencies for giving instruction to teachers already in service are numerous; and the normal schools and the colleges are capable of making prompt and successful efforts to supply the better trained and equipped teachers for whom the reports of the Conferences call.

Many recommendations will be found to be made by more than one Conference. Thus, all the Conferences on foreign languages seem to agree that the introduction of two foreign languages in the same year is inexpedient; and all of them insist on practice in reading the foreign language aloud, on the use of good English in translating, and on practice in translating the foreign language at sight, and in writing it. Again, all the Conferences on scientific subjects dwell on laboratory work by the pupils as the best means of instruction, and on the great utility of the genuine laboratory note-book; and they all protest that teachers of science need at least as thorough a special training as teachers of languages or mathematics receive. In reading the reports, many instances will be noticed in which different Conferences have reached similar conclusions without any consultation, or have followed a common line of thought.

Your Committee now proceed to give summaries of the most important recommendations made by the Conferences as regards topics and methods, reserving the subject of time-allotment. But in so doing, they desire to say that the reading of these summaries should not absolve anyone interested in the general subject from reading with care the entire report of every Conference. The several reports are so full of suggestions and recommendations concisely and cogently stated that it is impossible to present adequate abstracts of them.

1. LATIN.

An important recommendation of the Latin Conference is the recommendation that the study of Latin be introduced into American schools earlier than it now is. They recommend that translation at sight form a constant and increasing part of the examinations for admission to college and of the work of preparation. They next urge that practice in writing Latin should not be dissociated from practice in reading and translating; but, on the contrary, that the two should be carried on with equal steps. The Conference desire the schools to adopt a greater variety of Latin authors for beginners, and they give good reasons against the exclusive use of Caesar's Gallic War. They object to the common practice of putting the teaching of beginners into the hands of the youngest teachers, who have the slenderest equipment of knowledge and experience. They dwell on the importance of attending to pronunciation and reading aloud, to forms, vocabulary, syntax, and order, and to the means of learning to understand the Latin before translating it; and they describe and urge the importance of a higher ideal in translation than now prevails in secondary schools. The formal recommendations of the Conference, fourteen in number, will be found concisely stated in numbered paragraphs at the close of their report.

2. GREEK.

The Conference on Greek agree with the Conference on Latin in recommending the cultivation of reading at sight in schools, and in recommending that practice in translation into the foreign language should be continued throughout the school course. They urge that three years be the minimum time for the study of Greek in schools; provided that Latin be studied four years. They would not have a pupil begin the study of Greek without a knowledge of the elements of Latin. They recommend the substitution of portions of the Hellenica for two books of the Anabasis in the requirements for admission to college, and the use of some narrative portions of Thucydides in schools. They urge that Homer should continue to be studied in all schools which provide instruction in Greek through three years, and they suggest that the Odyssey is to be preferred to the Iliad. They regret "that so few colleges through their admission examinations encourage reading at sight in schools." Like the Latin Conference, the Greek Conference urge that the reading of the text be constantly practiced by both teacher and pupil, "and that teachers require from their pupils no less intelligent reading of the text than accurate translation of the same." The Greek Conference also adopted a vote "to concur with the Latin Conference as to the age at which the study of Latin should be begun." The specific recommendations of the Conference will be found in brief form in the paragraphs at the head of the eleven numbered sections into which their report is divided.

3. ENGLISH.

The Conference on English found it necessary to deal with the study of English in schools below the high school grade as well as in the high school. Their opening recommendations deal with the very first years of school, and one of the most interesting and admirable parts of their report relates to English in the primary and the grammar schools.

The Conference are of the opinion that English should be pursued in the high school during the entire course of four years; but in making this recommendation the Conference have in mind both study of literature and training in the expression of thought. To the study of rhetoric they assign one hour a week in the third year of the high school course. To the subject of historical and systematic grammar they assign one hour a week in the fourth year of the high school course. The intelligent reader of the report of this Conference will find described in it the means by which the study of English in secondary schools is to be made the equal of any other study in disciplinary or developing power. The Conference claim for English as much time as the Latin Conference claim for Latin in secondary schools; and it is clear that they intend that the study shall be in all respects as serious and informing as the study of Latin. One of the most interesting opinions expressed by the Conference is "that the best results in the teaching of English in high schools cannot be secured without the aid given by the study of some other language; and that Latin and German, by reason of their fuller inflectional system, are especially suited to this end." In the case of high schools, as well as in schools of lower grade, the Conference declare that every teacher, whatever his department, should feel responsible for the use of good English on the part of his pupils. In several passages of this report the idea recurs that training in English must go hand in hand with the study of other subjects. Thus the Conference hope for the study of the history and geography of the English-speaking people, so far as these illustrate the development of the English language. They mention that "the extent to which the study of the sources of English words can be carried in any school or class will depend on the acquaintance the pupils possess with Latin, French, and German." They say that the study of words should be so pursued as to illustrate the political, social, intellectual, and religious development of the English race; and they urge that the admission of a student to college should be made to depend largely on his ability to write English, as shown in his examination books on other subjects. It is a fundamental idea in this report that the study of every other subject should contribute to the pupil's training in English; and that the pupil's capacity to write English should be made available, and be developed, in every other department. The very specific recommendations of the Conference as to English requirements for admission to colleges and scientific schools are especially wise and valuable.

4. OTHER MODERN LANGUAGES.

The most novel and striking recommendation made by the Conference on Modern Languages is that an elective course in German or French be provided in the grammar school, the instruction to be open to children at about ten years of age. The Conference made this recommendation "in the firm belief that the educational effects of modern language study will be of immense benefit to all who are able to pursue it under proper guidance." They admit that the study of Latin presents the same advantages; but living languages seem to them better adapted to grammar school work. The recommendations of this Conference with regard to the number of lessons a week are specific. They even construct a table showing the time which should be devoted to modern languages in each of the last four years of the elementary schools and in each year of the high school. They plead that "all pupils of the same intelligence and the same degree of maturity be instructed alike, no matter whether they are subsequently to enter a college or scientific school, or intend to pursue their studies no farther." The Conference also state with great precision what in their judgment may be expected of pupils in German and French at the various stages of their progress. An important passage of the report treats of the best way to facilitate the progress of beginners;—pupils should be lifted over hard places; frequent reviews are not to be recommended; new texts stimulate interest and enlarge the vocabulary. Their recommendations concerning translation into English, reading aloud, habituating the ear to the sounds of the foreign language, and translating into the foreign language, closely resemble the recommendations of the Conferences on Latin, Greek, and English regarding the best methods of instruction in those languages. In regard to college requirements, the Conference agree with several other Conferences in stating "that college requirements for admission should coincide with the high school requirements for graduation." Finally, they declare that "the worst obstacle to modern language study is the lack of properly equipped instructors; and that it is the duty of universities, states, and cities to provide opportunities for the special preparation of modern language teachers."

5. MATHEMATICS.

The form of the report of the Conference on Mathematics differs somewhat from that of the other reports. This report is subdivided under five headings:—1st, General Conclusions. 2nd, The Teaching of Arithmetic. 3rd, The Teaching of Concrete Geometry. 4th, The Teaching of Algebra. 5th, The Teaching of Formal or Demonstrative Geometry.

The first general conclusion of the Conference was arrived at unanimously. The Conference consisted of one government official and university professor, five professors of mathematics in as many colleges, one principal of a high school, two teachers of mathematics in endowed schools, and one proprietor of a private school for boys. The professional experience of these gentlemen and their several fields of work were various, and they came from widely separated parts of the country; yet they were unanimously of opinon "that a radical change in the teaching of arithmetic was necessary." They recommend "that the course in arithmetic be at once abridged and enriched; abridged by omitting entirely those subjects which perplex and exhaust the pupil without affording any really valuable mental discipline, and enriched by a greater number of exercises in simple calculation, and in the solution of concrete problems." They specify in detail the subjects which they think should be curtailed, or entirely omitted; and they give in their special report on the teaching of arithmetic a full statement of the reasons on which their conclusion is based. They map out a course in arithmetic which, in their judgment, should begin about the age of six years, and be completed at about the thirteenth year of age.

The Conference next recommend that a course of instruction in concrete geometry with numerous exercises be introduced into the grammar schools; and that this instruction should, during the earlier years, be given in connection with drawing. They recommend that the study of systematic algebra should be begun at the age of fourteen; but that, in connection with the study of arithmetic, the pupils should earlier be made familiar with algebraic expressions and symbols, including the method of solving simple equations. "The Conference believe that the study of demonstrative geometry should begin at the end of the first year's study of algebra, and be carried on by the side of algebra for the next two years, occupying about two hours and a half a week." They are also of opinion "that if the introductory course in concrete geometry has been well taught, both plane and solid geometry can be mastered at this time." Most of the improvements in teaching arithmetic which the Conference suggest "can be summed up under the two heads of giving the teaching a more concrete form, and paying more attention to facility and correctness in work. The concrete system should not be confined to principles, but be extended to practical applications in measuring and in physics."

In regard to the teaching of concrete geometry, the Conference urge that while the student's geometrical education should begin in the kindergarten, or at the latest in the primary school, systematic instruction in concrete or experimental geometry should begin at about the age of ten for the average student, and should occupy about one school hour a week for at least three years. From the outset of this course, the pupil should be required to express himself verbally as well as by drawing and modelling. He should learn to estimate by the eye, and to measure with some degree of accuracy, lengths, angular magnitudes, and areas; to make accurate plans from his own measurements and estimates; and to make models of simple geometrical solids. The whole work in concrete geometry will connect itself on the one side with the work in arithmetic, and on the other with elementary instruction in physics. With the study of arithmetic is therefore to be intimately associated the study of algebraic signs and forms, of concrete geometry, and of elementary physics. Here is a striking instance of the interlacing of subjects which seems so desirable to every one of the nine Conferences.

Under the head of teaching algebra, the Conference set forth in detail the method of familiarizing the pupil with the use of algebraic language during the study of arithmetic. This part of the report also deals clearly with the question of the time required for the thorough mastery of algebra through quadratic equations. The report on the teaching of demonstrative geometry is a clear and concise statement of the best method of teaching this subject. It insists on the importance of elegance and finish in geometrical demonstration, for the reason that the discipline for which geometrical demonstration is to be chiefly prized is a discipline in complete, exact, and logical statement. If slovenliness of expression, or awkwardness of form, is tolerated, this admirable discipline is lost. The Conference therefore recommended an abundance of oral exercises in geometry—for which there is no proper substitute—and the rejection of all demonstrations which are not exact and formally perfect. Indeed throughout all the teaching of mathematics the Conference deem it important that great stress be laid by the teacher on accuracy of statement and elegance of form as well as on clear and rigorous reasoning. Another very important recommendation in this part of the report is to be found in the following passage,—"As soon as the student has acquired the art of rigorous demonstration, his work should cease to be merely receptive. He should begin to devise constructions and demonstrations for himself. Geometry cannot be mastered by reading the demonstrations of a text-book; and while there is no branch of elementary mathematics in which purely receptive work, if continued too long, may lose its interest more completely, there is also none in which independent work can be made more attractive and stimulating." These observations are entirely in accordance with the recent practice of some colleges in setting admission examination papers in geometry which demand of the candidates some capacity to solve new problems, or rather to make new application of familiar principles.

6. PHYSICS, CHEMISTRY, AND ASTRONOMY.

The Conference on this subject were urgent that the study of simple natural phenomena be introduced into elementary schools; and it was the sense of the Conference that at least one period a day from the first year of the primary school should be given to such study. Apparently the Conference entertained the opinion that the present teachers in elementary schools are ill prepared to teach children how to observe simple natural phenomena; for their second recommendation was that special science teachers or superintendents be appointed to instruct the teachers of elementary schools in the methods of teaching natural phenomena. The Conference was clearly of opinion that from the beginning this study should be pursued by the pupil chiefly, though not exclusively, by means of experiments and by practice in the use of simple instruments for making physical measurements. The report dwells repeatedly on the importance of the study of things and phenomena by direct contact. It emphasizes the necessity of a large proportion of laboratory work in the study of physics and chemistry, and advocates the keeping of laboratory note-books by the pupils, and the use of such note-books as part of the test for admission to college. At the same time the report points out that laboratory work must be conjoined with the study of a text-book and with attendance at lectures or demonstrations; and that intelligent direction by a good teacher is as necessary in a laboratory as it is in the ordinary recitation or lecture room. The great utility of the laboratory note-book is emphatically stated. To the objection that the kind of instruction described requires much time and effort on the part of the teacher, the Conference reply that to give good instruction in the sciences requires of the teacher more work than to give good instruction in mathematics or the languages; and that the sooner this fact is recognized by those who have the management of schools the better for all concerned. The science teacher must regularly spend much time in collecting materials, preparing experiments, and keeping collections in order; and this indispensable labor should be allowed for in programmes and salaries. As regards the means of testing the progress of the pupils in physics and chemistry, the Conference were unanimously of opinion that a laboratory examination should always be combined with an oral or written examination, neither test taken singly being sufficient. There was a difference of opinion in the Conference on the question whether physics should precede chemistry, or chemistry physics. The logical order would place physics first; but all the members of the Conference but one advised that chemistry be put first for practical reasons which are stated in the majority report. A sub-committee of the Conference has prepared lists of experiments in physics and chemistry for the use of secondary schools,—not, of course, as a prescription, but only as a suggestion, and a somewhat precise indication of the topics which the Conference had in mind, and of the limits of the instruction.

7. NATURAL HISTORY.

The Conference on Natural History unanimously agreed that the study of botany and zoölogy ought to be introduced into the primary schools at the very beginning of the school course, and be pursued steadily, with not less than two periods a week, throughout the whole course below the high school. In the next place they agreed that in these early lessons in natural science no text-book should be used; but that the study should constantly be associated with the study of literature, language, and drawing. It was their opinion that the study of physiology should be postponed to the later years of the high school course; but that in the high school, some branch of natural history proper should be pursued every day throughout at least one year. Like the report on Physics, Chemistry, and Astronomy, the report on Natural History emphasizes the absolute necessity of laboratory work by the pupils on plants and animals; and would have careful drawing insisted on from the beginning of the instruction. As the laboratory note-book is recommended by the Conference on Physics, so the Conference on Natural History recommends that the pupils should be made to express themselves clearly and exactly in words, or by drawings, in describing the objects which they observe; and they believe that this practice will be found a valuable aid in training the pupils in the art of expression. They agree with the Conference on Physics, Chemistry, and Astronomy that science examinations should include both a written and a laboratory test, and that the laboratory note-books of the pupils should be produced at the examination. The recommendations of this Conference are therefore very similar to those of the sixth Conference, so far as methods go; but there are appended to the general report of the Conference on Natural History sub-

reports which describe the proper topics, the best order of topics, and the right methods of instruction in botany for schools below the high school, and for the high school itself, and in zoölogy for the secondary schools. Inasmuch as both the subject matter and the methods of instruction in natural history are much less familiar to ordinary school teachers than the matter and the methods in the languages and mathematics, the Conference believed that descriptive details were necessary in order to give a clear view of the intentions of the Conference. In another sub-report the Conference give their reasons for recommending the postponement to the latest possible time of the study of physiology and hygiene. Like the sixth Conference, the Conference on Natural History protest that no person should be regarded as qualified to teach natural science who has not had special training for this work,—a preparation at least as thorough as that of their fellow teachers of mathematics and the languages.

8. HISTORY, CIVIL GOVERNMENT, AND POLITICAL ECONOMY.

The Conference on History, Civil Government, and Political Economy had a task different in some respects from those of other Conferences. It is now-a-days admitted that language, natural science, and mathematics should each make a substantial part of education; but the function of history in education is still very imperfectly apprehended. Accordingly, the eighth Conference were at pains to declare their conception of the object of studying history and civil government in schools, and their belief in the efficiency of these studies in training the judgment, and in preparing children for intellectual enjoyments in after years, and for the exercise at maturity of a salutary influence upon national affairs. They believed that the time devoted in schools to history and the allied subjects should be materially increased; and they have therefore presented arguments in favor of that increase. At the same time, they state strongly their conviction that they have recommended "nothing that was not already being done in some good schools, and that might not reasonably be attained wherever there is an efficient system of graded schools." This Conference state quite as strongly as any other their desire to associate the study of their particular subject with that of other subjects which enter into every school programme. They declare that the teaching of history should be intimately connected with the teaching of English; that pupils should be encouraged to avail themselves of their knowledge of ancient and modern languages; and that their study of history should be associated with the study of topography and political geography, and should be supplemented by the study of historical and commercial geography, and the drawing of historical maps. They desire that historical works should be used for reading in schools, and that subjects of English composition should be drawn from the lessons in history. They would have historical poems committed to memory, and the reading of biographies and historical novels encouraged. While they are of opinion that political economy should not be taught in secondary schools, they urge that, in connection with United States history, civil government, and commercial geography, instruction should be given in the most important economic topics. The Conference would therefore have the instruction in history made contributory to the work in three other school departments, namely, English, geography, and drawing. The subject of civil government they would associate with both history and geography. They would introduce it into the grammar school by means of oral lessons, and into the high school by means of a text-book with collateral reading and oral lessons. In the high school they believe that the study of civil government may be made comparative,—that is, that the American method may be compared with foreign systems.

Although the Conference was made up of very diverse elements, every member of the Conference was heartily in favor of every vote adopted. This remarkable unanimity was not obtained by the silence of dissentients, or the withdrawal of opposition on disputed points. It was the natural result of the strong conviction of all the members, that history, when taught by the methods advocated in their report, deserves a position in school programmes which would give it equal dignity and importance with any of the most favored subjects, and that the advantages for all children of the rational study of history ought to be diffused as widely as possible. On one point they made a clearer declaration than any other Conference; although several other Conferences indicate similar opinions. They declared that their interest was chiefly "in the school children who have no expectation of going to college, the larger number of whom will not even enter a high school," and that their "recommendations are in no way directed to building up the colleges, or increasing the number of college students." Like every other Conference, they felt anxious about the qualifications of the teachers who are to be entrusted with the teaching of history, and they urged that only teachers who have had adequate special training should be employed to teach history and civil government. In their specific recommendations they strongly urge that the historical course be made continuous from year to year, and extend through eight years, and in this respect be placed upon the same footing with other substantial subjects.

The answers of this Conference to the questions contained in the memorandum sent to the Conferences by the Committee of Ten were specific and clear. They will be found in an appendix to the report of the Conference.

In regard to the time to be devoted to history in school programmes, this Conference ask for not less than three periods a week throughout a course of eight years; and they suggest that some of this time can be found by contracting the course in arithmetic, and using for history a part of the time now given to political geography and to language study. Of these eight years they suggest that four should be in the high school and four in the grammar school. They "especially recommend such a choice of subjects as will give pupils in the grammar schools an opportunity of studying the history of other countries, and to the high schools one year's study on the intensive method."

A large portion of the report is necessarily taken up with the description of what the Conference consider the most suitable historical topics and the best methods of teaching history. This portion of the report does not admit of any useful presentation in outline; it must be read in full.

With regard to examinations in history for admission to college, the Conference protest "against the present lax and inefficient system," and seem to sum up their own desires on this subject in the statement that "the requirements for college ought to be so framed that the methods of teaching best adapted to meet them will also be best for all pupils."

Like the Conferences on scientific subjects the Conference on History insist on note-books, abstracts, special reports, and other written work, as desirable means of teaching. If the recommendations of the nine Conferences should be carried out in grammar and high schools, there would certainly be at least one written exercise a day for every pupil,—a result which persons interested in training children to write English deem it important to accomplish.

The observations of the Conference on geographical training in connection with history are interesting and suggestive, as are also the recurring remarks on the need of proper apparatus for teaching history, such as maps, reference-libraries, historical pictures, and photographs. It is not the natural sciences alone which need school apparatus.

9. GEOGRAPHY.

Considering that geography has been a subject of recognized value in elementary schools for many generations, and that a considerable portion of the whole school time of children has long been devoted to a study called by this name, it is somewhat startling to find that the report of the Conference on Geography deals with more novelties than any other report; exhibits more dissatisfaction with prevailing methods; and makes, on the whole, the most revolutionary suggestions. This Conference had but nine members present at its sessions; and before the final revision of its report had been accomplished, one of the most valued of its members died. Seven members sign the majority report, and the minority report is presented by one member. The dissenting member, however, while protesting against the views of the majority on many points, concurs with the majority in some of the most important conclusions arrived at by the Conference.

It is obvious on even a cursory reading of the majority and minority reports that geography means for all the members of this Conference something entirely different from the term geography as generally used in school programmes. Their definition of the word makes it embrace not only a description of the surface of the earth, but also the elements of botany, zoology, astronomy, and meteorology, as well as many considerations pertaining to commerce, government, and ethnology. "The physical environment of man" expresses as well as any single phrase can the Conference's conception of the principal subject which they wish to have taught. No one can read the reports without perceiving that the advanced instruction in geography which the Conference conceive to be desirable and feasible in high schools cannot be given until the pupils have mastered many of the elementary facts of botany, zoölogy, geometry, and physics. It is noteworthy also that this ninth Conference, like the seventh, dealt avowedly and unreservedly with the whole range of instruction in primary and secondary schools. They did not pretend to treat chiefly instruction in secondary schools, and incidentally instruction in the lower schools; but, on the contrary, grasped at once the whole problem, and described the topics, methods, and apparatus appropriate to the entire course of twelve years. They recognized that complete descriptions would be necessary in all three branches of the subject,—topics, methods, and equipment; and they have given these descriptions with an amplitude and force which leave little to be desired. More distinctly than any other Conference, they recognized that they were presenting an ideal course which could not be carried into effect everywhere or immediately. Indeed at several points they frankly state that the means of carrying out their recommendations are not at present readily accessible; and they exhibit the same anxiety which is felt by several other Conferences about training teachers for the kind of work which the Conference believe to be desirable. After the full and interesting descriptions of the relations and divisions of geographical science, as the Conference define it, the most important sections of their report relate to the methods and means of presenting the subject in schools, and to the right order in developing it. The methods which they advocate require not only better equipped teachers, but better means of illustrating geographical facts in the schoolroom, such as charts, maps, globes, photographs, models, lantern slides, and lanterns. Like all the other Conferences on scientific subjects, the ninth Conference dwell on the importance of forming from the start good habits of observing correctly and stating accurately the facts observed. They also wish that the instruction in geography may be connected with the instruction in drawing, history, and English. They believe that meteorology may be taught as an observational study in the earliest years of the grammar school, the scholars being even then made familiar with the use of the thermometer, the wind-vane, and the rain-gauge; and that it may be carried much farther in the high school years, after physics has been studied, so that the pupils may then attain a general understanding of topographical maps, of pressure and wind charts, of isothermal charts, and of such complicated subjects as weather prediction, rainfall and the distribution of rain, storms, and the seasonal variations of the atmosphere. Their conception of physiography is a very comprehensive one. In short, they recommend a study of physical geography which would embrace in its scope the elements of half-a-dozen natural sciences, and would bind together in one sheaf the various gleanings which the pupils would have gathered from widely separated fields. There can be no doubt that the study would be interesting, informing, and developing, or that it would be difficult and in every sense substantial.

It already appears that the nine Conferences have attended carefully to three out of the five subjects which it was the in-

Table I.

Subject	Elementary Grades—Primary and Grammar School								Secondary School—High School or Academy			
	1st Year Age 6-7	2d Year 7-8	3d Year 8-9	4th Year 9-10	5th Year 10-11	6th Year 11-12	7th Year 12-13	8th Year 13-14	9th Year 14-15	10th Year 15-16	11th Year 16-17	12th Year 17-18
1. Latin						Reasons given for beginning Latin earlier than is now the custom.			5 p. a wk.	5 p. a wk.	5 p. a wk.	5 p. a wk.
2. Greek							Latin to be begun a year before Greek.			5 p. a wk.	4 p. a wk.	4 p. a wk.
3. English	Pupils to reproduce orally stories told them, to invent stories and describe objects.		Supplementary reading begun—and continued through all the grades. Composition begun—writing narratives and descriptions—oral and written exercises on forms and the sentence.				From this grade no reader to be used.	Grammar, 3 p. a wk.	Literature, 3 p. a wk. Composition, 2 p. a wk.	Literature, 3 p. a wk. Composition, 2 p. a wk.	Literature, 3 p. a wk. Composition, 1 p. a wk. Rhetoric, 1 p. a wk.	Literature, 3 p. a wk. Composition, 1 p. a wk. Grammar, 1 p. a wk.
4. Modern Languages					Elective German or French, 5 p. a wk.	Elective German or French, 4 p. a wk.	Elective German or French, 3 p. a wk. at least.	Elective German or French, 3 p. a wk. at least.	The language begun below, 4 p. a wk.	The same language, 4 p. a wk. Second language, 4 p. a wk.	The same language, 4 p. a wk. Second language, 4 p. a wk.	The same language, 4 p. a wk. Second language, 4 p. a wk.

	First eight years						
5. MATHEMATICS.	Arithmetic during first eight years, with algebraic expressions and symbols and simple equations—no specific number of hours being recommended.	Concrete Geometry, 1 p. a wk. / Concrete Geometry, 1 p. a wk. / Concrete Geometry, 1 p. a wk.	Algebra, 5 p. a wk.	Algebra or Book-keeping and Commercial Arithmetic, 2½ p. a wk. Geometry, 2½ p. a wk.	Algebra or Book-keeping and Commercial Arithmetic, 2½ p. a wk. Geometry, 2½ p. a wk.	Trigonometry and higher Algebra for candidates for scientific schools.
6. PHYSICS, CHEMISTRY, AND ASTRONOMY	Study of natural phenomena 5 p. a wk. through first eight years by experiments, including physical measurements and the recommendations of Conferences 7 and 9.			Elective Astronomy, 5 p. a wk. .. 12 wks.	Chemistry, 5 p. a wk.	Physics, 5 p. a wk.
7. NAT. HISTORY	Through first eight years 2 p. a wk. of not less than 30 minutes each, devoted to plants and animals; the instruction to be correlated with language, drawing, literature, and geography.		One yr. (which yr. not specified) for botany or zoölogy. Half-yr. (late in course) anatomy, physiology, and hygiene, 5 p. a wk.			
8. HISTORY	Biography & Mythology, 3 p. a wk.	American History and elements of civil government, 3 p. a wk.	Greek and Roman History, 3 p. a wk.	French History, 3 p. a wk.	English History, 3 p. a wk.	American History, 3 p. a wk.	A special period intensively, and civil government, 3 p. a wk.
9. GEOGRAPHY	Time alloted in first eight years to equal that given to number work. The subject—the earth, its environment and inhabitants, including the elements of astronomy, meteorology, zoölogy, botany, history, commerce, races, religions, and governments.	Physical Geography.	(Physiography, geology, or meteorology at some part of the high school course. Possibly more than one of these where election is allowed.)		Elective Meteorology, ½ this year or next.	Elective geology or physiography, ½ yr.

Abbreviations: p. = a recitation period of 40–45 minutes; wk. = week; yr. = yr.

tention of the National Council of Education that they should examine. They have discussed fully the proper limits of the several subjects of instruction in secondary schools, the best methods of instruction, and the best methods of testing pupils' attainments. The Conferences were equally faithful in discussing the other two subjects committed to them by the Council, namely, the most desirable allotment of time for each subject, and the requirements for admission to college.

The next subject which the Committee of Ten, following the guidance of the Conferences, desire to present to the Council is, therefore, the allotment of school time among the various subjects of study. It is the obvious duty of the Committee, in the first place, to group together in tabular form the numerous suggestions on this subject made by the Conferences. Having exhibited the programme-time suggestions of the Conferences, it will remain for the Committee to construct a flexible and comprehensive schedule of studies, based on the recommendations of the Conferences.

The preceding table exhibits the demands for programme time made by all the Conferences. It will be seen at once that this table does not yield, without modification, a practical programme. The nine Conferences acted separately, and were studying each its own needs, and not the comparative needs of all the subjects. It was not for them to balance the different interests, but for each to present strongly one interest. It will further be noticed that some of their demands are not specific,—that is, they do not call for any specified number of recitation periods for a definite number of weeks during a stated number of years. The Conferences on Languages and History are the most definite in their recommendations, the Conferences on Mathematics and the Sciences being much less definite. Table 1 is therefore not a programme, but the materials from which serviceable programmes may be constructed.

The Committee of Ten deliberately placed in this one table the recommendations of the Conferences for the elementary grades and the recommendations for secondary schools, in order that the sequence of the recommendations for each subject might be clearly brought out. The recommendations made for the secondary schools presuppose in many cases that the recommendations made for the elementary schools have been fulfilled; or, at least, in many cases the Conferences would have made different recommendations for the secondary schools, if they had been compelled to act on the assumption that things must remain just as they are in the elementary schools.

At this point it is well to call attention to the list of subjects which the Conferences deal with as proper for secondary schools. They are: 1. languages—Latin, Greek, English, German, and French, (and locally Spanish); 2. mathematics—algebra, geometry, and trigonometry; 3. general history, and the intensive study of special epochs; 4. natural history—including descriptive astronomy, meteorology, botany, zoölogy, physiology, geology, and ethnology, most of which subjects may be conveniently grouped under the title of physical geography; and 5. physics and chemistry. The Committee of Ten assent to this list, both for what it includes and for what it excludes, with some practical qualifications to be mentioned below.

Table II exhibits the total amount of instruction (estimated by the number of weekly periods assigned to each subject) to be given in a secondary school during each year of a four years' course, on the supposition that the recommendations of the Conferences are all carried out.

The method of estimating the amount of instruction offered in any subject by the number of recitation periods assigned to it each week for a given number of years or half years is in some respects an inadequate one, for it takes no account of the scope and intensity of the instruction given during the periods; but so far as it goes, it is trustworthy and instructive. It represents with tolerable accuracy the proportional expenditure which a school is making on a given subject, and therefore the proportional importance which the school attaches to that subject. It also represents roughly the proportion of the pupil's entire school time which he can devote to a given subject, provided he is free to take all the instruction offered in that subject. All experience shows that subjects deemed important get a large

247

TABLE II.

1ST SECONDARY SCHOOL YEAR

Latin	5 p.
English Literature, 3 p.	
" Composition, 2 p.	} 5 p.
German or French	4 p.
Algebra	5 p.
History	3 p.
	22 p.

2ND SECONDARY SCHOOL YEAR

Latin	5 p.
Greek	5 p.
English Literature, 3 p.	
" Composition, 2 p.	} 5 p.
German	4 p.
French	4 p.
Algebra,* 2½ p.	
Geometry, 2½ p.	} 5 p.
Astronomy (12 weeks)	5 p.
Botany or Zoölogy	5 p.
History	3 p.
	37½ p.

* Option of book-keeping and commercial arithmetic.

3RD SECONDARY SCHOOL YEAR

Latin	5 p.
Greek	4 p.
English Literature, 3 p.	
" Composition, 1 p.	} 5 p.
Rhetoric, 1 p.	
German	4 p.
French	4 p.
Algebra*	2½ p.
Geometry	2½ p.
Chemistry	5 p.
History	3 p.
	35 p.

* Option of book-keeping and commercial arithmetic.

4TH SECONDARY SCHOOL YEAR

Latin	5 p.
Greek	4 p.
English Literature, 3 p.	
" Composition, 1 p.	} 5 p.
" Grammar, 1 p.	
German	4 p.
French	4 p.
Trigonometry, 2 p. ½ yr.	
Higher Algebra, 2 p. ½ yr.	} 2 p.
Physics	5 p.
Anatomy, Physiology, and	
Hygiene, ½ yr.	5 p.
History	3 p.
Geol. or Physiography,	
3 p. ½ yr.	} 3 p.
Meteorology, 3 p. ½ yr.	
	37½ p.

number of weekly periods, while those deemed unimportant get a small number. Moreover, if the programme time assigned to a given subject be insufficient, the value of that subject as training cannot be got, no matter how good the quality of the instruction.

Every one of these years, except the first, contains much more instruction than any one pupil can follow; but, looking at the bearing of the table on the important question of educational expenditure, it is encouraging to observe that there are already many secondary schools in this country in which quite as many subjects are taught as are mentioned in this table, and in which there are more weekly periods of instruction provided for separate classes than are found in any year of the table. In some urban high schools which provide from five to nine different courses of three to five years each, and in some endowed secondary schools which maintain two or three separate courses called Classical, Latin-scientific, and English, or designated by similar titles, the total number of weekly periods of unrepeated instruction given to distinct classes is even now larger than the largest total of weekly periods found in Table II. The annual expenditure in such schools is sufficient to provide all the instruction called for by Table II. The suggestions of the Conferences presuppose that all the pupils of like intelligence and maturity in any subject study it in the same way and to the same extent, so long as they study it at all,—this being a point on which all the Conferences insist strongly. No provision is made, therefore, for teaching Latin, or algebra, or history to one portion of a class four times a week, and to another portion of the same class only thrice or twice a week. Such provisions are very common in American schools; but the recommendations of the Conferences, if put into effect, would do away with all expenditures of this sort.

It clearly appears from Table II that the recommendations of the Conferences on scientific subjects have been moderate so far as the proposed allotment of time to them is concerned. The Conferences on Physics, Chemistry and Astronomy, Natural History, and Geography held one combined session in Chicago, and passed a resolution that one-fourth of the whole high school course ought to be devoted to natural science, their intention doubtless being that each pupil should devote one quarter of his time to science; yet if all the time asked for in secondary schools by the scientific Conferences be added together, it will appear, first, that the rare pupil who should take all the scientific instruction provided would need for it only one quarter of his time, and secondly, that less than one-sixth of the whole instruction to be given in accordance with the combined recommendations of all the Conferences is devoted to subjects of natural science. The first year of the secondary school course according to Table II. will contain no science at all; and it is only in the last year of the secondary school that the proportion of natural science teaching rises to one-fourth of the whole instruction.

In studying these two tables which result from the recommendations of the Conferences, the Committee of Ten perceived at once, that if the recommendations are to be carried out, so far as offering the instruction proposed is concerned, a selection of studies for the individual pupil must be made in the second, third, and fourth years of the secondary school course. This selection will obviously be made in different ways in different schools. Any school principal may say,—"With the staff at my command I can teach only five subjects out of those proposed by the Conferences in the manner proposed. My school shall therefore be limited to these five." Another school may be able to teach in the thorough manner proposed five subjects, but some or all of these five may be different from those selected by the first school. A larger or richer school may be able to teach all the subjects mentioned, and by the methods and with the apparatus described. In the last case, each pupil, under the supervision of the teachers, and with the advice of parents or friends, may make choice between several different four-years' courses arranged by the school; or, if the school authorities prefer, the pupil may be allowed to make year by year a carefully guided choice among a limited number of subjects; or these two methods may be combined. Selection for the individual is necessary to thoroughness, and to the imparting of power as distinguished from information; for any large subject whatever, to yield its training value, must be pursued through several years and be studied from three to five times a week, and if each subject studied is thus to claim a considerable fraction of the pupil's school time, then clearly the individual pupil can give attention to only a moderate number of subjects.

In Table II the number of weekly periods assigned to a single subject varies from two to five, about half of the assignments being made for five periods a week. There is an obvious convenience in the number five because it ordinarily gives one period a day for five days in the week; but there is also an obvious disadvantage in making too free use of the number five. It practically limits to three or, at most, four, the number of subjects which the individual pupil may pursue simultaneously; and this limit is inexpedient in a four years' programme.

The Committee have therefore prepared the following modification of Table II, using four as the standard number of weekly periods, except in the first year of a new language, and in the few cases in which the Conferences advise a number smaller than four. By this means the total number of periods is somewhat reduced, except in the first year, and the numbers of periods allotted to different subjects are made more consonant, each with the others. The result is only a correlation and adjustment of the recommendations of the Conferences, no judgment or recommendation of the Committee being expressed in it.

The adoption of the number four as the standard number of weekly periods will not make it impossible to carry into effect the fundamental conception of all the Conferences, namely,— that all the subjects which make part of the secondary school course should be taught consecutively enough and extensively enough to make every subject yield that training which it is best fitted to yield,—provided that the proposed correlation and association of subjects are carried out in practice. With regard to the arrangement or sequence of subjects, the Committee follow in this table the recommendations of the Conferences with only slight modifications. They insert in the first year applied geography, using the term in the sense in which it is used by the Conference on Geography; and they make this insertion in order that natural science may be represented in the programme of that year, and that a complete break of continuity, as regards science subjects, between the eighth grade and the second year of the secondary school may be avoided.

They have felt obliged to put physics into the third year, and chemistry into the fourth, in order that the subject of physics may precede meteorology and physiography; and they have slightly increased the number of lessons in astronomy. With regard to the proportions of school time to be devoted to the different subjects, Table III reduces somewhat the proportional time devoted to Latin, English, and mathematics, and increases the proportional time to be devoted to natural science. In a secondary school which teaches all the subjects recommended by the Conferences, and to the extent contemplated in Table III, nearly one-fifth of the whole instruction given will be devoted to natural science.

The Committee regard Table III not, of course, as a feasible programme, but as the possible source of a great variety of good secondary school programmes. It would be difficult to make a bad programme out of the materials contained in this table, unless indeed the fundamental principles advocated by the Conferences should be neglected. With some reference to Table I, excellent six years' and five years' programmes for secondary schools can readily be constructed by spreading the subjects contained in Table III over six or five years instead of four,—of course with some changes in the time-allotment.

The details of the time-allotment for the several studies which enter into the secondary school programme may seem to some persons mechanical, or even trivial—a technical matter to be dealt with by each superintendent of schools, or by each principal of a secondary school, acting on his own individual experience and judgment; but such is not the opinion of the Committee of Ten. The Committee believe that to establish just proportions between the several subjects, or groups of allied subjects, on which the Conferences were held, it is essential that each principal subject shall be taught thoroughly and extensively, and therefore for an adequate number of periods a week on the school programme. If twice as much time is given in a school to Latin as is given to mathematics, the attainments of the pupils in Latin ought to be twice as great as they are in mathematics, provided that equally good work is done in the

Table III.

1st Secondary School Year

Latin	5 p.
English Literature, 2 p. } " Composition, 2 p. }	4 p.
German [or French]	5 p.
Algebra	4 p.
History of Italy, Spain, and France	3 p.
Applied Geography (European political—continental and oceanic flora and fauna)	4 p.
	25 p.

2nd Secondary School Year

Latin	4 p.
Greek	5 p.
English Literature, 2 p. } " Composition, 2 p. }	4 p.
German, continued	4 p.
French, begun	5 p.
Algebra,* 2 p. } Geometry, 2 p. }	4 p.
Botany or Zoölogy	4 p.
English History to 1688	3 p.
	33 p.

* Option of book-keeping and commercial arithmetic.

3rd Secondary School Year

Latin	4 p.
Greek	4 p.
English Literature, 2 p. " Composition, 1 p.	4 p.
Rhetoric, 1 p.	
German	4 p.
French	4 p.
Algebra,* 2 p. } Geometry, 2 p. }	4 p.
Physics	4 p.
History, English and American	3 p.
Astronomy, 3 p. 1st ½ yr. } Meteorology, 3 p. 2nd ½ yr. }	3 p.
	34 p.

* Option of book-keeping and commercial arithmetic.

4th Secondary School Year

Latin	4 p.
Greek	4 p.

English Literature, 2 p. }
    " Composition, 1 p. }
    " Grammar, 1 p. }
	4 p.

German	4 p.
French	4 p.
Trigonometry, } Higher Algebra, }	2 p.
Chemistry	4 p.
History (intensive) and Civil Government	3 p.

Geology or Physiography, }
    4 p. 1st ½ yr. }
Anatomy, Physiology, and }
    Hygiene, 4 p. 2nd ½ yr. }
	4 p.

	33 p.

two subjects; and Latin will have twice the educational value of mathematics. Again, if in a secondary school Latin is steadily pursued for four years with four or five hours a week devoted to it, that subject will be worth more to the pupil than the sum of half a dozen other subjects, each of which has one sixth of the time allotted to Latin. The good effects of continuous study in one subject will be won for the pupil through the Latin, and they will not be won through the six other subjects among which only so much time as is devoted to the single language has been divided. If every subject studied at all is to be studied thoroughly and consecutively, every subject must receive an adequate time-allotment. If every subject is to provide a substantial mental training, it must have a time-allotment sufficient to produce that fruit. Finally, since selection must be exercised by or on behalf of the individual pupil, all the subjects between which choice is allowed should be approximately equivalent to each other in seriousness, dignity, and efficacy. Therefore they should have approximately equal time-allotments. The Conferences have abundantly shown how every subject which they recommend can be made a serious subject of instruction, well fitted to train the pupil's powers of observation, expression, and reasoning. It remains for makers of school programmes to give every subject the chance of developing a good training capacity by giving it an adequate time-allotment.

The schedule of studies contained in Table III permits flexibility and variety in three respects. First, it is not necessary that any school should teach all the subjects which it contains, or any particular set of subjects. Secondly, it is not necessary that the individual pupil should everywhere and always have the same number of periods of instruction per week. In one school the pupils might have but sixteen periods a week, in another twenty; or in some years of the course the pupils might have more periods a week than in other years. Within the schedule many particular arrangements for the convenience of a school, or for the welfare of an individual pupil would be possible. Thirdly, it is not necessary that every secondary school should begin its work at the level which is assumed as the starting point of secondary instruction in Tables I, II, and III. If in any community the high school has no such grammar school foundation beneath it as is imagined in Table I it will simply have to begin its work lower down in the table. The sequence of studies recommended by the Conferences would still serve as a guide; but the demarcation between the elementary schools and the high school would occur in that community at a lower point. From this point of view, Tables I, II, and III may be considered to set a standard towards which secondary schools should tend; and not a standard to which they can at once conform.

The adoption of a programme based on Table III would not necessarily change at all the relation of a school to the colleges or universities to which it habitually sends pupils. Any such programme would lend itself either to the examination method of admission to college, or to the certificate method; and it could be slightly modified in such a way as to meet the present admission requirements of any college in the country. Future changes in admission requirements might fairly be made with a view to the capabilities of programmes based on Table III.

As samples of school programmes constructed within the schedules of Table III, the Committee present the following working programmes, which they recommend for trial wherever the secondary school period is limited to four years. All four combined might, of course, be tabulated as one programme with options by subject.

These four programmes taken together use all the subjects mentioned in Table III, and usually, but not always, to about the amounts there indicated. History and English suffer serious contraction in the Classical programme. All four programmes conform to the general recommendations of the Conferences, that is,—they treat each subject in the same way for all pupils with trifling exceptions; they give time enough to each subject to win from it the kind of mental training it is fitted to supply; they put the different principal subjects on an approximate equality so far as time-allotment is concerned; they omit all short information courses; and they make sufficiently continuous the instruction in each of the main lines, namely, language, science, history and mathematics. With slight modifications, they would prepare the pupils for admission to appropriate courses in any American college or university on the existing requirements; and they would also meet the new college requirements which are suggested below.

In preparing these programmes, the Committee were perfectly aware that it is impossible to make a satisfactory secondary school programme, limited to a period of four years, and founded on the present elementary school subjects and methods. In the opinion of the Committee, several subjects now reserved for high schools,—such as algebra, geometry, natural science, and foreign languages,—should be begun earlier than now, and therefore within the schools classified as elementary; or, as an alternative, the secondary school period should be made to begin two years earlier than at present, leaving six years instead of eight for the elementary school period. Under the present organization, elementary subjects and elementary methods are, in the judgment of the Committee, kept in use too long.

The most striking differences in the four programmes will be found, as is intimated in the headings, in the relative amounts of time given to foreign languages. In the Classical programme the foreign languages get a large share of time; in the English programme a small share. In compensation, English and history are more developed in the English programme than in the Classical.

Many teachers will say, at first sight, that physics comes too early in these programmes and Greek too late. One member of the Committee is firmly of the opinion that Greek comes too late. The explanation of the positions assigned to these subjects is that the Committee of Ten attached great importance to two general principles in programme making:—In the first place they endeavored to postpone till the third year the grave choice between the Classical course and the Latin-Scientific. They believed that this bifurcation should occur as late as possible, since the choice between these two roads often determines for life the youth's career. Moreover, they believed that it is possible to make this important decision for a boy on good grounds, only when he has had opportunity to exhibit his quality and discover his tastes by making excursions into all the principal fields of knowledge. The youth who has never studied any but his native language cannot know his own capacity for linguistic acquisition; and the youth who has never made a chemical or physical experiment cannot know whether or not he has a taste for exact science. The wisest teacher, or the most observant parent, can hardly predict with confidence a boy's gift for a subject which he has never touched. In these considerations the Committee found strong reasons for postponing bifurcation, and making the subjects of the first two years as truly representative as possible. Secondly, inasmuch as many boys and girls who begin the secondary school course do not stay in school more than two years, the Committee thought it important to select the studies of the first two years in such a way that linguistic, historical, mathematical, and scientific subjects should all be properly represented. Natural history being represented by physical geography, the Committee wished physics to represent the inorganic sciences of precision. The first two years of any one of the four programmes presented above will, in the judgment of the Committee, be highly profitable by themselves to children who can go no farther.

Although the Committee thought it expedient to include among the four programmes, one which included neither Latin nor Greek, and one which included only one foreign language (which might be either ancient or modern), they desired to affirm explicitly their unanimous opinion that, under existing conditions in the United States as to the training of teachers and the provision of necessary means of instruction, the two programmes called respectively Modern Languages and English must in practice be distinctly inferior to the other two.

In the construction of the sample programmes the Committee adopted twenty as the maximum number of weekly periods, but with two qualifications, namely, that at least five of the twenty periods should be given to unprepared work, and that laboratory subjects should have double periods whenever that prolongation should be possible.

The omission of music, drawing, and elocution from the

programmes offered by the Committee was not intended to imply that these subjects ought to receive no systematic attention. It was merely thought best to leave it to local school authorities to determine, without suggestions from the Committee, how these subjects should be introduced into the programmes in addition to the subjects reported on by the Conferences.

The Committee were governed in the construction of the first three programmes by the rule laid down by the language Conferences, namely, that two foreign languages should not be begun at the same time. To obey this rule is to accept strict limitations in the construction of a four years' Classical programme. A five years' or six years' programme can be made much more easily under this restriction. The Committee were anxious to give five weekly periods to every foreign language in the year when it was first attacked; but did not find it possible to do so in every case.

The four programmes can be carried out economically in a single school; because, with a few inevitable exceptions, the several subjects occur simultaneously in at least three programmes and with the same number of weekly periods.

Numerous possible transpositions of subjects will occur to every experienced teacher who examines these specimen programmes. Thus, in some localities it would be better to transpose French and German; the selection and order of science subjects might be varied considerably to suit the needs or circumstances of different schools; and the selection and order of historical subjects admit of large variety.

Many subjects now familiar in secondary school courses of study do not appear in Table III or in the specimen programmes given above; but it must not be supposed that the omitted subjects are necessarily to be neglected. If the recommendations of the Conference were carried out, some of the omitted subjects would be better dealt with under any one of the above programmes than they are now under familiar high school and academy programmes in which they figure as separate subjects. Thus, drawing does not appear as a separate subject in the specimen programmes; but the careful reader of the Conference reports will notice that drawing, both mechanical and free-hand, is to be used in the study of history, botany, zoölogy, astronomy, meteorology, physics, geography, and physiography, and that the kind of drawing recommended by the Conferences is the most useful kind,—namely, that which is applied to recording, describing, and discussing observations. This abundant use of drawing might not prevent the need of some special instruction in drawing, but it ought to diminish the number of periods devoted exclusively to drawing. Again, neither ethics nor economics, neither metaphysics nor aesthetics appear in the programmes; but in the large number of periods devoted to English and history there would be some time for incidental instruction in the elements of these subjects. It is through the reading and writing required of pupils, or recommended to them, that the fundamental ideas on these important topics are to be inculcated. Again, the industrial and commercial subjects do not appear in these programmes; but book-keeping and commercial arithmetic are provided for by the option for algebra designated in Table III; and if it were desired to provide more amply for subjects thought to have practical importance in trade or the useful arts, it would be easy to provide options in such subjects for some of the science contained in the third and fourth years of the "English" programme.

The Committee of Ten think much would be gained if, in addition to the usual programme hours, a portion of Saturday morning should be regularly used for laboratory work in the scientific subjects. Laboratory work requires more consecutive time than the ordinary period of recitation affords; so that an hour and a half is about the shortest advantageous period for a laboratory exercise. The Committee venture to suggest further that, in addition to the regular school sessions in the morning, one afternoon in every week should be used for out-of-door instruction in geography, botany, zoölogy, and geology, these afternoon and Saturday morning exercises being counted as regular work for the teachers who conduct them. In all laboratory and field work, the Committee believe that it will be found profitable to employ as assistants to the regular teachers,

—particularly at the beginning of laboratory and field work in each subject,—recent graduates of the secondary schools who have themselves followed the laboratory and field courses; for at the beginning the pupil will need a large amount of individual instruction in the manipulation of specimens, the use of instruments, and the prompt recording of observations. One teacher without assistants cannot supervise effectively the work of thirty or forty pupils, either in the laboratory or in the field. The laboratory work on Saturday mornings could be maintained throughout the school year; the afternoon excursions would of course be difficult, or impossible, for perhaps a third of the school year.

In general, the Committee of Ten have endeavored to emphasize the principles which should govern all secondary school programmes, and to show how the main recommendations of the several Conferences may be carried out in a variety of feasible programmes.

One of the subjects which the Committee of Ten were directed to consider was requirements for admission to college; and particularly they were expected to report on uniform requirements for admission to colleges, as well as on a uniform secondary school programme. Almost all the Conferences have something to say about the best mode of testing the attainments of candidates at college admission examinations; and some of them, notably the Conferences on History and Geography, make very explicit declarations concerning the nature of college examinations. The improvements desired in the mode of testing the attainments of pupils who have pursued in the secondary schools the various subjects which enter into the course will be found clearly described under each subject in the several Conference reports; but there is a general principle concerning the relation of the secondary schools to colleges which the Committee of Ten, inspired and guided by the Conferences, feel it their duty to set forth with all possible distinctness.

The secondary schools of the United States, taken as a whole, do not exist for the purpose of preparing boys and girls for colleges. Only an insignificant percentage of the graduates of these schools go to colleges or scientific schools. Their main function is to prepare for the duties of life that small proportion of all the children in the country—a proportion small in number, but very important to the welfare of the nation—who show themselves able to profit by an education prolonged to the eighteenth year, and whose parents are able to support them while they remain so long at school. There are, to be sure, a few private or endowed secondary schools in the country, which make it their principal object to prepare students for the colleges and universities; but the number of these schools is relatively small. A secondary school programme intended for national use must therefore be made for those children whose education is not to be pursued beyond the secondary school. The preparation of a few pupils for college or scientific school should in the ordinary secondary school be the incidental, and not the principal object. At the same time, it is obviously desirable that the colleges and scientific schools should be accessible to all boys or girls who have completed creditably the secondary school course. Their parents often do not decide for them, four years before the college age, that they shall go to college, and they themselves may not, perhaps, feel the desire to continue their education until near the end of their school course. In order that any successful graduate of a good secondary school should be free to present himself at the gates of the college or scientific school of his choice, it is necessary that the colleges and scientific schools of the country should accept for admission to appropriate courses of their instruction the attainments of any youth who has passed creditably through a good secondary school course, no matter to what group of subjects he may have mainly devoted himself in the secondary school. As secondary school courses are now too often arranged, this is not a reasonable request to prefer to the colleges and scientific schools; because the pupil may now to through a secondary school course of a very feeble and scrappy nature—studying a little of many subjects and not much of any one, getting, perhaps, a little information in a variety of fields, but nothing which can be called a thorough training. Now the recommendations of the nine Conferences, if well carried out, might fairly be held to make all the main subjects taught in the secondary schools of equal rank for the purposes of admission to college or scientific school. They would all be taught consecutively and thoroughly, and would all be carried on in the same spirit; they would all be used for training the powers of observation, memory, expression, and reasoning; and they would all be good to that end, although differing among themselves in quality and substance. In preparing the programmes of Table IV, the Committee had in mind that the requirements for admission to colleges might, for schools which adopted a programme derived from that table, be simplified to a considerable extent, though not reduced. A college might say,—We will accept for admission any groups of studies taken from the secondary school programme, provided that the sum of the studies in each of the four years amounts to sixteen, or eighteen, or twenty periods a week,—as may be thought best,—and provided, further, that in each year at least four of the subjects presented shall have been pursued at least three periods a week, and that at least three of the subjects shall have been pursued three years or more. For the purposes of this reckoning, natural history, geography, meteorology, and astronomy might be grouped together as one subject. Every youth who entered college would have spent four years in studying a few subjects thoroughly; and, on the theory that all the subjects are to be considered equivalent in educational rank for the purposes of admission to college, it would make no difference which subjects he had chosen from the programme—he would have had four years of strong and effective mental training. The Conferences on Geography and Modern Languages make the most explicit statement to the effect that college requirements for admission should coincide with high-school requirements for graduation. The Conference on English is of opinion "that no student should be admitted to college who shows in his English examination and his other examinations that he is

very deficient in ability to write good English." This recommendation suggests that an ample English course in the secondary school should be required of all persons who intend to
enter college. It would of course be possible for any college to
require for admission any one subject, or any group of subjects,
in the table, and the requirements of different colleges, while
all kept within the table, might differ in many respects; but the
Committee are of opinion that the satisfactory completion of
any one of the four years' courses of study embodied in the fore-
going programmes should admit to corresponding courses in
colleges and scientific schools. They believe that this close articulation between the secondary schools and the higher institutions would be advantageous alike for the schools, the colleges, and the country.

Every reader of this report and of the reports of the nine
Conferences will be satisfied that to carry out the improvements proposed more highly trained teachers will be needed
than are now ordinarily to be found for the service of the
elementary and secondary schools. The Committee of Ten desire to point out some of the means of procuring these better
trained teachers. For the further instruction of teachers in actual service, three agencies already in existence may be much
better utilized than they now are. The Summer Schools which
many universities now maintain might be resorted to by much
larger numbers of teachers, particularly if some aid, such as the
payment of tuition fees and travelling expenses, should be
given to teachers who are willing to devote half of their vaca-
tions to study, by the cities and towns which these teachers
serve. Secondly, in all the towns and cities in which colleges and
universities are planted, these colleges or universities may use-
fully give stated courses of instruction in the main subjects used
in the elementary and secondary schools to teachers employed
in those towns and cities. This is a reasonable service which the
colleges and universities may render to their own communities.
Thirdly, a superintendent who has himself become familiar
with the best mode of teaching any one of the subjects which

TABLE IV.

YEAR	CLASSICAL Three foreign languages (one modern)		LATIN-SCIENTIFIC Two foreign languages (one modern)	
I	Latin	5 p.	Latin	5 p.
	English	4 p.	English	4 p.
	Algebra	4 p.	Algebra	4 p.
	History	4 p.	History	4 p.
	Physical Geography	3 p.	Physical Geography	3 p.
		20 p.		20 p.
II	Latin	5 p.	Latin	5 p.
	English	2 p.	English	2 p.

	*German [or French]
	  begun
		4 p.	German [or French]
			  begun
				4 p.

	Geometry	3 p.	Geometry	3 p.
	Physics	3 p.	Physics	3 p.
	History	3 p.	Botany or Zoölogy	3 p.
		20 p.		20 p.
III	Latin	4 p.	Latin	4 p.
	*Greek	5 p.	English	3 p.
	English	3 p.	German [or French]	4 p.
	German [or French]	4 p.	Mathe- { Algebra 2 matics { Geometry 2 }	4 p.
	Mathe- { Algebra 2 matics { Geometry 2 }	4 p.	Astronomy ½ yr. & Meteorology ½ yr.	3 p.
		20 p.	History	2 p.
				20 p.
IV	Latin	4 p.	Latin	4 p.
	Greek	5 p.	English { as in Classical 2 { additional 2 }	4 p.
	English	2 p.	German [or French]	3 p.
	German [or French]	3 p.	Chemistry	3 p.

	Chemistry	3 p.	Trigonometry & Higher
			  Algebra
			    or
			  History }
				3 p.

	Trigonometry &
	  Higher Algebra
	    or
	  History }
		3 p.	Geology or Physiog-
			  raphy ½ yr.
			    and
			  Anatomy, Physiology,
			  & Hygiene ½ yr. }
				3 p.

		20 p.		20 p.

* In any school in which Greek can be better taught than a modern language, or in which local public opinion or the history of the school makes it desirable to teach Greek in an ample way, Greek may be substituted for German or French in the second year of the Classical programme.

TABLE IV. (*continued*).

YEAR	MODERN LANGUAGES Two foreign languages (both modern)		ENGLISH One foreign language (ancient or modern)	
I	French [*or* German] begun English Algebra History Physical Geography	5 p. 4 p. 4 p. 4 p. 3 p. 20 p.	Latin, or German, or French English Algebra History Physical Geography	5 p. 4 p. 4 p. 4 p. 3 p. 20 p.
II	French [*or* German] English German [*or* French] begun Geometry Physics Botany or Zoölogy	4 p. 2 p. 5 p. 3 p. 3 p. 3 p. 20 p.	Latin, or German, or French English Geometry Physics History Botany or Zoölogy	5 or 4 p. 3 or 4 p. 3 p. 3 p. 3 p. 3 p. 20 p.
III	French [*or* German] English German [*or* French] Mathe- { Algebra 2 matics { Geometry 2 } 4 p. Astronomy ½ yr & Meteorology ½ yr. History	4 p. 3 p. 4 p. 3 p. 2 p. 20 p.	Latin, or German, or French English { as in others 3 { additional 2 } 5 p. Mathe- { Algebra 2 matics { Geometry 2 } 4 p. Astronomy ½ yr. & Meteorology ½ yr. History { as in the Latin-Scientific 2 { additional 2 } 4 p.	4 p. 3 p. 20 p.
IV	French [*or* German] English { as in Classical 2 { additional 2 } 4 p. German [*or* French] Chemistry Trigonometry & Higher Algebra 3 or History } 3 p. Geology or Physiography ½ yr. and Anatomy, Physiology, & Hygiene ½ yr. } 3 p.	3 p. 4 p. 3 p. 20 p.	Latin, or German, or French English { as in Classical 2 { additional 2 } 4 p. Chemistry Trigonometry & Higher Algebra History Geology or Physiography ½ yr. and Anatomy, Physiology, & Hygiene ½ yr. } 3 p.	4 p. 3 p. 3 p. 3 p. 20 p.

enter into the school course can always be a very useful instructor for the whole body of teachers under his charge. A real master of any one subject will always have many suggestions to make to teachers of other subjects. The same is true of the principal of a high school, or other leading teacher in a town or city. In every considerable city school system the best teacher in each department of instruction should be enabled to give part of his time to helping the other teachers by inspecting and criticising their work, and showing them, both by precept and example, how to do it better.

In regard to preparing young men and women for the business of teaching, the country has a right to expect much more than it has yet obtained from the colleges and normal schools. The common expectation of attainment for pupils of the normal schools has been altogether too low the country over. The normal schools, as a class, themselves need better apparatus, libraries, programmes, and teachers. As to the colleges, it is quite as much an enlargement of sympathies as an improvement of apparatus or of teaching that they need. They ought to take more interest than they have heretofore done, not only in the secondary, but in the elementary schools; and they ought to take pains to fit men well for the duties of a school superintendent. They already train a considerable number of the best principals of high schools and academies; but this is not sufficient. They should take an active interest, through their presidents, professors, and other teachers, in improving the schools in their respective localities, and in contributing to the thorough discussion of all questions affecting the welfare of both the elementary and the secondary schools.

Finally, the Committee venture to suggest, in the interest of secondary schools, that uniform dates—such as the last Thursday, Friday, and Saturday, or the third Monday, Tuesday, and Wednesday of June and September—be established for the admission examinations of colleges and scientific schools throughout the United States. It is a serious inconvenience for secondary schools which habitually prepare candidates for several different colleges or scientific schools that the admission examinations of different institutions are apt to occur on different dates, sometimes rather widely separated.

The Committee also wish to call attention to the service which Schools of Law, Medicine, Engineering, and Technology, whether connected with universities or not, can render to secondary education by arranging their requirements for admission, as regards selection and range of subjects, in conformity with the courses of study recommended by the Committee. By bringing their entrance requirements into close relation with any or all of the programmes recommended for secondary schools, these professional schools can give valuable support to high schools, academies, and preparatory schools.

> *Charles W. Eliot,*
> *William T. Harris,*
> *James B. Angell,*
> *John Tetlow,*
> *James M. Taylor,*
> *Oscar D. Robinson,*
> *James H. Baker,*
> *Richard H. Jesse,*
> *James C. Mackenzie,*
> *Henry C. King.*

4 December, 1893.

Minority Report

President Baker signs the above report, but adds the following statement:—

I beg leave to note some exceptions taken to parts of the Report of the Committee of Ten. Had the Committee not been limited in time, doubtless fuller discussion would have resulted in modifying some statements embodied in the report. The great value of the reports of the Conferences upon the subjects referred to them, as to matter, place, time, methods, adequate and continuous work for each subject, and identity of work in different courses, and the masterly summary and tabulation of their recommendations, made by the Chairman of the Committee of Ten, can but invite cordial commendation. Objections are raised to parts of the special work of the Committee.

1. I cannot endorse expressions that appear to sanction the idea that the choice of subjects in secondary schools may be a matter of comparative indifference. I note especially the following sentences, referring the reader to their context for accurate interpretation.

"Any school principal may say:—'With the staff at my command I can teach only five subjects out of those proposed by the Conferences in the manner proposed. My school shall, therefore, be limited to these five.' Another school may be able to teach in the thorough manner proposed five subjects, but some or all of these five may be different from those selected by the first school."

"If twice as much time is given in a school to Latin as is given to mathematics, the attainments of the pupils in Latin ought to be twice as great as they are in mathematics, provided that equally good work is done in the two subjects; and Latin will have twice the educational value of mathematics."

"The schedule of studies contained in Table III permits flexibility and variety in three respects. First, it is not necessary that any school should teach all the subjects which it contains, or any particular set of subjects."

"Every youth who entered college would have spent four years in studying a few subjects thoroughly; and on the theory that all the subjects are to be considered equivalent in educational rank for the purpose of admission to college, it would make no difference which subjects he had chosen from the programme—he would have had four years of strong and effective mental training."

All such statements are based upon the theory that, for the purposes of general education, one study is as good as another, —a theory which appears to me to ignore Philosophy, Psychology and Science of Education. It is a theory which makes education formal and does not consider the nature and value of the content. Power comes through knowledge; we can not conceive of observation and memory in the abstract. The world which offers to the human mind several distinct views is the world in which our power that comes through knowledge is to be used, the world which we are to understand and enjoy. The relation between the subjective power and the objective—or subjective —knowledge is inseparable and vital. On any other theory, for general education, we might well consider the study of Egyptian hieroglyphics as valuable as that of physics, and Choctaw as important as Latin. Secondary school programmes can not well omit mathematics, or science, or history, or literature, or the culture of the ancient classics. An education which gives a view in all directions is the work of elementary and secondary schools. Such an education is the necessary preparation for the special work of the university student. If I rightly understood, the majority of the Committee rejected the theory of equivalence of studies for general education.

Studies vary in value for the training of the different powers, and for this additional reason the choice can not be regarded as a matter of indifference.

The training of "observation, memory, expression and reasoning" (inductive) is a very important part of education, but is not all of education. The imagination, deductive reasoning, the rich possibilities of emotional life, the education of the will through ethical ideas and correct habit, all are to be considered in a scheme of learning. Ideals are to be added to the scientific method.

The dilemma which appears on an examination of the time demands of the various conferences offers to the programme maker the alternatives of omitting essential subjects and of a rational adjustment of the time element, while retaining all essential subjects. Reason and experience point toward the latter alternative. By wise selection of matter within the lines of study adequate and consecutive time can be given to each.

2. The language of the second paragraph following Table ii might be misconstrued to mean that the Committee favor the multiplication of courses with a loss of the thoroughness attainable when the teaching force is devoted to one or two courses. Intension rather than extension of effort, both in respect to the number of courses and in respect to the number of studies or topics under each principal subject, is to be strongly recommended.

3. It may seem trivial to offer criticism of the specimen programmes made by the Committee, and yet I believe that each member felt that with ample deliberation results somewhat different would have been reached. Note for instance that in some of the programmes history is entirely omitted in the second year, and physics is given only three hours per week,—no more time than is allowed for botany or zoölogy. There are many symmetrical seecondary school programmes in actual operation today which furnish continuous instruction in all important subjects throughout the four years, allowing to each an amount of time adequate to good results. For most high schools the first, the Classical programme, and the last programme, the one offering one foreign language, will commend themselves because they are economical, and they combine a good finishing course with adequate college preparation.

4. On the basis of the tabulated results of the Conferences I

believe that by earnest scientific examination a scheme of work can be formulated that will meet the views of the members of the Committee and of most educators. As an afterthought it may be an occasion for regret that the strength of the discussion was not devoted to Table III. Instead of considering the work of the Committee as ended, I would recommend that the National Council hold itself responsible for further examination of the data furnished by the Conferences. I have not presumed to offer a substitute report, because I believe that the importance of the work demands further effort of an entire Committee.

Respectfully submitted,

James H. Baker.

BIBLIOGRAPHY

That the *Report* of the Committee of Ten has received no close attention from historians is somewhat surprising, considering the importance of the document. The most perceptive writing on the topic was roughly contemporaneous with the publication of the *Report,* and, while scores of term papers in courses in the history of American education have undoubtedly been written about the Ten, few scholars have given it, until recently, any study in depth. This neglect is related to the larger problem of education and its history. The new profession of educators, after, roughly, 1910, was so intent on looking forward, on "action" as they said, that they forgot to look back, except when history could serve their particular ends. The *Report* of the Committee of Ten, written as it was by academicians, avoided the sociological and demographic problems which so consumed the energies of the new educators. Only recently, with the shift in emphasis described in the final chapter above, have the deliberations and recommendations of the Ten shown themselves to be of more than passing importance and even of possible help for practitioners today. Until recently, then, little work of merit has been done on the schools of the 1890s; the gap can be seen by a glance at the dates of the references that follow this essay. Secondary works on the *Report* are few; but there are important bodies of primary material.

Of manuscript sources, enough remain to recreate the formation of the Committee and the details of its deliberations. Most useful are the C. W. Eliot Papers in the Harvard University Archives. Much correspondence to and from Eliot is missing, but what remains is important. The W. T. Harris Papers at the Library of Congress are vast—over 13,000 items are catalogued—but disappointing. Most of the material can be found in printed form elsewhere, and much is tediously repetitious. Another source of Harris' papers is the Bureau of Education Records in the United States Archives, stored, incongruously, in the Labor and Transportation Branch of that institution. These records—letterpress copies of a great deal of correspondence of the various Commissioners—are uncatalogued and poorly preserved in unsorted boxes. This sadly neglected source of information about the early days of the Bureau has been almost wholly overlooked by historians. The role played by the Bureau and by the Department of the Interior in disseminating the *Report* of the Committee is fully revealed in Harris' correspondence there. Future historians will also find other information on topics from Florence Nightingale's interest in the training of American nurses to the sale of reindeer meat in Alaska (long the responsibility of the Commissioner of Education).

The James C. Mackenzie Papers, most of which are now at the Lawrenceville School (the balance remain with the Mackenzie family but will eventually go to the school), comprise a small but extremely useful collection. The dimensions of the classicists' opposition to Eliot is found in letters preserved there. The John Tetlow Papers, in the Houghton Library at Harvard, are less useful but give important information about Eliot's role in the formation of the Committee, information that contradicts much of our present understanding, which comes largely from Nicholas Murray Butler. Butler's Papers are at Columbia and are a good source of evidence as to the scope and nature of his activity in the interests of the Committee.

In the James B. Angell Papers in the Michigan Historical Collections at the University of Michigan, there are a number of relevant letters. Oscar Robinson eased the historian's job by publishing some of his correspondence with Eliot ("The Work of the Committee of Ten.")[1]

1. Full titles follow in the list of References.

There is a wealth of published primary material illustrative of the schools of the 1890s. Most important are the reports of state and local school boards and superintendents. These documents, many of them voluminous, are full of statistics and discussion of the operation of the schools. They vary enormously in usefulness; often the most voluminous are the least helpful. The slim biennial volumes of the Wisconsin superintendent, for example, are superior to those of many of his more garrulous colleagues. The Connecticut school report of 1880 gives a clear picture of the fight for free secondary education. The St. Louis reports from the time when Harris was Commissioner through the '90s are full of valuable data. The footnotes in the text record the reports most useful for this present study.

The proceedings of the various educational associations provide excellent evidence of the thinking of the leading schoolmen of their day. Too much reliance can be put on them, however; what was said at NEA meetings, in particular, did not always reflect accurately either the condition in the schools or the general currents of opinion among teachers. What Harris, Eliot, Nightingale, and Greenwood thought did not always correspond with the ideas of the teachers in small schools in Georgia, Michigan, and Vermont. Proceedings, then, must be read with a bias in mind; so read, they are revealing. Since the Committee of Ten was an NEA project, the *Addresses and Proceedings* of that organization are of the first importance. Several key speeches were also made before the American Institute of Instruction. The regional associations dealt with the *Report*, particularly the New England Association of Colleges and Preparatory Schools, which held a special meeting in 1894 on that subject alone. The views of the members of the Committee and the Conferences are largely preserved in these volumes of proceedings of the various societies and associations.

Several of the many special reports published on education in the 1880s and 90s are valuable, most of them prepared under the aegis of the NEA. The so-called "Canfield Report" ("The Opportunities of the Rural Population for Higher Education") in 1889 is most perceptive. Less helpful are the series of reports by the NEA's Committee on Secondary Education during the 80s. *The Report of the Committee of Fifteen on Elementary Education* and of the *Committee on College Entrance Requirements* are essential documents for the period. The American Philological Association's "Report of the Committee of Twelve on Courses of Study in Latin and Greek for Secondary Schools" is the best example of classicists' resistance to the proposals of the Ten. And, finally, the various documents published by the NEA Commission for the Reorganization of Secondary Education, especially the "Cardinal Principles of Education," show the extent of the shift away from the philosophy of 1893.

Statements by the leaders of the schools appear also in the various journals of the day. Well-known lay publications like *Harper's Weekly, Atlantic Monthly, Arena, Century, Nation, Outlook,* and *Independent* irregularly carried articles about education; but all carried statements about the *Report* of the Committee of Ten. Of the professional journals, the most important was Butler's *Educational Review.* While its editor's bias is obvious, the Committee is fully and enthusiastically reported in its pages. Schurman's *School Review* also published some key articles. Kasson's *Education* and Winship's *Journal of Education,* journals written for schoolteachers rather than for men like Eliot and Butler, have a markedly different bias. One must read the editorial reaction to the *Report* in both the *Educational Review* and the *Journal of Education* to see accurately the two points of view. There are a host of smaller journals, now often difficult to find even in large libraries, which are useful in that they implicitly demonstrate the intellectual level of their readers, the teachers, and the conditions in the schools, primarily the elementary institutions. Some of these were state-wide publications—the *Colorado School Journal,* the *Indiana School Journal,* the *Ohio Educational Monthly and National Teacher*—while others were regional, such as the *Southwestern Journal of Education* and the *Western School Journal.*

A small number of important articles from these various journals, reports, and proceedings should be noted. For an understanding of the background of the Committee, Eliot's three influential speeches are essential, "The Gap between the Elementary Schools and the Colleges," "Shortening and Enriching the Grammar School Course," and "Undesirable and Desirable Uniformity in Schools." Addis ("Ten Years of Education in the United States") gives a convenient general summary of the situation. Hewes' "The Public Schools of the United States" is a thorough study of the statistical story. Shaw covers ground indicated in his article's title, "Compulsory Education in the United States. "

Articles about the Committee and its *Report* are numerous, and the published views of the Ten themselves important. Most perceptive is Mackenzie's "The Feasibility of Modifying the Programs." Baker's long summary, "Review of the Report of the Committee of Ten," gives some indication as to what the Ten thought was novel in their document. Eliot's and Harris' articles ("The Report of the Committee of Ten" and "The Committee of Ten on Secondary Schools") in *Educational Review* are rather uninspired. Robinson's critical article, "The Work of the Committee of Ten," in *School Review* is revealing.

Of statements in favor of the *Report*'s recommendations, those by Butler in the editorial columns of *Educational Review* are interesting, both for their content and as evidence of his involvement with the Committee. E. P. Seaver's 1894 Boston school report is another praise-filled review of the *Report*. Of hostile opinion, the best examples, each of a different color, are the editorials in *Education* and the *Journal of Education*, Burke Hinsdale's "The Dogma of Formal Discipline," and the relevant sections in the second volume of G. Stanley Hall's *Adolescence*. Other discussions of the document are found conveniently in the New York Regents' *Bulletin* record of the thirty-second University convocation of that state. All shades of opinion, save that of the rural teacher, are seen in this source. Also worthy of attention are the series of articles in *Educational Review* on the Committee, especially that by Charles DeGarmo, and Jacob Schurman's study in *School Review*. Three articles written after release of the *Report* are revealing: Eliot's "Recent Changes in Secondary Education," Andrew West's "A New Revival," and Edwin Dexter's "Ten Years' Influence of the Report of the Committee of Ten."

Secondary material on the *Report* and on the schools of its day is plentiful in quantity but short on quality. More than sixteen texts can be consulted concerning the history of education in America during this period. The best general history was written by a contemporary of the members of the Committee, Elmer E. Brown. He, E. G. Dexter, and J. B. Brown really should be considered primary sources, for they were contemporary critics. Elwood P. Cubberley's *Changing Conceptions of Education* and *Public Education in the United States* mark a change in attitude of scholars toward the *Report,* and Cubberley's sharp words of criticism have been generally accepted for several decades. Educational historians, in their textbooks of the present moment, are still somewhat in disagreement over the extent of the *Report*'s effect.

Four relatively contemporary studies of the Ten have been made. The earliest and least satisfactory is by Thomas H. Briggs, "The Committee of Ten." Bernard Mehl's unpublished dissertation at the University of Illinois covers the entire decade of the 90s, though somewhat unevenly. Lawrence Cremin in a short article, "The Revolution in American Secondary Education, 1893–1918" sketches in the change in the schools in those two and a half decades. And Jones, Keppel, and Ulich cover much the same ground, again in a limited way. Edward Krug's collection of a number of Eliot's writings on "popular education," including a portion of the *Report* of the Committee of Ten, is also useful.

There are many histories of education for particular states or regions, most of them of limited usefulness. The best is probably Aurner's three-volume study of Iowa's schools. Inglis and Martin are of some help with the early Massachusetts' high schools but do not touch on the 1890s. Eby on Texas, Gifford on New York, Putnam on Michigan, and Ryan on the South are of mixed quality, but often revealing.

There are a number of excellent studies of the 90s and their schools. Of the many general intellectual histories, two stand out—Commager's *The American Mind* and Hofstadter's *Social Darwinism in American Thought.* The former succinctly sketches in the intellectual climate of the day, arguing that the 1890s were indeed a "watershed" in American development. The latter deals with science and its effects, describing a movement that greatly affected members of the Committee of Ten. More specifically on education is Oscar Handlin's short book *John Dewey's Challenge to Education.* Handlin comes to grips with the sorry condition of the schools with a clarity and vigor not seen in earlier writers. Henry Seidel Canby's memoirs, *The Age of Confidence,* bear Handlin out, and in a lucid and biting style. Also enlightening is the second volume in Mark Sullivan's series, *Our Times,* entitled *America Finding Herself.* Sullivan describes schools and particularly school readers with whimsy and affection.

A word should be said of sources revealing of the members of the Ten. *The Dictionary of American Biography* deals with no less than eight of them; only Robinson and Tetlow are excluded. None of Eliot's several biographies deals with his contributions to the lower schools, a shocking oversight, but James' two-volume study is still by far the best source of information about the Chairman's life. Eliot also published two useful collections of his speeches, many of which deal with education: *Educational Reform* and *A Late Harvest.* Shirley Smith's biography of Angell gives little attention to his contributions to primary and secondary education, and Angell's own *Reminiscences* do not correct this fault. Kurt Leidecker has prepared a biography of Harris, and Mosier and Roberts have both dealt with the Commissioner's views on education, but none of these three works is distinguished. Harris still is best seen through his vast and scattered array of articles. A sketchy mimeographed biography of Jesse exists, written by Henry O. Severance. King is blessed with an excellent biography by Donald O. Love of Oberlin. Taylor's biography by Elizabeth Haight is again neglectful of the Vassar president's activities in the schools and in the various regional associations.

Mulford's *History of the Lawrenceville School* pays much attention to Mackenzie, including his early years prior to his headmastership at the school. While no biographies exist for Baker, Tetlow, and Robinson, it still remains remarkable that, with only their exception, the Ten have received such attention by historians. One must admit that several of the biographies of the college men were written by dutiful and often uncritical alumni, who could not or chose not to see the effect of their heroes beyond the confines of their campuses, but at the same time one sees again that the membership of the Ten was by any standard a highly respected, publicly prominent one. New biographies are needed, especially of Eliot and the remarkable Mackenzie.

A number of special areas of education have been covered by historians. Most recently two brilliant studies have appeared: Lawrence Cremin's *The Transformation of the School* (1961), a history of Progressive Education, and Frederick Rudolph's lucidly written *The American College and University: A History* (1962). Elsbree's *The American Teacher* describes teachers and the condition of teaching from colonial times to the 1930s. Broome's 1902 study of college admission requirements simplifies a confused and confusing area. Two studies of the secondary school curriculum are available. Stout has made a statistical study of curricula in the north central states from 1860 to 1918, which is useful only insofar as the course titles he operates with truly represent what was taught. Latimer's recent study using the Commissioner of Education's *Reports* has flaws that were noted above, page 188. The National Educational Association is treated in three works, Wesley's *NEA: The First Hundred Years*, Fenner's "The National Education Association, 1892–1942" (and its shortened, published version), and McKenna's "Policy Evolution in the National Education Association."

Finally, a word should be said about relevant bibliographies. General sources for the history of American education need no repeating; they are fully listed in Brickman's *Guide to Research in Educational History* and Bailyn's *Education in the*

280

Forming of American Society. The complicated apparatus of the American Historical Association's *Writings on American History* is an invaluable device. Walkeley's study of publications dealing with school-college articulation was published in 1914 and covers its select ground well. Monroe's 1897 bibliography and E. E. Brown's and J. F. Brown's textbooks all provide excellent references. Nelson's bibliography of N.E.A. *Proceedings* and publications and the similar reviews published for the U.S. Commissioner of Education are essential. Two bibliographies on the Committee of Ten itself were published shortly after the *Report,* one in the *Educational Review* and the other in the *Report* of the Commissioner of Education for 1892–93. Both of these, however, tend to list only the favorable articles and reviews.

The list of references following contains the most important titles. A complete list of sources used in this study may be found in my unpublished doctoral dissertation, "The Committee of Ten" (1961), available in the Archives of the Harvard College Library.

REFERENCES

Addis, Wellford, "Ten Years of Education in the United States," *School Review, 1* (1893), 339–53.

Ambler, Charles H., *A History of Education in West Virginia,* Huntington, 1951.

American Institute of Instruction, *Addresses and Proceedings,* 1881–96.

American Philological Association, "Report of the Committee of Twelve on Courses of Study in Latin and Greek for Secondary Schools," APA *Transactions* (1899), pp. lxxvii–cxxi.

Angell, James B., "The Relation of the University, College, and Higher Technical Schools to the Public System of Instruction," National Educational Association, *Addresses and Proceedings* (1887), pp. 146–51.

——— *The Reminiscences of James Burrill Angell,* New York, 1911.

Association of Colleges and Preparatory Schools in the Middle States and Maryland, *Addresses and Proceedings,* 1893–1900.

Association of Colleges and Preparatory Schools in the Southern States, *Addresses and Proceedings,* 1895–1902.

Aurner, Clarence Ray, *History of Education in Iowa,* 3 vols. Iowa City, 1914–20.

Bailyn, B., *Education in the Forming of American Society,* Chapel Hill, 1960.

Baker, James H., "The High School as a Finishing-School," National Educational Association, *Addresses and Proceedings* (1890), pp. 633–40.

——— "Practical Education: The Psychological View," National Educational Association, *Addresses and Proceedings* (1888), pp. 166–73.

——— "Review of the Report of the Committee of Ten," National Educational Association, *Addresses and Proceedings* (1894), pp. 645–60.

Bancroft, Cecil F. P., "Report of the Committee of Ten, from the Point of View of an Endowed Academy," *Educational Review, 7* (1894), 280–85.

"Bibliography" (on the Committee of Ten), *Report* of the Commissioner of Education (1892–93), *2*, 1491–94.

—— in "Editorial," *Educational Review, 8* (1894), 103–04.

Bolton, Frederick E., and Thomas W. Bibb, *History of Education in Washington*, U.S. Office of Education, Bulletin 90, Washington, 1935.

Boone, R. G., *Education in the United States*, New York, 1889.

Boston, *Fourteenth Annual Report of the Superintendent of Public Schools* (1894).

Bradley, John E., "The Report of the Committee of Ten, from the Point of View of the Smaller Colleges," *Educational Review, 7* (1894), 370–74.

Brickman, William W., *Guide to Research in Educational History*, New York, 1949.

Briggs, Thomas H., "The Committee of Ten," *Junior-Senior High School Clearing House, 6* (1931), 134–41.

Broome, E. C., "A Historical and Critical Discussion of College Admission Requirements," Columbia University Contributions to Philosophy, Psychology, and Education, *11* (New York, 1902), 3–4.

Brown, E. E., *The Making of Our Middle Schools*, New York, 1903.

Brown, John Franklin, *The American High School*, New York, 1909.

Burrell, B. J., and R. H. Eckelberry, "The High School Question before the Courts in the Post-Civil-War Period." *School Review, 42* (1934), 255–65.

Butler, Nicholas Murray, *Across the Busy Years*, 2 vols. New York, 1935.

—— Education in the United States, 2 vols. Albany, 1900.

—— "The Function of the Secondary School," *Academy, 5* (1890), 131–48.

—— "An Important Educational Conference," *Harper's Weekly, 37* (1893), 1109–10.

—— "Manual Training," American Institute of Instruction, *Addresses and Proceedings* (1888), pp. 214–34.

—— "Open Letter," *The Century, 48* (1894), 314–16.

―― "The Reform of High School Education," *Harper's Weekly, 38* (1894), 42–43.

―― "The Reform of Secondary Education in the United States," *Atlantic Monthly, 73* (1894), 372–84.

―― "Status of Education at the Close of the Century," National Educational Association, *Addresses and Proceedings* (1900), pp. 188–203.

Canby, Henry S., *The Age of Confidence: Life in the Nineties,* New York, 1934.

Canfield, James H., "The Opportunities of the Rural Population for Higher Education," Report of the Committee on Secondary Education, National Council of Education, National Educational Association, *Addresses and Proceedings* (1889), pp. 370–93.

Clark, John S., "Art in Secondary Education—an Omission of the Committee of Ten." *Educational Review, 7* (1894), 374–81.

Cloud, Roy W., *Education in California,* Stanford, 1952.

Collar, William C., "The Action of the Colleges upon the Schools," *Educational Review, 2* (1891), 422–41.

College Association of the Middle States and Maryland, *Proceedings* (1889–92).

Commager, Henry Steele, *The American Mind: An Interpretation of American Thought and Character since the 1880s,* New Haven, 1950.

Conant, James B., *The Revolutionary Transformation of the American High School,* Cambridge, 1959.

"Confessions of Three School Superintendents," *Atlantic Monthly, 82* (1898), 644–53.

Cremin, Lawrence A., "The Progressive Movement in Education: A Perspective," *Harvard Educational Review, 27* (1957), 251–70.

―― "The Revolution in American Secondary Education, 1893–1918," *Teachers College Record, 56* (1955), 295–308.

―― *The Transformation of the School,* New York, 1961.

Cubberley, Ellwood P., *Changing Conceptions of Education,* Boston, 1909.

——— *Public Education in the United States,* rev. ed. Boston, 1934.

DeGarmo, Charles, "Report of the Committee of Ten, from the Point of View of Educational Theory," *Educational Review,* 7 (1894), 275–80.

Dexter, Edwin G., *A History of Education in the United States,* New York, 1906.

——— "Ten Years' Influence of the Report of the Committee of Ten," *School Review, 14* (1906), 254–69.

Eby, Frederick, *The Development of Education in Texas,* New York, 1925.

Eliot, C. W., "American Education since the Civil War," Rice Institute Pamphlet, 9, No. 1 (1922), 1–25.

——— *Educational Reform,* New York, 1898.

——— "The Function of Education in Democratic Society," *Outlook, 57* (1897), 570–75.

——— "The Fundamental Assumptions in the Report of the Committee of Ten (1893)," *Educational Review, 30* (1905), 325–43.

——— "The Gap between the Elementary Schools and the Colleges," National Educational Association, *Addresses and Proceedings* (1890), pp. 522–42.

——— "The Grammar School of the Future," *Journal of Education, 38* (1893), 379.

——— *A Late Harvest,* Boston, 1924.

——— "Recent Changes in Secondary Education," *Atlantic Monthly, 84* (1899), 433–44.

——— "The Report of the Committee of Ten," *Educational Review,* 7 (1894), 105–10.

——— "Requirements for Admission to Colleges and Scientific Schools," Address to the New York Schoolmasters' Association, New York, 1897.

——— "The School," *Atlantic Monthly, 92* (1903), 577–86.

——— "Secondary School and College," *Educational Review, 13* (1897), 465–68.

——— "Secondary School Programs, and the Conferences of December 1892," New England Association of Colleges and

Preparatory Schools, *Addresses and Proceedings* (1893), pp. 19–33.

—— "Shortening and Enriching the Grammar School Course," National Educational Association, *Addresses and Proceedings* (1892), pp. 617–25.

—— "Tendencies of Secondary Education," *Educational Review, 14* (1897), 417–27.

—— "Undesirable and Desirable Uniformity in Schools," National Educational Association, *Addresses and Proceedings* (1892), pp. 82–95.

—— "The Unity of Educational Reform," American Institute of Instruction, *Addresses and Proceedings* (1894), pp. 151–73.

—— "What Has Been Gained in Uniformity of College Admission Requirements in the Past Twenty Years," *School Review, 12* (1904), 757–81.

—— "Wherein Popular Education Has Failed," *Forum, 14* (1892–93), 411–28.

Elsbree, Willard S., *The American Teacher,* New York, 1939.

Emerson, Henry P., "Bearing of the Report on Elementary Education," New York Regents *Bulletin, 28* (1894), 283–86.

Fenner, Mildred Sandison, "The National Education Association, 1892–1942," unpublished dissertation, George Washington University, 1942.

—— *NEA History,* Washington, 1945.

Ferrier, William Warren, *Ninety Years of Education in California, 1846–1936,* Berkeley, 1937.

Gifford, W. J., *Historical Development of the New York State High School System,* New York, 1922.

Greenough, James Jay, "The Present Requirements for Admission to Harvard College," *Atlantic Monthly, 69* (1892), 671–77.

Greenwood, J. M., "The Report of the Conferences," *Western School Journal, 10* (1894), 77–79, 98–100.

Griffin, Orwin B., *Evolution of the Connecticut State School System,* Contributions to Education, Teachers College, Columbia University, 293 (New York, 1928).

Haight, Elizabeth Hazelton, *The Life and Letters of James Monroe Taylor: The Biography of an Educator,* New York, 1919.

Hall, G. Stanley, *Adolescence,* 2 vols. New York, 1904.

Handlin, Oscar, *John Dewey's Challenge to Education,* New York, 1959.

—— "Rejoinder to the Critics of John Dewey," New York *Times Magazine* (June 15, 1958), 13 ff.

Harris, William Torrey, "The Committee of Ten on Secondary Schools," *Educational Review, 7* (1894), 4–10.

—— "The Curriculum for Secondary Schools," National Educational Association, *Addresses and Proceedings* (1894), pp. 496–508.

—— "Education in the United States," in N. S. Shaler, *The United States of America* (New York, 1894), pp. 294–359.

—— "Excessive Helps in Education," *Education, 9* (1888–89), 215–20.

—— "The Intellectual Value of Tool-Work," National Educational Association, *Addresses and Proceedings* (1889), pp. 92–98.

—— "Latin and Greek in Modern Education," *Journal of the Women's Education Union, 8* (1880).

—— "My Pedagogical Creed," *School Journal, 54* (1897), 813 ff.

—— "The New Education," *Arena, 17* (1896–97), 353–60.

—— "The Old Psychology versus the New," Massachusetts Schoolmasters' Club, Boston, 1895.

—— "On the Necessity of Colleges to Supplement the High Schools," *Ohio Educational Monthly and National Teacher* (August 1888), pp. 434–51.

—— "On the Relation of the College to the Common School," American Institute of Instruction, *Addresses and Proceedings* (1883), pp. 139–71.

—— "The Pendulum of School Reform," *Education, 8* (1888), 347–50.

—— "The Present Status of Education in the United States," National Educational Association, *Addresses and Proceedings* (1891), pp. 136–43.

——— "Report of Committee to Report a Course of Study for all Grades," National Educational Association, *Addresses and Proceedings* (1876), pp. 58–70.

——— *A Statement of the Theory of Education in the United States of America as Approved by Many Leading Educators,* Washington, 1874.

——— "What Shall the Public Schools Teach?" *Forum, 4* (1887–88), 573–81.

Harrison, Caskie, "Letter" to *The Dial, 14* (1894), 102–03.

Hertzler, Silas, *The Rise of the High School in Connecticut,* Baltimore, 1930.

Hewes, F. W., "Common Schools in the United States," *Harper's Weekly, 38* (1894), 138–40.

——— "The Public Schools of the United States," *Harper's Weekly, 39* (1895), 1017–18, 1040–41, 1068–69, 1093–95, 1112–16, 1141, 1164–65.

Hill, Frank A., "The Report of the Committee of Ten," American Institute of Instruction, *Addresses and Proceedings* (1895), pp. 174–87.

Hinsdale, Burke A., "The Dogma of Formal Discipline," National Educational Association, *Addresses and Proceedings* (1894), 625–35.

——— "President Eliot on Popular Education," *Intelligence, 13* (1893), 52 ff.

Hofstadter, Richard, *The Age of Reform,* New York, 1955.

——— *Social Darwinism in American Thought,* Philadelphia, 1945.

Huling, Ray Greene, "The Reports on Secondary School Studies," *School Review, 2* (1894), 268–80.

Hyde, William DeWitt, "Educational Values as Assessed by the Committee of Ten," New England Association of Colleges and Preparatory Schools, *Addresses and Proceedings* (1894), pp. 38–55.

——— "President Eliot as an Educational Reformer," *Atlantic Monthly, 83* (1899), 348–57.

Inglis, A. J., *The Rise of the High School in Massachusetts,*

Contributions to Education, Teachers College, Columbia University, 50 (New York, 1911).

James, Henry, *Charles W. Eliot,* 2 vols. Boston, 1930.

Jesse, Richard D., "What Constitutes a College and What a Secondary School," North Central Association of Colleges and Secondary Schools, *Proceedings* (1896), pp. 24–46.

—— "Some Helpful Educators," *Educational Review, 42* (1911), 20–22.

Jones, H. M., F. Keppel, and R. Ulich, "On the Conflict between the 'Liberal Arts' and the 'Schools of Education,'" American Council of Learned Societies, *Newsletter, 5* (1954), 17–38.

Kennedy, John, "Report of the Committee of Ten," New York Regents *Bulletin, 28* (1894), 273–82.

Keyes, Charles H., "The Modifications of Secondary School Course Most Demanded by the Conditions of To-day, and Most Ignored by the Committee of Ten," National Educational Association, *Addresses and Proceedings* (1895), pp. 731–41.

Koerner, James D., ed., *The Case for Basic Education,* Boston, 1959.

Krug, Edward A., ed., *Charles W. Eliot and Popular Education,* New York, 1962.

Latimer, John Francis, *What's Happened to Our High Schools?* Washington, 1958.

Leidecker, Kurt F., *Yankee Teacher,* New York, 1946.

Lignon, Moses Edward, *A History of Public Education in Kentucky,* Bulletin of the Bureau of School Service, College of Education, University of Kentucky, *14,* No. 4 (1942).

Love, Donald O., *Henry Churchill King of Oberlin,* New Haven, 1956.

McKenna, F. R., "Policy Evolution in the National Education Association," unpublished dissertation, Harvard University, 1954.

Mackenzie, James Cameron, "The Course for Academies and High Schools Recommended by the Committee of Ten," *Independent, 46* (1894), 983–84.

—— "The Feasibility of Modifying the Programs of the Elementary and Secondary Schools to meet the Suggestions in the Report of the Committee of Ten," National Educational Association, *Addresses and Proceedings* (1894), pp. 143–51.

—— "The Report of the Committee of Ten," *School Review,* 2 (1894), 146–55.

—— "Supervision of Private Schools by the State or Municipal Authorities," National Educational Association, *Addresses and Proceedings* (1893), pp. 183–90.

Martin, George, *The Evolution of the Massachusetts Public School System,* New York, 1894.

Mehl, Bernard, "The High School at the Turn of the Century: A Study of the Changes in the Aims and the Programs of Public Secondary Education in the U.S., 1890–1900," unpublished dissertation, University of Illinois, 1954.

—— "The Committee of Ten: a Re-evaluation," *Progressive Education, 33* (1956), 105–09.

—— "The Conant Report and the Committee of Ten: A Historical Appraisal," *Educational Research Bulletin* (Ohio State University), *39* (1960), 29–38, 56.

Middlekauff, Robert, *Ancients and Axioms: Secondary Education in Eighteenth-Century New England,* New Haven, 1963.

Monroe, Will S., *Bibliography of Education,* New York, 1897.

Moore, E. C., *Fifty Years of American Education,* Boston, 1917.

Morison, Samuel E., *Three Centuries of Harvard, 1636–1936,* Cambridge, 1936.

Mosier, Richard David, "The Educational Philosophy of William T. Harris," *Peabody Journal of Education, 29* (1951), 24–33.

Mulford, Roland J., *History of the Lawrenceville School, 1810–1935,* Princeton, 1935.

National Education Association, Commission on the Reorganization of Secondary Education, *Cardinal Principles of Education,* Bureau of Education, *Bulletin, 35* (Washington, 1918).

—— *Addresses and Proceedings* (1870–1900).

—— *Report of the Committee of Fifteen on Elementary Education*, New York, 1895.

—— *Report of Committee on College Entrance Requirements*, Chicago, 1899.

—— "Report of Committee on Secondary Education: The Place and Function of the Academy," *Addresses and Proceedings* (1885), pp. 447–58.

—— "Report of Committee on Secondary Education: the Relation of High Schools to Colleges," *Addresses and Proceedings* (1887), pp. 282–88.

—— "Report of Committee on Secondary Education: Uniformity in Requirements for Admission to College," *Addresses and Proceedings* (1891), pp. 306–16.

—— *Report of the Committee on Secondary School Studies Appointed at the Meeting of the National Educational Association, July 9, 1892; with the Reports of the Conferences Arranged by This Committee, and Held December 28–30, 1892*, Bureau of Education, Document 205 (Washington, 1893).

—— "Report on Preparation for College," *Addresses and Proceedings* (1884), pp. 36–42.

National Society for the Study of Education, "Curriculum-Making: Past and Present," Twenty-Sixth *Yearbook*, Part I, Bloomington, 1926.

Nelson, Martha F., *Index by Authors, Titles, and Subjects to the Publications of the National Educational Association for Its First Fifty Years, 1857–1906*, Winona, Minn., 1907.

New England Association of Colleges and Preparatory Schools, *Addresses and Proceedings* (1885–1900).

New York, University of the State of, Regents' *Bulletin, 28:* Thirty-Second University Convocation (1894).

Nightingale, A. F., "The Claims of the Classics," National Educational Association, *Addresses and Proceedings* (1887), pp. 397–416.

North Central Association of Colleges and Secondary Schools, *Proceedings* (1896–1900).

Orr, Dorothy, *A History of Education in Georgia,* Chapel Hill, 1950.

Parker, Francis W., "The Report of the Committee of Ten— Its Use for the Improvement of Teachers Now at Work in the Schools," National Educational Association, *Addresses and Proceedings* (1894), pp. 442–51.

Putnam, Daniel, *The Development of Primary and Secondary Public Education in Michigan,* Ann Arbor, 1904.

"Reference on the Report of the Committee of Ten . . . prepared for the 32nd University Convocation of the State of New York . . ." *School Review,* 2 (1894), 558–60.

Rice, Joseph Mayer, *The Public School System of the United States,* New York, 1893.

—— "Why Teachers Have No Professional Standing—Some Suggestions to the National Educational Association," *Forum,* 27 (1899), 452–63.

Roberts, John S., *William Torrey Harris: A Critical Study of His Educational and Related Philosophical Views,* Washington, 1924.

Robinson, O. D., "The Report from the Point of View of the Large Mixed High School," New York Regents' *Bulletin,* 28 (1894), 287–91.

—— "Should Electives in the High Schools Be by Courses or by Subjects?" National Educational Association, *Addresses and Proceedings* (1895), pp. 586–91.

—— "The Work of the Committee of Ten," *School Review,* 2 (1894), 366–72.

Ross, James A., "President King of Oberlin College," *Education,* 23 (1903), 467–70.

Royce, Josiah, "Is There a Science of Education?" *Educational Review,* 1 (1891), 15–25, 121–32.

Rudolph, Frederick, *The American College and University: A History,* New York, 1962.

Ryan, Will Carson, et al., *Secondary Education in the South,* Chapel Hill, 1946.

Sachs, Julius, "The Report of the Committee of Ten, from the

Point of View of the College Preparatory School," *Educational Review, 8* (1894), 75–83.

Schurman, J. G., "The Report on Secondary School Studies," *School Review, 2* (1894), 83–95.

Scott, F. N., "The Report of the Committee of Ten on English Teaching," in *Annual Report of the Superintendent of Public Instruction of Michigan,* Part II (1894), 44–49.

Severance, Henry O., *Richard Henry Jesse: President of the University of Missouri* (mimeograph), Columbia, Mo., 1937.

Shaw, William B., "Compulsory Education in the United States," *Educational Review, 3* (1892), 444–49; *4* (1892), 47–52, 129–41.

Shinn, Josiah H., *History of Education in Arkansas,* Bureau of Education, Circular of Information, 1 (Washington, 1900).

Sizer, Theodore R., *The Age of the Academies,* New York, 1964.

Smith, Shirley W., *James Burrill Angell: An American Influence,* Ann Arbor, 1954.

Smith, Timothy L., "Progressivism in American Education, 1880–1900," *Harvard Educational Review, 31* (1961), 168–93.

Stephens, Frank F., *A History of the University of Missouri,* Columbia, 1962.

Stout, J. E., *The Development of High School Curricula in the North Central States from 1860 to 1918,* University of Chicago Supplementary Educational Monographs, 3, No. 3 (Chicago, 1921).

Sullivan, Mark, *Education of an American,* New York, 1938.

—— *Our Times: America Finding Herself,* New York, 1929.

Sumner, William Graham, "Our Colleges before the Country," in *War and Other Essays,* New Haven, 1911.

Sweet, Julia J., "The Report of the Committee of Ten," *Proceedings* of the Iowa State Teachers Association (1894), pp. 123–24.

Taylor, J. M., "The Report of the Committee of Ten," *School Review, 2* (1894), 193–99.

Ulich, Robert, *Professional Education as a Humane Study,* New York, 1956.

United States Commissioner of Education, *Reports* (1890–1900)

Welter, Rush, *Popular Education and Democratic Thought in America,* New York, 1962.

Wesley, Edgar B., *NEA: The First Hundred Years,* New York, 1957.

West, Andrew F., "A New Revival," *Educational Review, 18* (1899), 252–62.

Willcox, M. A., "The Program of the Committee of Ten," *Education, 15* (1894–95), 257–63.

INDEX

(Federal, Regional, State, and Municipal school laws and systems are indexed under those headings.)